Also edited by Richard Aldous and Sabine Lee

HAROLD MACMILLAN AND BRITAIN'S WORLD ROLE

Also by Sabine Lee

AN UNEASY PARTNERSHIP: British–German Relations between 1955 and 1961

Harold Macmillan
Aspects of a Political Life

Edited by

Richard Aldous
Lecturer in Modern History
University College, Dublin

and

Sabine Lee
Lecturer in German History
University of Birmingham

Foreword by Alistair Horne

First published in Great Britain 1999 by
MACMILLAN PRESS LTD
Houndmills, Basingstoke, Hampshire RG21 6XS and London
Companies and representatives throughout the world

A catalogue record for this book is available from the British Library.

ISBN 0–333–71373–7

First published in the United States of America 1999 by
ST. MARTIN'S PRESS, INC.,
Scholarly and Reference Division,
175 Fifth Avenue, New York, N.Y. 10010

ISBN 0–312–21906–7

Library of Congress Cataloging-in-Publication Data
Harold Macmillan : aspects of a political life / edited by Richard
Aldous, Sabine Lee.
p. cm.
Includes bibliographical references and index.
ISBN 0–312–21906–7
1. Macmillan, Harold, 1894–   . 2. Great Britain—Politics and
government—1945–1964.   3. Prime ministers—Great Britain–
–Biography.   I. Aldous, Richard.   II. Lee, Sabine.
DA566.9.M33H373   1998
941.085'5'092—dc21
[B]   98–38450
                                                                          CIP

This book is printed on paper suitable for recycling and made from fully managed and
sustained forest sources.

10   9   8   7   6   5   4   3   2   1
08   07   06   05   04   03   02   01   00   99

Printed and bound in Great Britain by
Antony Rowe Ltd, Chippenham, Wiltshire

Contents

Foreword
Alistair Horne

In July 1996 I had the greatest good fortune to be invited to attend the oration to the joint Houses of Parliament by Nelson Mandela in St Stephen's Hall. During it I reflected how, as a young journalist, I had had the equal good fortune to listen to President de Gaulle, in the same place and on the last such auspicious occasion, when he had been invited by Harold Macmillan in 1960. Looking round the great hall, I reckoned that I was probably one of a very small handful privileged to have been at both. In his remarkable speech, Mandela singled out Macmillan and 'The wind of change' as one of the few British statesmen deserving of any praise. De Gaulle, in his speech, duly lauded Macmillan and British institutions; then returned home to slam the door on Macmillan's application to join the EEC less than three years later!

The bracketing of those two red-letter events reminded me last summer of the remarkable range covered by Harold Macmillan's seven years in office. From the turmoil which accompanied Eden's resignation in 1956, from Suez to the Cuban Missile Crisis, to the frenzy that surrounded Macmillan's resignation in 1963, these years covered some of the most dramatic events in recent British history.

His first four years were triumphant – he established closest relations with both Presidents Eisenhower and Kennedy; as first peacetime PM to visit Moscow, in 1959, with Khrushchev he began to break the log-jam of the Cold War; and, that same year, he returned the Tories to power with a hundred majority. From then on, events conspired against him; the economy turned sour; he recognized the 'wind of change' in Africa, but failed to resolve the crisis in Rhodesia; and, in 1963, de Gaulle vetoed his application to join the EEC. That same year the Profumo scandal came close to destroying him. But his premiership was redeemed by his pioneering the Nuclear Test Ban with the Soviets, which presaged the Gorbachev–Reagan accords of the 1980s. In October 1963, a sudden prostatectomy forced his retirement – in all probability, unnecessarily.

December 1996 marked the tenth anniversary of Macmillan's death, and therefore it seems to me most timely and apposite that this conference should have been set up in Christ's College, Cambridge, in September of that year to re-examine his career.

Political reputations have a curious way of advancing and receding with almost indecent speed. Who can now recall how once the British popular press trumpeted Nigel Lawson, following his famous tax-slash budget, as the 'greatest Chancellor since . . .'; since *who . . .*? Indeed, perhaps, there may be British schoolchildren in a decade's time unable to recall who, and wherefore, was the 'Iron Lady'?

When he died, in the middle of the Thatcher epoch, Harold Macmillan was covered in laurels. Perhaps it was because he was regarded, romantically, as some kind of king-over-the-water antithesis to Thatcherdom. Now, derided once again as the 'old actor-manager', his reputation seems to lie at the other end of the scale.

In the 1980s, the years of his extreme old age, Harold Macmillan emerged into a kind of new golden age. Though the Enoch Powells and the Tebbits may have growled, his maiden speech in the Lords, with its highly emotive appeal about the miners and the dangers of a divided society received widest acclaim. So did his less well-judged, rather mischievous subsequent sally about 'selling off the family silver'. In December 1986 he died venerated as the grand old man of British politics, in affection and respect.

Yet, had he died in 1996 one feels he might almost have shuffled off the scene the forgotten Prime Minister, if not actively misprized (especially by the 'young fogeys' of Tory journalism) as the progenitor of all our current woes. Why this sudden reversal in his fortunes? Could it be that at the peak of Monetarism, people yearned for those halcyon days of 'You've never had it so good'? That we reached towards 'Supermac' as a kind of antidote to Maggie? That in contrast, perhaps, the less confrontational, more 'middle-road', world of John Major's resembled a little too closely Macmillan's own?

There are some rather tendentious parallels. If Macmillan had come back to earth around the time of the sacking of Norman Lamont, he might well have thought that – with all the talk about soaring unemployment, high interest rates, inflation, and a sluggish economy – Selwyn Lloyd was still at the Treasury, and long overdue for a 'night of the long knives'. (Except, of course, that Selwyn would have gone without such a frightful, undignified howl as Norman! Times change.)

Selfishly, this official biographer comes out of this swing in reputations as an extremely lucky man. Had my two volumes appeared in the 1990s instead of the 1980s, I have little doubt that they would have almost disappeared without trace, relegated to the dustier shelves of Hatchards!

Often one is asked – now that the 30-year rule has released most of the papers for the Macmillan years, and other material has emerged – would you have changed much? My answer: some details, some fine-tuning possibly, but otherwise not a great deal; tactics versus strategy. Since the *Aldington v. Tolstoy* case, I would now be a good deal *less* harsh in apportioning blame to Macmillan for the repatriation of the Cossacks in 1945; in fact I would absolve him almost entirely. I would be harsher on him for the cover-up over Calder Hall in 1957 – which I certainly missed in writing my biography; and I think I would be harsher over his whole handling of the EEC business. *Pace* the reproofs of the young fogeys, I do not think I would be any more severe with Macmillan over his handling of the economy, or the trades unions, than I have been already. Perusal of the Public Record Office documents for 1963 showed little to change one's recounting of the Profumo Affair. Nevertheless, doubtless time will show that there are still nuggets to be found – missed by an idle and incompetent official biographer!

But what does change, has changed, is the *point of view.*

When writing an 'update' on Macmillan back in 1993 (to mark the thirtieth anniversary of his resignation), I interviewed a number of survivors from his entourage – including the late Lord Thorneycroft (who, however, remained unforgiving, and critical, of the 'little local difficulties' of 1958 and the reasons behind his own resignation). Most agreed on four scores: with the one aberration of the 'Night of the Long Knives' (when he sacked a third of his Cabinet in July 1962), he was superb in his appointments, and particularly in the 'team' which ran his inner office. Secondly, his reputation as a thinker survives intact. (Part of the duties of his 'team' was to protect the space he created for himself in which to think – and read.) None of his successors can challenge his claim to have been Britain's best-read PM. Thirdly, and not least, 'Supermac' did have that elusive, indefinable quality of style; nobody can take this away from him, and with him it vanished from Westminster forever.

And, fourthly, he and the Tory Party of his times could reckon on – what seems today – an amazing degree of traditional loyalty, in both directions. Sacked ministers did not immediately sit down and pen whingeing, *sua culpa* (and generally unreadable) memoirs. Even Rab Butler – disloyal and indiscreet as he could be on occasions – would never have become a Norman Lamont!

The Macmillan diaries reveal, underneath the often flippant exterior, a most penetrating mind which asked all the key questions of our times. The tragedy was – in common with some of his successors – the answers all too often just eluded him. 'Events, events', as he once sighed.

Frequently in his conversations with me in the 1970s and 1980s, Macmillan would reckon that his greatest success had been the Nuclear Test Ban he had signed with Kennedy and Khrushchev in 1963; 'partial' only, but it led to the 'SALT' [Strategic Arms Limitation Talks] agreements of the 1980s. Perhaps, today, he would rate his highest achievement as that of keeping the Tory Party together in face of the EEC challenge. But maybe, also, Macmillan's Tory government of 1963 can be viewed as sharing one thing with John Major's: did it in fact 'overstay its leave', to become – in the words of that octogenarian party loyalist Bill Deedes – 'like a horse carrying more lead than it can manage?'

As I remarked earlier, facts don't change; what does change, has changed, is the *point of view.* By way of an example, last year I was invited by BBC2 to act as 'adviser' on a programme dealing with Macmillan's career, under a series entitled 'Reputations'. I said I would only do it if there would be no 'trivialization' – i.e. the prevailing mode. I was assured it would be an in-depth, serious representation. The researchers seemed respectable and highly diligent. Yet, just before screening, I was told that the producer had decided it needed 'livening up'. Instantly my heart sank! In the event it hit the small screen entitled *The Macmillans.* Approximately three-quarters dealt with Lady Dorothy and her affair with Bob Boothby; onty seventeen minutes out of sixty related to the Macmillan premiership; and the whole programme managed to get by without once mentioning Khrushchev, the Cuban Missile Crisis, or the Nuclear Test Ban of 1963 (which, after all, Macmillan did consider to be his greatest contribution – and indeed history may well prove him to have been right).

In sum, the BBC's performance was much more revealing of our times, our attitudes and points of view, than Harold Macmillan's. If nothing else, it proved – once again – the paramount importance of rewriting history and biography regularly, by trained historians and biographers, and not leaving it to the media whizz-kids and associated Paxmanism.

For this reason alone, I am particularly delighted that this conference should be taking place, and most flattered to start the ball rolling.

The above were, approximately, the remarks I made from the Chair when introducing the Macmillan Conference on 5 September 1996, reconstituted from my scribbled notes. Not being possessed of clair-voyance, however, I could not then anticipate the excellent stan-dard of most of the ensuing contributions. Given alt the distortions of the media over past years, what was particularly gratifying to me was the objectivity of the younger participants, who would not have been around in Macmillan's day. They were not led astray by the beguiling images of the grouse-moor, dukeries or Old Etonians, which gave *Private Eye* so much fun in those days (in fact, its first *raison d'être)* but were able to get – most critically – at the *real* Macmillan within, his mistakes and his achievements. I personally came away strongly impressed, and encouraged, and look forward to publication of this book as a serious contribution to the histori-cal record.

Acknowledgements

This volume is based on a conference held at Christ's College, Cambridge, in September 1996. The editors would like to thank the Centre of International Studies, Cambridge, the Department of Modern History, University College, Dublin, and the School of History, University of Birmingham for their financial support, and the Masters and Fellows of Christ's College, Cambridge, for their splendid hosting of the conference. The editors would like to express their gratitude to Professor Corelli Barnett, Dr Peter Caterrell, Dr Alan Clark MP, Dr Ian Clark, Professor Ronan Fanning, Dr Anthony Howard, Dr Philip Towle, Professor D. C. Watt and Dr Nevil Wylie for their advice and invaluable contribution to the conference. Finally, they would like to thank Annabelle Buckley of Macmillan Press, who has been helpful as ever in seeing the publication of the volume through all its critical stages.

Notes on the Contributors

Richard Aldous is College Lecturer in Modern History at University College, Dublin. He co-edited, with Sabine Lee, *Harold Macmillan and Britain's World Role* (1996) and is currently writing a biography of Sir Malcolm Sargent.

Nigel Ashton is Lecturer in International History at the London School of Economics. Previously he held posts at the University of Liverpool and the University of Salford. He is the author of *Eisenhower, Macmillan and the Problem of Nasser: Anglo-American Relations and Arab Nationalism, 1955-59* (1996), and is currently working on a book looking at Anglo-American relations in the early 1960s, to be published under the title *Kennedy and Macmillan: A Very Special Relationship?*

S. J. Ball is Lecturer in Modern History at the University of Glasgow. Educated at Brasenose College, Oxford, and Christ's College, Cambridge, he is the author of *The Bomber in British Strategy* (Oxford, 1995) and *The Cold War* (London, 1997).

N. J. Crowson undertook his doctoral research at Southampton University. He became Fellow of the Department of Politics, Queen's University, Belfast, before joining the Institute of Contemporary British History as Director of Research. Currently he is Lecturer in Modern and Contemporary British History at the University of Birmingham. He is author of *Facing Fascism: The Conservative Party and the European Dictators, 1935–1940.*

Alistair Horne was educated in Switzerland, the United States and Jesus College, Cambridge. Over the last four decades he has published widely on a wide variety of historical subjects. His publications include the prize-winning titles *The Prize of Glory: Verdun, 1916* (1992), *A Savage War of Peace: Algeria, 1954–62* (1977), *The French Army and Politics, 1870–1970* (1984), *How Far from Austerlitz: Napoleon, 1805–1815* (1996), and the widely acclaimed official biography of Harold Macmillan (1988/9).

Lewis Johnman is Quintin Hogg Research Fellow in History at the University of Westminster. He is author, with Anthony Gorst, of *The Suez Crisis* (1996).

Sir Curtis Keeble joined the Diplomatic Service in 1947 and held several overseas appointments including Berlin and Washington before taking charge of the Foreign Office Department responsible for the first round of EEC entry negotiations. In 1974 he was appointed first British Ambassador to the German Democratic Republic, in 1976 Deputy Under Secretary of State in the Foreign and Commonwealth Office and in 1978 Ambassador to the Soviet Union. His publications include *Britain and the Soviet Union* (1990).

Richard Lamb was educated at Downside and Merton College, Oxford. He is author of several books on contemporary history including *The Macmillan Years,* which was the first publication to use the official documents on Macmillan's premiership. He has recently published *Mussolini and the British* and is currently editing for the Public Record Office the CD ROM on the Macmillan documents covering 1957–63.

Sabine Lee was educated at the Universities of Düsseldorf and Cambridge. She completed her PhD with a thesis on British–German relations. She worked as Lecturer in Modern European History at the University of Hull and is currently Lecturer in German History at the University of Birmingham. Her publications include *An Uneasy Relationship: British–German Relations between 1955 and 1961* (1995) and, co-edited with Richard Aldous, *Harold Macmillan and Britain's World Role* (1996).

W. Scott Lucas is Head of American and Canadian Studies at the University of Birmingham. He is the author of numerous books and articles on British and US foreign policy after 1945. His next book, *Freedom's War: The US Crusade against the Soviet Union, 1945–1956,* will be published in early 1999.

N. Piers Ludlow was educated in Italy and Belgium before reading modern history at Trinity College, Oxford. His doctorate from St Antony's College, Oxford, examined European reactions to Britain's first EEC application. He is the author of *Dealing with Britain: The Six and the First UK Application to the EEC.* He is currently Lecturer in International History at the London School of Economics.

Charles Lysaght studied politics and economics at University College, Dublin, before proceeding to Christ's College, Cambridge. In 1964 he succeeded Kenneth Clarke and Norman Lamont as President of the Cambridge Union. He was subsequently called to the Bar and has worked as barrister, lecturer and legal adviser in Dublin. He is author of a biography of Brendan Bracken.

Donette Murray studied modern and contemporary history at the University of Ulster and has recently completed her PhD with a thesis on Anglo-American defence relations during the Kennedy Presidency. She is currently Lecturer at the Queen's University of Belfast.

John Subritzky is a graduate of the Universities of Auckland and Cambridge. He is currently completing a book on the Malaysian–Indonesian confrontation. He currently works as policy officer in New Zealand's Ministry of Foreign Affairs.

Sir Oliver Wright was educated at Solihull School and Christ's College, Cambridge. After four years in the Royal Navy, he joined the Diplomatic Service in 1945. He has held numerous overseas appointments including New York, Bucharest, Singapore, Berlin, and South Africa. Between 1960 and 1963 he was Private Secretary to the Foreign Secretary, from 1964 to 1966 to the Prime Minister. He served as Ambassador to Copenhagen, Bonn and Washington between 1966 and 1986.

1 Introduction
Richard Aldous and Sabine Lee

Shirley Williams, the former Labour Cabinet Minister, once re-marked that the most important quality required for political suc-cess is stamina. This was a trait Harold Macmillan possessed in abundance. Behind the panache and elegant wit lay a dogged re-lentlessness in the face of disappointment. Like a heavyweight boxer who will not fall down, Macmillan absorbed punch after punch throughout his career but always kept going. In the end it was not scandal or political embarrassment for failed policies that saw him off. Harold Macmillan only relinquished his grip on power because he thought he was dying. Only days after offering his resignation to the Queen he knew it was a mistake and regretted it until his death twenty-three years later.

For almost fifty years it seemed unlikely that Harold Macmillan would succeed at the highest level. Macmillan was not one of the stars of his generation. Of his Etonian contemporaries, Macmillan lacked the good looks and intellectual arrogance of Eden or the blue-blooded sense of purpose of 'Bobberty' Cecil. Between 1894 and 1939, despite opportunities and privilege, Macmillan exuded failure and mediocrity. He was a sickly child at Eton and displayed little academic or sporting accomplishment. At Oxford, he arrived (after private tuition) as a promising Exhibitioner, yet gained only a second-class degree. Real achievements seemed to pass unno-ticed. He fought courageously and was wounded in the First World War but was not decorated. Success in entering the House of Com-mons at a relatively young age was dissipated by becoming a mav-erick within his own party. Many considered his beliefs on welfare and poverty to be more akin to Socialism than Toryism. His vocal opposition to appeasement confirmed his image as a disaffected 'crank'. When he burnt an effigy of the Prime Minister, Neville Chamberlain, at Birch Grove on Bonfire Night it symbolized not only the dissatisfaction with his own party but also his impotence within it.

Macmillan's professional failure was not helped by the appalling circumstances of his private life. He did not have the dashing good looks or sparkling wit to make him a ladies' man. Some historians have even tried, without much conviction, to imply that Macmillan was homosexual. Closer to the truth is that Macmillan as a young man was extremely shy with women and showed little inclination to woo. Working for the Duke of Devonshire after the First World War brought him into contact with the duke's teenage daughter, Lady Dorothy, who made all the running for him. A horsy girl with little in the way of looks or brains, she had spent most of her childhood in rural Ireland. She knew very little of men and less of sex. They married in 1920 but Dorothy quickly bored of him. Matters were not helped by her family. Her sisters found Macmillan dull and middle-class. Before dinner at Chatsworth they would draw lots to see who had to suffer his company. Slights of this kind might have been endured if his wife had remained true. In fact, the marriage was a disaster. After years of promiscuity during the early part of their marriage, Dorothy took a regular lover in 1929 and kept him until her death in 1966. Her choice could hardly have been more vicious. Bob Boothby, Conservative MP, was one of Macmillan's closest friends and political allies. This was a cuckolding of the most spectacular and humiliating kind.

Politically and privately, therefore, Macmillan's life until the outbreak of the Second World War was not happy. We might speculate that had Lord Halifax kept his nerve against Churchill in May 1940 and replaced Chamberlain as Prime Minister, Harold Macmillan might well have disappeared into political obscurity. It was the Second World War that made Macmillan. He gained preferment from Churchill and demonstrated that he had the capability to be a government minister. More importantly he came to believe that politics was a game in which he could win. The transformation was dramatic, not least on the outside. The badly cut tweed suits were replaced by something altogether sharper. Snagged teeth were capped and straightened. The glasses were removed for the cameras and a bushy moustache trimmed. Even the personality seemed changed. Earnest, bookish, dull-dog Macmillan was replaced by a witty raconteur whose dry humour made him amusing company and apparently unflappable in a crisis.

The set-backs continued to come. Macmillan forfeited his seat in 1945 and lost ground to Rab Butler in setting the agenda for post-war Conservatism. Back in the Commons in 1951, he was disappointed only to be offered the Ministry of Housing by Churchill who, anyway, did not have the paternal affection for him that Macmillan desired. Nevertheless, he later acknowledged that it was his public relations triumph at Housing and not his record in higher offices that eventually made him prime minister. Success at Housing was followed by a disastrous spell at the Ministry of Defence and a frustratingly short time at the Foreign Office. As Chancellor of the Exchequer, Macmillan badly misjudged American attitudes to British action at the Suez canal and, having been a leading hawk before the campaign, abruptly became first of the 'bolters' on the eve of victory. And yet from the political carnage of the Suez crisis, it was to the barnstorming, media-friendly Harold Macmillan that the Conservative party turned for salvation. A lifetime of withstanding embarrassment and disappointment had finally resulted in Harold Macmillan reaching the top of the 'greasy pole'.

Macmillan's transformation from shambolic wreck to elegant statesman has done little to help his historical reputation. The sense that he was 'all style and no substance' was already established in 1963 and remains to this day. Papers from his Premiership now available under the Thirty-Year Rule enable essays in this collection to attempt a more considered judgement of Macmillan's political legacy.

It is immediately clear that, as Prime Minister, foreign affairs dominated Macmillan's thinking, a fact he acknowledged in his memoirs. The late 1950s and early 1960s were times of international tension and danger. Macmillan, like other world statesmen, assumed he was the best man to deal with the difficulties of the Cold War. He had a measure of success in re-establishing a special relationship with American presidents if not the US foreign policy-making establishment itself. Personal diplomacy was Macmillan's favoured approach although it was also one in which he frequently failed, particularly in European affairs. An over-estimation of his own personal standing as well as misjudgement of Britain's bargaining power with the Six led to a souring of relations with his most significant European partners. In particular Britain's policy hampered a good understanding with France and damaged that with the other key European player, Germany. Strain in the relationship between Adenauer and Macmillan was exacerbated by the latter's attempts at personal diplomacy with the Soviet leader, Nikita Khrushchev. Macmillan's visit to Moscow in 1959 shortly after Khrushchev's Berlin ultimatum did much to undermine the cohesion of the Western camp and was even more detrimental for Anglo-German relations.

There is no doubt about Macmillan's enthusiasm for European co-operation and Britain's role in a wider economic grouping.

Whether his attempt at getting Britain into the European club was a symbol of his own political success is more debatable. Macmillan did not succeed in securing entry to the EEC for Britain during his premiership. He only alienated de Gaulle and frustrated negotiators at Brussels with the 'conditional application' in 1961. Nevertheless, he initiated a major reversal in British thinking about the virtues of European integration and Britain's place in Europe. Perhaps without this radical reappraisal of policy Britain would not have joined after de Gaulle's downfall.

Macmillan's shift in European policy necessitated a corresponding re-evaluation of colonial commitments. Despite the enthusiastic, even radical, rhetoric of the 'Wind of Change' speech, Macmillan's attitude towards Empire was of pragmatism in the face of a wider problem in redesigning Britain's world role (as the case of Malaysia demonstrates only too clearly). Macmillan was too preoccupied with summiteering, joining the Common Market and guaranteeing Britain's status as a nuclear power to deal with colonial affairs. Despite this fundamental lack of interest, Macmillan did knowingly initiate a process which would bring about an end to British rule in Africa that was dignified and relatively peaceful.

Despite Macmillan's obsession with foreign affairs, some of his most important successes lay in the hard reality of electoral politics and the management of his party's affairs. He succeeded in rebuilding the government and his party after the humiliation of the Suez Crisis. Few would have predicted in January 1957 that the Conservatives would win the next general election. The lion's share of the credit for the 1959 victory went to Harold Macmillan, not least because he had displayed such ruthlessness and singlemindedness in achieving a hundred seat majority. He convinced the electorate that they had 'never had it so good' at home and lived in a country once again taken seriously on the world stage. In the process SUPERMAC was born. Could he have won again in 1964? By the time of his resignation in 1963, the Profumo crisis had been seen through and the deadwood of a party in power since 1951 had been cut back in the 'Night of the Long Knives'. In reality, the Conservatives in 1964 came within four seats of victory when led by a man easily ridiculed for his matchstick economics and eighteenth-century demeanour. Whether the more populist and flamboyant Macmillan would have found one more electoral rabbit to pull out of the hat must remain an unanswered question. It would not have been his first such trick.

In the end, perhaps Macmillan's most important legacy is not so much what he achieved but what was put in train. He took the important first step towards redefining Britain's relations with western Europe and initiated a dignified process of decolonization in Africa. In *The Middle Way* and as Chancellor and Prime Minister, he showed a willingness to reform, even revolutionize, Britain's spending priorities, most notably in the defence budget. And he always gave himself time to think – perhaps unusual for a politician – about long-term policy. The Future Policy Committee and the Grand Design are indicative of Macmillan's determination that government should not simply be a question of management but also of vision and strategy. Perhaps it is this belief in the intellectual nature of politics (notwithstanding an eye for the main chance) that distinguishes him from those who followed. From his days as a young man in the trenches fulminating against Irish nationalists to his speeches as Lord Stockton about selling off the 'family silver', Macmillan adored thinking about politics in its historical and philosophical context. In his maiden speech in the House of Lords he acknowledged that his time in politics had not always been successful and that he had often been regarded with 'dislike by the leaders of my party' (although, he continued, 'I was, fortunately, able to deal with the matter fairly soon by becoming the leader of the party myself'). The battle for Macmillan's historical reputation continues and this volume makes a contribution to the debate. But whatever judgements await Harold Macmillan, there can be no doubting that his was a magnificent political life.

2 Macmillan: a View from the Foreign Office

Sir Oliver Wright

One of the many pleasures of taking part in the Macmillan Conference was to go back to Alistair Horne's splendid two-volume biography of him who was known affectionately to his staff as Uncle Harold, to refresh memory and sort out fact from accrued fiction. Indeed, one judges a book about someone who, like Harold Macmillan, played a central role in one's professional life, by whether the author gets right, in fact and judgement, the events of which one has first-hand experience. By this test Horne gets a Triple A rating. His accounts – for example of the Cuban missile crisis, of Nassau and Polaris, of de Gaulle's first veto – strike me as being bang on target. One has confidence that if he is right about things one knows about, he is not likely to be wrong on matters which one doesn't.

I first came in contact with Mr Macmillan at the 4-Power Foreign Ministers' Conference in Geneva in October 1955 on 'The Reunification of Germany'. He was somewhat less than half-way through his short stint as Foreign Secretary. I was a very junior diplomat in Berlin, handling the affairs of what we still called the Soviet Zone of Germany, in the days before the Wall. They needed someone in Geneva to fill the British slot in the International Secretariat which was to produce the minutes of the Conference. It was a measure of the low expectations of the Conference that they should send to it someone as junior as myself.

Macmillan had in July accompanied Eden to an earlier 'Summit' on the same question. The summiteers – Khrushchev and Bulganin, Dulles, Faure and Eden – had in two days agreed on nothing except to refer the problem to their foreign ministers. What the Heads of Government had been unable to resolve in two days, the foreign ministers were unable to resolve in two weeks. There were two sessions daily, morning and afternoon, Monday to Friday; we listened to Mr Molotov say 'no' to German reunification in ten not very different ways. The only agreement that the International Secretariat had to record each evening was that the four foreign ministers would meet again the next day.

Macmillan had his own technique for surviving these bum-numbing sessions. When it was his turn to speak, Pat Hancock or Fred Warner, two accompanying officials from the Foreign Office, would pass up notes of 'points to make' and Macmillan would gracefuly improvise on these themes for 15 minutes or so. When it was not his turn to speak, he would encourage the time to pass more agreeably and more quickly by reading a book placed on his knees out of sight under the conference table. I remember being very shocked at first, thinking that our Foreign Secretary should be taking his work more seriously; but after a time, I realized how wise he was and only wished I could do the same.

Most evenings were passed in official entertainment, each Head of Delegation entertaining and being entertained by other Heads of Delegation, together with their entourages. The negotiating indigestion of the day was succeeded by the gastronomic indigestion of the evening. It is not often appreciated by the general public how much diplomats are obliged to ruin their digestions in the service of their country. One evening, when Macmillan had a night off, I was invited to have dinner with him and a few other members of his delegation. That was a bit of a shock too. I had rather expected to participate in, or at any rate listen to, a wise and witty survey of the Conference to date. Not a bit of it. Macmillan had switched off completely. The conversation was purely social from beginning to end; from soup to coffee not a word of shop. Afterwards I asked John Wyndham, who was Macmillan's sort of private secretary–boon companion and author of a delightful slim volume of memoirs, 'Wyndham and Children First', why I had been invited. 'No reason at all, dear chap; the PM just likes to have a new face or two around.' Alistair Horne gives less than a page to the two weeks of the 1955 Geneva Foreign Ministers' Conference. About right.

Macmillan's brief spell at the Foreign Office followed by his lengthy tenure of No. 10 Downing Street was a pretty fraught time in international affairs. The 1950s under Eden were, I suppose, the most disastrous period in British foreign policy since the Second World War; which is odd when you think that Eden's main strengths were held to lie in his knowledge of international affairs and his experience in diplomacy. The Suez adventure and the failure to realize the seriousness of purpose of the negotiations at Messina which led to the Treaty of Rome were unmitigated disasters.

At the time of Suez I was still stationed in Berlin. I and all my colleagues were particularly sickened that this barmy escapade at the end of the Mediterranean was distracting international attention from something far more heinous happening in our own back yard: the Soviet invasion of Hungary. In London the Chief Clerk of the Foreign Office, the person in charge of personnel, was deluged by letters of resignation from members of the Service who wanted nothing to do with this act of piracy. Eventually tempers calmed; Eden withdrew from Suez and colleagues withdrew their letters of resignation. Just as well, really; otherwise the nation would not have had enough diplomats to carry on the nation's diplomacy. Consciences were soothed when it was pointed out that the unwritten contract between public servants and their political masters states that civil servants advise, ministers decide and civil servants carry out ministers' decisions. After all, politicians are the elect of the people and are answerable to Parliament; civil servants are neither.

Suez marked a parting of the ways for Britain and France. Both were partners in the Suez débâcle. Both felt let down by the Americans. Each reacted in a totally different way. Macmillan's first priority when he became Prime Minister was to re-establish our relations with Washington. The French priority was to distance itself from the United States by giving full attention to the Treaty of Rome, creating a Common Market of the Six which France could and would lead, and setting the seal on the post-war reconciliation between France and Germany. Both were conspicuously successful. Both had enduring consequences. Unfortunately both successes and consequences proved to be mutually incompatible. Since Suez, France has enjoyed a difficult relationship with America and Britain has been unable to develop a satisfactory relationship with Europe.

That Macmillan was successful in restoring relations with the Americans and particularly where it mattered, the White House, is beyond dispute. And that the successful pursuit of this objective has been of great and long-lasting benefit to Britain is equally not in dispute. He was able to re-establish fairly quickly the friendship with Eisenhower which he had formed during the war years when he had been our man in North Africa and Ike had been Supreme Allied Commander in Europe. Ike was no doubt equally glad to be on good terms with his old friend again. The first fruits of this policy was the repeal in 1958 of the McMahon Act, which restored nuclear collaboration between Britain and the United States.

When Kennedy succeeded Eisenhower at the White House,

Macmillan was himself doubtful whether he would be able to establish the same relations of trust with this younger, charismatic figure as he had with his much older predecessor. He did so at first with a message of congratulations, which was also a message of ideas; a masterly survey of the world and a vision of what needed to be done. The draft underwent many revisions and crossed and re-crossed Downing Street many times. It struck a chord in Kennedy's mind and from their first meeting the two men found that they enjoyed each other's company and thought much along the same lines.

It was the Cuban Missile Crisis of late 1962 which cemented Macmillan's quasi-avuncular relationship with Kennedy. I well remember the morning that Hugh Stevenson, chairman of the Joint Intelligence Committee, came into the Private Office and asked to see the Secretary of State. He had brought with him a portfolio of photographs to show Lord Home aerial proof of the presence of Soviet missiles in Cuba. Gromyko had lied in his teeth when Home had pressed him on the subject at the UN, denying that any were there.

In the Private Office we were well aware of the nightly telephone calls between the White House and No. 10. Horne rightly describes them as something less than consultation, something more than information. Kennedy, not Macmillan, always placed the calls; he would not have done so if he had not wanted to; he would not have continued to do so if he had not felt them useful, even necessary. It is lonely at the top, any top; loneliest of all at a time of crisis when one false step might have meant war, nuclear war. And even presidents need someone outside the immediate circle, whose experience they acknowledge, whose sympathy they can rely on, whose judgement they value and whose discretion they can trust, to talk through the events of the day with and to help harness their thoughts for the morrow. Macmillan supplied this need; and of enormous benefit to Britain it was. I have heard this unique exchange described as 'international samaritanism', a remark which suggests a gift for phrasemaking unsupported by insight or judgement.

Macmillan got his reward and Britain its benefit perhaps sooner than expected, at Nassau in December 1962: the Polaris missile, when Kennedy overruled all his staff to give his friend what he needed. The benefit was of immediate and lasting value. Twenty years later, when I was in Washington, during the Reagan–Thatcher political love affair, the successor missile to Polaris, Trident, went through 'on the nod'.

The third important consequence of the Macmillan–Kennedy relationship was the Partial Nuclear Test Ban Treaty, signed for Britain by Lord Home in Moscow in August 1963. Macmillan, while convinced of the necessity of nuclear deterrence and of Britain's possessing its own deterrent, saw the complementary need for bringing these weapons of mass destruction under some sort of control. And he had from the start of his premiership been working on both Eisenhower and Kennedy, who, he realized, had to be the prime movers on the Western side. It was the Cuban missile crisis which made Kennedy finally receptive to his ideas. And so the first step was taken. The Nuclear Treaty was to be the last major foreign policy act of the Macmillan administration. It was also to be the forerunner of a whole series of later arms limitation treaties – SALT 1 and SALT 2 – and, in Reagan's day, of the abolition of a whole nuclear weapons system by the INF Treaty. Actions have consequences and they can be both beneficial and durable: Macmillan's transatlantic policy was both. The Campaign for Nuclear Disarmament (CND) ceased to be a serious political embarrassment thereafter.

It is a favourite pastime of sceptics to call the 'special relationship' into question. No practitioner would do so since it provides the background to the Embassy's daily work in Washington, DC. Indeed, it is perhaps the phrase itself which has become the main impediment to public acceptance of its reality. Of course, it is not exclusive; there are quite a number of special relationships among the nations of the world: the United States with Israel, for example; France with Germany; Britain with Ireland. The continuing intelligence and naval nuclear co-operation are but two of the on-going practical manifestations of this unique way of conducting business between our two nations. And, of course, it does not exclude flaming rows on occasion – Grenada, for example – which furnish the sceptics with proof that the special relationship is a thing of the past. None the less, it persists in persisting. America gave Britain the sort of help over the Falklands that it would have given to no other nation. Naturally, it works best when the personal chemistry of the people in charge and their national interests coincidence: Churchill and Roosevelt, Macmillan and both Eisenhower and Kennedy, Thatcher and Reagan. And as I know from personal experience, if the empathy is right at the top, it is right all the way down. Doors open, minds become receptive, deals are cut.

There is, not surprisingly, a downside to all this. It is Europe. After Suez, while Britain gave priority to the restoration of transatlantic relations, France deliberately turned her back on the Atlantic. For de Gaulle, America and Britain became indiscriminately 'les anglo-saxons' and virtually beyond the pale. France instead set about creating a continental Europe of the Six in her own image, using Europe to harness and control the re-emerging power of Germany and actively promoting Franco-German reconciliation, all of which Germany financed, a role in which Germany, burdened with history, acquiesced. Neither Eden nor Macmillan expected the negotiations at Messina to succeed or the Treaty of Rome to work. It was a catastrophic misjudgement. It fell to Macmillan to try to rectify the mistake. Negotiations for Britain to join in 1961 and 1962 went well, if laboriously, up to Edward Heath's level. They failed at the top. They came up against the insuperable rancour of de Gaulle, who had never recovered from the humiliation of France in 1940 and had always resented the fact that he had had to seek sanctuary in Britain and that Britain had given it. Churchill's 'Cross of Lorraine' pronounced his first veto in January 1963.

Macmillan also came up against the mutual dislike which had developed between himself and Adenauer. Adenauer, a Rhinelander, did not much care for Britain; indeed he did not have much reason to, having been dismissed at the end of the war from his position as Lord Mayor of Cologne by the British Town Major of the day. A summit in Bonn between Macmillan and Adenauer in 1962, which I attended, was a complete waste of time. Macmillan must have thought so too, for he took a nap during the after-lunch session and Alec Home had to keep the talks going. Adenauer soon got his revenge. Only days after de Gaulle's veto, he went to Paris and signed with de Gaulle the Franco-German Treaty of Friendship and Collaboration. The Treaty set the seal on Franco-German reconciliation. It also effectively put paid to any likelihood of Britain's being able to be 'at the heart of Europe'.

This legacy of Harold Macmillan's is also with us still. By taking his eye off the ball at Messina, Britain lost the chance of helping to build a Europe tailored to our tastes and taking account of our interests. We have been playing 'catch up' ever since and show no sign of winning, whichever party is in power.

The last time I was in Uncle Harold's company was in Sweden in August 1963, when for some reason best known to himself the PM had decided to accept the return hospitality of the Swedish Prime Minister, Tage Erlander. I had accompanied my own greatly revered boss, Lord Home, to Moscow for the signature of the Nuclear

Test Ban Treaty and we caught up with the Macmillans in Stockholm. We spent the weekend at the Swedish Chequers, Harpsund. It was crayfish time. We started the evening in a pavilion in the grounds of the main house eating crayfish and drinking akvavit. Very soon our Swedish hosts, led by their foreign minister, were merrily singing Swedish drinking songs, of which there are many. The British were acutely embarrassed. Then the deep diapason of a contralto voice could be heard above the hubbub: Aunt Dorothy had come to the rescue of British honour with the opening bars of 'Annie Laurie' and we all joined in. Next time it was our turn, Aunt Dorothy launched us into 'The Minstrel Boy'. And so it went on, Swedish drinking songs in antiphon with Scottish minstrel lays, with generous refills of akvavit the while.

The evening was not, however, at an end. We repaired to the main house, some of us unsteadily, for dinner. There, toasting the Macmillans, Erlander delivered, in faultless English, one of the wittiest after-dinner speeches I have ever heard and tears of laughter ran down our cheeks. When Uncle Harold got up to respond, he knew instinctively that it would be wrong to try to top that and that he had to come up with something quite different. So he pulled out the vox humana and plunged at once into variations, andante e maestoso, on the 'ties that bind'. Soon the tears of laughter changed to tears of deep felt emotion and the PM sat down to a satisfactory round of applause.

Afterwards, in the drawing room, I went up to him and in the sycophantic manner of which only Private Secretaries are masters, said: 'Prime Minister, you were in very good form tonight.' He looked at me from beneath those hooded eyelids and replied: 'Did you think so, my boy? I gave them my mood voice.' An actor indeed. But then, all successful politicians, indeed, all successful leaders – archbishops, field marshals, even in a modest way, ambassadors – have to be able to play their part when on stage. It goes with the leadership thing: 'be yourself – plus'.

The successful conduct of foreign policy depends to a certain extent on the personal chemistry between the Prime Minister of the day and the person he or she has appointed to the Foreign Office. It also depends on the degree of the PM's personal interest in 'the foreign'. Eden and Macmillan did not have a very satisfactory partnership, perhaps because both were strong personalities and both regarded themselves as experts in this field. Macmillan and Selwyn Lloyd were an uninspiring combination: there are horses for courses and Selwyn really found his metier as Speaker of the House of Commons.

Macmillan and Home were in many ways an ideal team. Both had been to Eton and Oxford. Macmillan had married the daughter of a duke and so was at ease with having an earl at the FO. Moreover, for the first four years of Macmillan's premiership, Home had been at the Commonwealth Office; the two men had come to trust each other's judgement and got on well together. Macmillan had suffered under Eden, learned from the experience and so handled the Foreign Office with a light touch. Home for his part always made certain that the PM knew what he was doing and was happy with it: five or ten minutes occasionally before or after Cabinet, fixed by the two Private Offices, was all that was necessary to keep the two men on the same wavelength and for Home to carry great weight in Cabinet, since he could always carry the PM with him.

Macmillan naturally kept '*haute politique*' for himself; Alec saw the value of his doing so and did not for a moment resent it. In any case there was plenty of other interesting work for him to cope with. There was a great deal of travelling in his programme – too much in Home's view – to keep the alliances in repair: NATO, SEATO and CENTO were all active, and if not all of them were particularly useful, they took up a good deal of time. The UN was very time-consuming as was the Laos problem. Moreover, Alec was never one to seek the limelight. He was happy to answer for the FO in the House of Lords and Their Lordships were delighted to have him in their midst. Down the corridor, Ted Heath handled the accession negotiations for Europe and answered in the House of Commons. So for three years all was sweetness and light between No. 10 and the FO. When Home retired, he always used to look back on his time at the Foreign Office as his 'golden years'. I, his Private Secretary, thought them just that too.

So I have always thought it strange that Macmillan, with all his gifts and his many and varied contributions to the safety of our nation and to our standing in the world, does not enjoy a reputation consistent with his merits. Perhaps it is a case of a prophet not being without honour save in his own country. Perhaps his character and personality do not appeal to later generations when the sound bite has superseded rational argument in politics. The delightful cartoon by Terry Jeffrey on the front of the programme of the Cambridge Conference encapsulates a good deal of the problem: Macmillan presents an old-fashioned appearance and is carrying an old-fashioned book.

Yet that languid face hid a complex personality and an acute political brain; the old-fashioned appearance belied a man with a forward-looking, even visionary concept of what he would like the world to be. The book correctly indicated a well-furnished mind, widely read in history and literature. He had a perspective in which to place the problems he had to deal with. He was an astute judge of human nature, particularly of political human nature: hence his addiction to Trollope. He saw things in depth.

When I followed Home to No. 10, a quotation from *The Gondoliers* written in Macmillan's own straggly hand, framed, stood on the broad window ledge to the left of the Principal Private Secretary's desk:

Quiet, calm deliberation untangles every knot.

If only that were so. Just because there is a problem does not mean that there is a solution to it. People, and nations, often need their problems more than they need solutions to them, for it is the problems that give them a sense of identity, a meaning to their lives. As de Toqueville correctly observed 150 years ago: 'Nations are like men; they prefer what flatters their passions to what serves their interests.'

It would seem that the world demands spectacular success before it is prepared to recognize greatness; and not always then. And one failure can undo many successes. It is interesting to speculate that had Macmillan been able to negotiate British entry into the European Community in 1963 he would have been buoyant enough in spirit to ride the scandals of that unhappy summer and would have taken his place among the great Prime Ministers of our country. As it was, de Gaulle's veto was a blow, political, psychological and physical, from which he never really recovered. And it showed. His illness was proof. For all that, he was a man who understood how the world we live in works, who knew what he wanted to do about it and achieved much of what he set out to do. For a practitioner, he was a statesman to admire, a politician to respect, a marvellous man to work for.

As a young diplomat I was grateful for my worm's eye view of the great man at work. Thirty-four years on, recollecting in tranquillity, my admiration grows for a unique person, unique in the number and magnitude of the problems he had to face and unique in the quiet, calm deliberation with which he brought his manifold gifts to bear upon them. In comparison, today's international scene, whilst abounding in insoluble problems and human misery, presents what are essentially second-order problems: the great issues of war and peace are thankfully not at stake as they were in Macmillan's day. So perhaps it does not matter that we seem only to have second-order personages to deal with them.

As for Macmillan, we shall not see his like again, nor, with a bit of luck, the magnitude of the problems he had to face. Life has moved on.

3 The Cost of Myth: Macmillan and the Illusion of the 'Special Relationship'[1]

W. Scott Lucas

In February 1993, British Prime Minister John Major travelled to Washington for talks with the new US President, Bill Clinton. The visit came at a particularly tense time for Anglo-American relations. There were divisions over policy in Bosnia, a US initiative to send an envoy to Northern Ireland, the development of trading relations through the North American Free Trade Area (NAFTA), and even the European development of the Airbus. Major's Conservative Party had not helped matters by indiscreetly advising Clinton's Republican opponents in the 1992 Presidential election. All of this paled, however, before the faith of the British press in the Anglo-American alliance. In the words of *The Times*, 'The special relationship between America and Britain, rarely evoked on the other side of the Atlantic and mentioned by British diplomats only in private whispers, remains a benchmark of London's influence on the international stage.'[2]

Very little was resolved during Major's visit, which lasted less than two days. The *Financial Times* struck a sceptical tone with the snide comment, 'The truth is that relationship is special above all in its lopsidedness.'[3] For the majority of the British press, however, the illusion remained:

> One meeting may say little about the future of the special relationship, but it has helped to confirm a common language. . . . There is still something to be said for a common language.[4]

The US journalist R. W. Apple joined the chorus: 'The special relationship between Britain and the US, whose obituary has been written so often, is alive and well. . . . It is language, shared experi-

16

ence and common political culture that make the bonds between Britain and the US so strong.'[5]

Even more striking is the perpetuation of these images by British historians. Alan Dobson, in a recent survey of Anglo-American relations in the twentieth century, ignores his own chronicle of divisions between London and Washington to assert blithely, 'In crisis after crisis . . . Britain and the USA have approached things similarly and in a partnership that is suggestive of there being further life in the relationship.'[6] Nicholas Cull, writing about Britain and the US during the Second World War, goes even further by stressing the permanent 'essence of the Anglo-American relationship, which is not purely a pragmatic creation of the elite but a confluence of culture and historical necessity'.[7]

In one sense, this rose-tinted vision was fostered by the image of a 'Grand Alliance', albeit one belatedly joined by the US, against the Axis in the Second World War. Yet Churchill's invocation of the 'special relationship of the English-speaking peoples' in the Iron Curtain speech of 1946 was buffeted throughout the early Cold War by tensions between British and American interests and policies, culminating in the traumatic division over the Suez War. It was Harold Macmillan, fighting for his new Government and his political reputation as well as any Anglo-American alliance, who enshrined the concept of an 'interdependence' across the North Atlantic.

No judgement need be made of Macmillan's manipulation of history and his persistent repackaging of the 'special relationship', both in his memoirs and in his recollections to biographers, to bolster his reputation. There was a great cost, however, in Macmillan's strategy of reliance, in rhetoric and in deed, on a London–Washington axis. In doing so, the Prime Minister added to the growing estrangement of Britain from 'Europe'. Six years later, when Macmillan belatedly tried to get Britain into the European Economic Community, the legacy of Atlantic 'interdependence' would help provoke a French veto.

Macmillan's account of his premiership, in his public statements, his memoirs and his testimony to his biographers, moves from tales of camaraderie with Dwight Eisenhower, his old buddy from the Second World War, to his extraordinary bond with John F. Kennedy.

Macmillan always harked back to his comment of 1943 that Britain played the Greeks to the Romans of the US, providing the brains to complement American brawn in the international contest with Soviet Communism.

The portrayal served both Prime Minister and country. His government would be marked by the ongoing contraction – military, economic and diplomatic – of Britain's global position, but Macmillan was loathe to shun the mantle of greatness. The illusion of the 'special relationship' offered a personal and national solution. Through the claim to partnership with Washington, Macmillan and Britain would still be players in superpower contests.

Any rigorous examination dispels the myth. Macmillan's account of a confederation of equals, on the personal or political level, is not corroborated by US evidence. After he left the presidency in 1961, Eisenhower only corresponded once with his 'old friend' Macmillan. His administration may have been concerned with the public portrayal of British support for the US at certain critical points, such as the aftermath of the Soviet launch of *Sputnik* in October 1957, but general strategy was not based on an Anglo-American partnership. To the contrary, in key areas such as the Middle East, Africa and Asia, the US was more concerned with establishing a policy 'independent' of British influence. What is striking about the records of Eisenhower's National Security Council is not how often Britain is mentioned but how rarely attention is paid to London's position.

Nor does Macmillan's 'special relationship' correspond with the logic of 'alliance'. Co-operation between London and Washington was not an unconditional emanation of a shared heritage. It was dependence upon organizational links and a convergence of interests. Where British support was unnecessary for the achievement of American goals, for example in Latin America, there was no special relationship. Where interests conflicted, as in the issue of relations with Communist China, there was perpetual tension in Anglo-American consultations, a tension resolved only when Macmillan abandoned Britain's freedom of action on the issue in 1957. The Foreign Office captured the nature of 'alliance' in February 1957, 'We should pursue a policy in step with that of the US. We have no alternative.'[8]

These simple but essential realities are obscured by the ability of Macmillan to manipulate the illusions of 'alliance' throughout his career. The son of Indiana's Nellie Belles, he later celebrated his own Anglo-American heritage for publicity's sake; in fact, his early life showed few signs of involvement with affairs across the Atlantic. Bonds forged in North Africa and Italy in the Second World War may have had a limited influence – Macmillan worked closely with Robert Murphy, who would eventually become the third-highest official in the State Department – but their long-term impact was mythological. Macmillan may have trumpeted his involvement with the Supreme Allied Commander, Dwight Eisenhower, for political advantage in the 1950s; however, there was little reciprocation. The future US President never elevated the wartime contacts beyond an acquaintance with Macmillan and his work.

Indeed, Macmillan's attentions in the decade after the Second World War would be devoted to domestic politics. Losing his seat in the 1945 election, he had to secure a sanctuary through a by-election in Bromley four months later. Entry into the Cabinet in 1951 in the relatively minor position of Minister of Housing had to be parlayed into the triumph of building 300,000 council houses in a year and his stay at the Ministry of Defence was abbreviated by Winston Churchill's departure.

When the Eden government finally yielded the prize of Foreign Secretary, Macmillan was far too pragmatic in his approach for a personal celebration of Anglo-American partnership. He sensibly allowed Eden to seek the plaudits from the Geneva Summit in July 1955, assuming the burdens of the subsequent Conference of Foreign Ministers. His relationship with US Secretary of State John Foster Dulles was a warm one, particularly given the undeclared state of war between Eden and Foster Dulles; however, its benefits came through the details of sustaining Britain's position on the Cyprus question, securing West Germany's entry into NATO, or negotiating Britain's export of copper wire to Communist countries. On occasion, the Foreign Secretary would even test the notion of 'alliance' while leaving himself a route for retreat if his plans went awry. He pressed for British occupation of the Buraimi oasis, an area disputed between British-backed sheikhdoms and Saudi Arabia, in defiance of US wishes. Far less successful was his venture to bring Jordan into the Baghdad Pact, an initiative which almost led to the overthrow of King Hussein and prompted Eisenhower to write, 'The British never had any sense in the Middle East.'[9] Macmillan was shrewd enough to distance himself from the débâcle and suffered no ill will from Washington. After Eden moved Macmillan to the Treasury weeks later, Foster Dulles wrote that he was 'terribly disappointed'. He added, 'I have come to have great trust and reliance in you and because of this I have looked toward the future with greater confidence.'[10]

It was the Suez Crisis, the watershed for so much of post-war British foreign policy, that ultimately shaped Macmillan's conception of the Anglo-American 'alliance'. Macmillan's priority during the affair was the assertion of British power in the Middle East, with or without US assent. He pressed the War Cabinet to co-operate with Israel in an attack upon Egypt. To reassure colleagues that Britain could afford a war, he misled them about the state of the foreign reserves. Most importantly, he lied to Prime Minister Eden about the US position. Macmillan, told directly by Foster Dulles that Washington was opposed to military action and given no indication of support by President Eisenhower, still informed Eden that the US 'quite realised that we might have to act by force. . . . Our threat of force was vital, whether we used it or not, to keep Nasser worried.'[11]

Yet, when the British collusion with France and Israel failed to topple Nasser quickly, when the foreign reserves drained away as the US exerted economic and diplomatic pressure for a cease-fire, Macmillan suddenly distanced himself from the operation and personally sought reconciliation with Washington. First he appealed for American loans and provision of oil supplies. Then, to negotiate behind the Prime Minister's back, he assured US contacts that Eden would soon resign. At the same time, political manoeuvring within the Conservative Party ensured that Macmillan would move into Number 10 if Eden stepped down.

Thus, when Macmillan's intrigues yielded him the premiership on 10 January 1957, he entered not with an inherent belief in a 'special relationship', but with a recognition of his dependence upon US power. His position as Prime Minister, as well as Britain's military and economic strength, rested upon transatlantic co-operation. Of course, it would be politically inexpedient to admit London's subservience to Washington, so Macmillan instead proclaimed a global partnership of equals. Speaking on television a week after his accession, he asserted:

The life of the free world depends upon the partnership between us. . . . We don't intend to part from the Americans, and we don't intend to be satellites.[12]

Macmillan was assisted by the assessment of US leaders, made even before the end of the Eden government, that 'alliance' must be sustained despite the traumas of Suez. Eisenhower, confronting advisers hostile to London, finally announced, 'We must face the question, what must we do in Europe and then the question, how do we square this with the Arabs?'[13] He also claimed, 'Nothing would please this country more nor, in fact, could help us more, than to see British prestige and strength renewed and rejuvenated in the Middle East.'[14]

These conclusions were reached not because of an a priori belief in 'alliance' but because of a pragmatic assessment of US interests. This was best captured by the British Ambassador to Washington, Harold Caccia:

> The new era is one of more strictly business relationships, with much sentiment cut out and our special position temporarily, at least, impaired, but not totally dissipated.
>
> The Americans will remain convinced that Communism is their principal enemy and challenge. They will need Allies and on the whole they like doing business with us, provided that we talk in plain and blunt business terms. We should avoid at all costs appealing to emotion and old associations when doing business.[15]

In Whitehall, the Official Committee on the Middle East added, 'One of the underlying objectives of US policy would ... be the continuance of oil supplies to NATO countries, and for this reason her policy was likely, in general, to coincide with our interests.'[16]

The litmus test for Macmillan was an arrangement on atomic weapons. A reduction in expenditure on conventional forces, a priority for Macmillan's economic plans, could only be achieved if Britain developed its bomber and missile capabilities.[17] This in turn rested upon access to US technology, access which had been restricted since the 1946 McMahon Act. In his memoirs, Macmillan spelled out the linkage between 'alliance' and nuclear co-operation:

> The most urgent, and at the same time most delicate, task which confronted me on becoming Prime Minister was to repair and eventually to restore our old relationships with Washington. With this was closely linked the new defence organisation and strategy for the United Kingdom, which must now take full account of the impact of nuclear weapons.[18]

Visiting Washington at the end of January, Minister of Defence Duncan Sandys tried to prepare the ground in discussions with his US counterpart, Charles Wilson. When Wilson assessed that US legislation 'could not be changed at the moment', Sandys did not challenge the statement but reminded Wilson that, if active forces were decreased, then the amount of firepower per soldier had to be increased. He also conceded that atomic bombs could remain in US custody if they were placed on British airfields, a point Wilson eagerly endorsed.[19]

On the eve of Macmillan's first summit with Eisenhower in Bermuda, *The Times* reiterated the link between the personal and strategic alliances:

> To complete the work of repair is, far and away, the most urgent task before the new Bermuda. Fortunately Mr Eisenhower and Mr Macmillan have known, liked and trusted each other in the past, and they can pick up the partnership without formalities. . . .
>
> [The task is] to ensure closer cooperation at all levels. A fuller exchange of atomic information could be the first welcome result: assurances in the past have not always led to action lower down.[20]

The summit at Bermuda and the subsequent meeting with Eisenhower in Washington in October appeared to be unmitigated vindication for Macmillan. The first summit was presented as a personal victory, with Macmillan writing to Cabinet colleagues:

> We have not been in the dock. On the contrary, the Americans have been rather apologetic about their position. . . . The personal relations between myself and the President have been established upon a level of confidence which is most gratifying.[21]

Australian Prime Minister Robert Menzies was assured that there was 'no doubt that, as far, as the President is concerned, things are back on old footing', although Foster Dulles 'lags a little behind his Head of State'.[22]

The Washington summit, held after the shock of the Soviet launch of *Sputnik*, was a purported triumph for the strategic relationship, as the Eisenhower Administration pledged to repeal the McMahon Act and provide technical information and material for nuclear warheads to Britain. The Americans also agreed to a Declaration of Common Purpose (although they rejected Macmillan's preferred label of a Declaration of Interdependence):

> The concept of self-sufficiency is now out of date. The countries of the free world are interdependent and only in genuine partnership, by combining their resources and sharing tasks in many fields, can progress and safety be founded. For our part, we have agreed that our two countries will henceforth act in accordance with this principle.[23]

Macmillan's skill at self-promotion, both at the time and subsequently, ensured that the nuclear deal achieved legendary status, but closer examination raises doubts about the British achievement. The preliminary agreement at Bermuda to station sixty US Thor intermediate-range ballistic missiles on British soil, ostensibly under a dual-key system, provided a secure base for American strategists. After the summit, Eisenhower thanked Macmillan profusely, 'We are pleased that you found your way clear to allow United Kingdom bases to be used for AQUATONE if it should at some time become necessary.'[24] The benefits of US nuclear technology soon paled in the face of mounting costs for a British deterrent; in the end, London would be dependent on the provision of US weaponry.

In 1955 Macmillan had foreseen the danger of relying on a US deterrent:

> I think this is a very dangerous doctrine. . . . Politically it surrenders our power to influence American policy and then, strategically and tactically, it equally deprives us of any influence over the selection of targets and the use of our vital striking forces. The one, therefore, weakens our prestige and our influence in the world, and the other might imperil our safety.[25]

Yet, in the end, Macmillan's 'success' was British dependence on the US. In January 1957 he admitted to the Defence Committee that Britain would not use strategic or tactical nuclear weapons 'except in wars in which the US were engaged as our Allies or were otherwise giving us their full support' although he held on to the fig leaf that 'we should . . . have within our control sufficient weapons to provide a deterrent influence independent of the United States'.[26] The British Chiefs of Staff were blunter in their assessment on the eve of the Washington agreement nine months later:

We must either accept that we were a junior partner of the US (in which case we should have an unbalanced programme ourselves) or we must stick to our balanced programme (which, it was clear, we had not the capacity to support). It was difficult to compromise between two alternatives and the Prime Minister was in favour of the first, although if we once accepted that position it would be extremely difficult ever to return to a balanced programme.[27]

Macmillan had achieved no more than 'a quid pro quo for ... the provision of "real estate" in the United Kingdom for such things as intermediate-range ballistic missile sites'.[28] As Geoffrey Crowther, the managing director of *The Economist*, had predicted in *Foreign Affairs* at the start of 1957, 'alliance' would be based on the US as the 'only member that has any substantial freedom to choose its course of action for itself'.[29]

Diplomatic concessions made by Macmillan to the Americans were even more significant. Ever since it had recognized Communist China in 1949, Britain had held out against giving up its 'independent' line on Peking, quarrelling with Washington over 'strategic' exports and China's admission to the United Nations. Macmillan agreed that Britain would now defer to US wishes. In the Middle East, Britain stood aside as the US took over the Western strategy of dealing with Gamal Abdel Nasser; Macmillan's wish to cut the Egyptian President down immediately was replaced by unilateral US activity, such as the initiative to overthrow the Syrian government. US freedom of action in Latin America and Southeast Asia was implicitly, if not explicitly, confirmed.

The most telling effect of Macmillan's quest for the Special Relationship was never mentioned at Bermuda. The Prime Minister, in effect, had chosen between an Anglo-American 'alliance' and a British relationship with the emerging EEC. Whitehall had remained aloof from talks about the EEC since 1955 – Macmillan, as Foreign Secretary, had overseen the policy of detachment – but in the aftermath of Suez, some British Ministers, supported by officials, sought a review of Britain's Atlanticist position.

On 9 January 1957, as the Six were negotiating the Treaty of Rome, Foreign Secretary Selwyn Lloyd put a memorandum before the Cabinet. He argued that Britain, diplomatically and militarily, should work through the Western European Union rather than NATO:

Such an association would not be a 'Third Force' between America and Russia. Its object would rather be to develop into one powerful group within the North Atlantic Treaty Organisation almost as powerful as America and perhaps in friendly rivalry with her.

Then Lloyd took a stance on the nuclear issue which would differ radically from Macmillan's later policy. Because Britain was ahead of other European powers in the nuclear field, the Foreign Secretary claimed, 'We should be in a strong position to see that the arrangements were made on our terms.' While present links with the US and Canada should be maintained 'in substantially their present form', Lloyd foresaw that Britain would 'enlist not only the resources and skill of our European neighbours, particularly the Germans, but also their finance'. He put the question to the Cabinet, 'Might it not be better ... to pool our resources with our European allies so that Western Europe as a whole might become a third nuclear power comparable with the US and the Soviet Union? ... A policy on these lines need not imply antagonism towards the US; it might well be developed in cooperation with them.'[30]

Lloyd's proposals were sharply challenged by senior Ministers. The Lord President, Lord Salisbury, asserted, 'Our main aim at the present time should be to repair the breach which had been made in Anglo-American relations by the Suez dispute.' He was supported by the Commonwealth Secretary, Lord Home, and Minister of Defence Antony Head, and there was general agreement that European co-operation should not be based on nuclear strategy.

Yet the Cabinet was far from dismissive of Lloyd's initiative, as 'strong support was expressed for the general concept of a closer association between the United Kingdom and Western Europe'. Some Ministers emphasised 'that there must be some change in the basis of Anglo-American relations' since 'it was doubtful whether the US would now be willing to accord to [Britain] alone the special position which we had held as their principal ally in the war'.

In the end, the Cabinet tried to have it every possible way, calling for political leadership in Europe, Commonwealth cohesion, and maintenance of the Anglo-American 'alliance'. Ministers agreed to resume consideration of Lloyd's memorandum. They also instructed the Foreign Secretary to communicate their views to Eden. It was an empty injunction, of course, since the Prime Minister was already preparing his resignation.

Unfortunately, Macmillan's position is not recorded in the Cabinet minutes. Nor is it clear whether Macmillan, anticipating Eden's departure, recognized that Lloyd's proposal would have to be taken up by a new government, possibly under his leadership. What is clear is that Macmillan, once in Number 10, moved quickly along the line proposed by Salisbury. Preparing for a summit in Paris which would feature discussion of the European common market, Macmillan stressed that the visit would be packaged 'primarily in an European context' as it was 'important that we should not give the impression that we are forming an Anglo-French front vis-à-vis the US before the Bermuda meeting'.[31] The British delegation would threaten 'that, unless greater consideration could be shown for our point of view in the future, it might well be that we should find it impossible to enter an European Free Trade Association'.[32]

By the time Macmillan returned from Bermuda, the die was cast. A Cabinet committee concluded, 'There is another feature of Britain's present position in the world which we must not allow ourselves to forget, we have accepted partnership and alliance with the United States as a basic fact of life. In the strategic sphere indeed we have accepted America as the major partner.'[33]

The Treasury foresaw the dangers of British isolation with the Six's completion of the Treaty of Rome, signed within days of Bermuda, noting:

This exposes the United Kingdom to a most dangerous situation. If the Customs Union comes into existence and there is no Free Trade Area, this will represent a very grave economic threat to the United Kingdom. Yet, once the Customs Union Treaty has come into effect, it will become increasingly difficult for us to be sure of attaining the Industrial Free Trade Area which we need to safeguard our interests.[34]

Macmillan claimed in his memoirs that he warned the Cabinet of the seriousness of the situation, saying he intended to speak frankly to West German Chancellor Konrad Adenauer, but he offered no concessions in his policy towards the US nor did he pick up Lloyd's renewed suggestion for the Grand Design of European nations.[35] Instead, the Cabinet maintained the curious illusion that, through the European Free Trade Area, it could sustain both the Atlantic alliance and association with the European Community. Discussing the Treasury memorandum, Ministers agreed:

We must . . . expect resistance to any action on our part which could be interpreted as an attempt to diminish the impetus of this movement or, by linking the new European grouping too closely with the Atlantic community, to make it less independent of the United States. Nevertheless, if this effort to establish a European 'Third Force' succeeded in its present form without our being associated in some positive fashion with the new alignment of power in Europe, the consequences would be grave. Our existing European policy would be undermined and our special relationship with the United States would be endangered if the United States believed that our influence was less than that of the European Community.[36]

Macmillan, throughout his wooing of Eisenhower, clung to this fantasy, even as the story wore thin. The official records of his meeting with Felix Gaillard, the French President du Conseil, in November 1957 cannot obscure the tension exacerbated by the Washington summit of the previous month. Macmillan insisted:

[I have] been most disappointed to find that Anglo-American intentions had been misinterpreted and that [I] and the President were suspected of a conspiracy in Washington to advance an Anglo-American hegemony. The statements in the Declaration of Interdependence were quite to the contrary. The United States and United Kingdom had not worked out anything. There were no cut-and-dried plans for presentation to NATO or anyone else.

Gaillard's reply was acidic:

The NATO Alliance consisted, on the one hand, of people residing outside the Continent of Europe who were brought into the war and, on the other hand, of people who had been invaded and humiliated. The latter had a complex. They considered themselves to be a most advanced people and would not accept to be cast in the role of infantry of footsloggers in the next war.

It was no use saying: 'Let us share the task of making a car,' and then asking France and Germany to make the windscreen and the wipers, while the United States and the United Kingdom did the technical work of making the engine, chassis, and coachwork.

When Gaillard suggested closer Anglo-French co-operation on nuclear issues, Macmillan had to face the consequences of his decision. The American commitment to repeal the McMahon Act on exchange of nuclear information extended only to Britain; there was no hope of getting the Eisenhower Administration, let alone Congress to extend the offer to France. The Prime Minister finally told Gaillard that he did 'not want to run any risk of jeopardising the amendment' of the McMahon Act. Even Gaillard's suggestion of co-operation on civil nuclear matters was turned away by Macmillan.[37]

The British government was committed to its gamble on the Special Relationship. Dependence on the United States would be paraded as interdependence, economic and military limitations would be transformed into strengths, and the tricky question of Europe would be set aside. Macmillan told a television audience in February 1958:

> The independent contribution . . . gives us a better position in the world, it gives us a better position with respect to the United States. It puts us where we ought to be, in the position of a great power. The fact that we have it makes the United States pay a greater regard to our point of view, and that is of great importance.[38]

About the same time, Paul Gore-Booth, the Deputy Under-secretary for Economic Affairs in the Foreign Office, warned, 'In order to ward off the danger of our becoming a satellite we must balance our relationship with America by a closer relationship with our other friends, particularly in Europe. . . . In general we want the United States to remain involved as firmly as possible all round the world, but at the same time there are United Kingdom interests in defence of which we still need to retain the right and ability to act for ourselves.'[39] Such counsel would go unheard until it was far too late.

Of course Macmillan's emphasis on the Special Relationship in 1957 was not solely responsible for Britain's exclusion from Europe in the 1960s. The policy of limited co-operation with the Messina Conference had already damaged London's position before Macmillan's accession to power. Still, the new Prime Minister's decision to put his future and that of his government in the hands of the Anglo-American 'alliance' confirmed the divergence between Britain and Europe. Even Macmillan's reverent biographer Alistair Horne notes this, although without considering the implications:

> Macmillan's diary... reveals a fundamental parting of the ways in Franco-British relations. Britain henceforth would pursue the road of the Special Relationship; France would go separately and – implicitly – on a lower level, to Washington. Macmillan clearly and consciously gave the London–Washington entente priority over relations with Europe.[40]

Even after Macmillan belatedly tried and failed to bring Britain into Europe, his vain equation of a personal relationship with the President with an immutable Anglo-American alliance would be the overriding priority. As he wrote to John F. Kennedy after their last meeting in July 1963:

> I felt that it was a wonderful example of the way in which countries, and perhaps even more individuals, who trust each other can work rapidly and effectively together.... It has been a great pride to me to feel that in that at least we have been in part equal to the Churchill–Roosevelt relationship at the most critical moment of history.[41]

Alistair Horne blithely accepts this contention and effuses, 'One is entitled to speculate what [Macmillan and Kennedy] might have gone on jointly to achieve, had not both been removed prematurely.'[42] To the contrary, advance in Britain's relations with Europe could only be achieved after the impediment of Macmillan's 'Special Relationship' had been removed. It was in 1973, when a later Conservative government would bring Britain into the EEC, that Macmillan could give the Europe-first strategy the fullest support in the concluding page of his memoirs:

> It is in the new unity of Europe that we may, with full loyalty to our Commonwealth responsibilities, play our part to meet whatever unknown dangers and to exploit whatever new possibilities the next 50 years may bring.[43]

NOTES

1. I am grateful to Nick Gray, a postgraduate student at the University of Birmingham, for access to his research on the Macmillan government and to Alistair Morey, a PhD candidate at the University of Birmingham, for his comments on the draft.
2. 'Common Interest', *The Times*, 26 February 1993, p. 15.
3. 'Not So Special', *Financial Times*, 26 February 1993, p. 14.
4. 'Common Interest', *The Times*, p. 15.
5. R. W. Apple, 'Just Good Friends, Nothing Special', *The Times*, 26 February 1993, p. 14.
6. Alan Dobson, *Anglo-American Relations in the Twentieth Century* (London: Routledge, 1995), p. 177.
7. Nicholas J. Cull, 'Churchill, and the Myth of a Special Relationship', *Parliamentary Brief*, October 1995, p. 88.
8. Draft to UK delegation to Southeast Asian Treaty Organization, 14 February 1957, Public Record Office (hereafter cited as PRO), FO371/127748/V1051/40.
9. Eisenhower minute, 16 December 1955, DDE, Ann Whitman Series, Ann Whitman Diary, Box 7.
10. Foster Dulles to Macmillan, 20 December 1955, DDE, John Foster Dulles Papers, Subject, Alphabetical, Box 11, Eden–Macmillan–Lloyd Correspondence (2).
11. Macmillan to Eden, 26 September 1956, PRO, PREM11/1102.
12. Harold Macmillan, *Riding the Storm* (London: Macmillan, 1971), p. 196.
13. Eisenhower to Humphrey, 21 November 1956, DDE, Ann Whitman Series, DDE Diaries, Box 19, November 1956 Telephone Calls.
14. Eisenhower to Churchill, 27 November 1956, DDE, Ann Whitman Series, International, Box 18, Winston Churchill.
15. Washington to Foreign Office, Despatch 411, 28 December 1956, PRO, PREM11/2189.
16. OME (57)3, 2 February 1957, PRO, CAB134/2338.
17. D (57)2, 18 January 1957, PRO, CAB131/18.
18. Macmillan, *Riding the Storm*, p. 240.
19. Record of Sandys–Wilson meeting, 28 January 1957, PRO, FO371/129306.
20. *The Times*, 21 March 1957, 11.
21. Quoted in Horne, p. 26.
22. Macmillan to Menzies, 25 March 1957, PRO, PREM11/1789.
23. Macmillan, *Riding the Storm*, p. 757.
24. Eisenhower to Macmillan, 23 March 1957, PRO, PREM11/1763.
25. Quoted in Andrew Pierre, *Nuclear Politics: The British Experience with an Independent Strategic Force* (London: Oxford University Press, 1972), p. 93.
26. D (57) 2nd meeting, 27 January 1957, PRO, CAB131/18.
27. COS (57) 81st meeting, 21 October 1957, PRO, DEFE4/101.
28. Joint Planning Staff, JP (57) Note 12, 'Common Defence Policy for UK/US', 21 October 1957, PRO, DEFE6/45.

29. Geoffrey Crowther, 'Rebuilding the Alliance', *Foreign Affairs*, January 1957, p. 173.
30. CP (57) 6, 'The Grand Design', 5 January 1957, PRO, CAB129/84; CM 3 (57), 9 January 1957, PRO, CAB128/30.
31. Foreign Office to Paris, Cable 473, 27 February 1957, PRO, FO371/130646.
32. GEN580/1, 'The Common Market and the Free Trade Association', 8 March 1957, PRO, CAB13/123.
33. OI (57) 23, 26 March 1957, PRO, CAB134/2319.
34. Thorneycroft memorandum, CP (57)106, 30 April 1957, PRO, CAB129/84.
35. Macmillan, *Riding the Storm*, p. 435; Lloyd to Macmillan, 28 May 1957, PRO, PREM11/1841.
36. CC (57) 37, 2 May 1957, PRO, CAB128/31.
37. Record of Macmillan–Gaillard meeting, 25 November 1957, PRO, FO371/130646.
38. Quoted in Pierre, *Nuclear Politics*, p. 178.
39. Gore-Booth memorandum, 12 February 1958, PRO, FO371/132330.
40. Horne, p. 22.
41. Quoted in Horne, p. 518.
42. Horne, p. 526.
43. Harold Macmillan, *At the End of the Day* (London: Macmillan, 1973), p. 523.

4 Opportunity Knocks: Macmillan at the Treasury, 1955–7

Lewis Johnman

The fundamental dilemma of providing any assessment of the tenure of Harold Macmillan at the Treasury lies in his short-term occupation of the office of Chancellor of the Exchequer, and in the difficulty of separating any discernible economic policy that bore Macmillan's own stamp from the use of the office itself as a springboard to the Premiership. It is worth remembering just how minor a position Macmillan held in the Churchill Cabinet of 1951; not figuring at all in the initial list and eventually appearing as the third most junior member in a Cabinet of sixteen.[1] As his official biographer has noted, 'the road upwards looked effectively blocked... to an ambitious politician'.[2] It was to be a remarkable rise from Minister of Housing in 1952 via the Ministry of Defence, Foreign Secretaryship and Chancellorship, to be Prime Minister by January 1957. Given that his Premiership has recently been described by one commentator as 'by far the best of Britain's Post-war Prime Ministers, and that his administration performed considerably better than any of their successors', his 'attitude to the economy' being such that it 'would have prevented the galloping inflation of the late 1960s and 1970s', it is perhaps time that some analysis was given to Macmillan's occupation of the Treasury in both economic and political terms.[3] It was, however, to be a Chancellorship neatly divided between the inherited economic policy of the previous administration and the developing Suez Crisis; the latter providing what John Turner has perceptively referred to as 'the opportunity'.[4]

Macmillan inherited the post of Chancellor of the Exchequer from R. A. Butler, who had held the office for four years, in December 1955. Although there exists a range of accounts of the Cabinet re-shuffle of late 1955 – not least by the protagonists themselves – many are at odds and the one insight that can be made with any certainty is that the process was very poorly handled and left plenty of room for the development of strong political resentments, envies and ambitions.[5] This position had, in its turn, been strongly overshadowed by the prolonged clinging to office of Churchill, which had provoked in his successor, Eden, the desire to stamp his own authority by means of a general election, but paradoxically failure to carry this through by a major reconstruction of the government either before or after the May 1955 election. When such a major re-shuffle was not undertaken, the result, as Eden's official biographer remarked, was one of 'discontent, concern and criticism', with one Cabinet colleague remarking that 'Anthony never built a Cabinet in his own mould. He inherited one, and then tinkered with it.'[6] What is clear is that Eden's desire to replace Butler at the Treasury was provoked more by his desire to get Macmillan out of the Foreign Office and replace him with a Foreign Secretary who was more inclined to do the Prime Minister's bidding than was Macmillan. Despite the fact that the Chancellor of the Duchy of Lancaster, Lord Woolton, had told Eden to 'get rid of Butler' and had received the reply 'You are so wise', it was more Eden's distrust of Macmillan's independence of mind, than the fact that the election had had to be followed by packages of deflationary measures and an Autumn Budget, that prompted the move.[7]

Indeed, Eden and Macmillan had clashed most notably over the issue of Europe – where Macmillan had urged a far more positive approach to the Messina Conference than Eden was prepared to make – and, intriguingly, over the situation developing in Egypt, when Eden floated the idea of an international military force to protect the Suez Canal in the event of war between Egypt and Israel, only to be told that Macmillan did 'not propose to pursue' the idea.[8] Certainly, Butler did not demure from Eden's request in the summer of 1955 that he leave the Treasury, asking only that the Prime Minister delay the move, although this made something of a mockery of Eden's declaration in November 1955 in the House of Commons that 'In all his work my Right Hon. Friend, the Chancellor of the Exchequer, will continue to have my full support.'[9] In contrast to Butler's acceptance of the change, Macmillan was furious at Eden's proposal, seeing poisoned chalices all around. Concerning the move from the Foreign Office, Lord Woolton noted that 'Macmillan wondered whether his departure from the Foreign Office at a time when things were not going very well – he described them as "Eden's chickens coming home to roost" – would not give the appearance of failure', whereas on arrival at the Treasury,

Macmillan himself was to note that 'The position is much worse than I had expected. Butler had let things drift, and the reserves are steadily falling. If and when they are all expended, we have total collapse, under Harold Macmillan!'[10] Eden had, however, confided in, of all people Butler, as to how awkward he found Macmillan to deal with as Foreign Secretary. As Butler himself somewhat waspishly noted, 'The PM is an artist far more able and resolute than the newspapers give him credit for. He had, he said sedulously attempted to avoid interference with the Foreign Office. Having been there so long he found it difficult to work with so strong a character as Harold Macmillan.'[11] Whilst Butler went with relative quiescence, although not without some considerable admonishment from his friends, the irate Macmillan was to drive a very hard bargain with Eden. In Macmillan's view there was 'no point in my leaving the Foreign office to be an orthodox Chancellor of the Exchequer. I must be, if not a revolutionary, something of a reformer.' But more sinisterly, at least for Butler, if not at this stage, Eden, he insisted that he must be the 'undisputed head of the Home Front', occupying a position that was 'not inferior' to Butler, and that the latter should not be termed the 'Deputy Prime Minister'. This was a strident posture, but Eden was determined enough to affect the change that he agreed a form of words with Macmillan in that Butler 'in the absence of the Prime Minister ... will continue as hitherto to preside over meetings of the Cabinet'.[12] The rise from third junior spot in the 1951 Cabinet had been meteoric indeed, and lest Eden felt that the manoeuvring had helped his own position, there was always Macmillan's statement to Woolton that 'he saw no reason why if he was going to take over all the troubles of the Treasury, he should be ruled out of the succession for the Premiership in order to ease in Butler', to disabuse him.[13] The opportunity to ditch Eden and elbow Butler aside was not to be long in arriving, but firstly Macmillan had to contend with the peculiar frailty of the British economy.

The policy which Macmillan inherited from Butler was familiar; the maintenance of full employment, stable prices, economic growth, balance of payments equilibrium and moving the pound towards convertibility. The problem lay in squaring the aims of strong economic growth and full employment – it was Butler, after all, who had predicted the doubling of the British standard of living in the next twenty-five years at the 1954 Tory party conference – with stable prices, low inflation and a steady currency.[14] Butler's April

Budget of 1955 has been termed 'a serious blunder . . . handing out £135 million of tax reliefs in the middle of a raging boom'.[15] Certainly Butler's sentiments in February 1955 would not have indicated a 'give away' budget. In minutes to Eden, prior to the February Statement on the economy, Butler was commenting on a deteriorating balance of payments position, largely caused by excessive demand sucking in imports, and he suggested 'a tighter monetary policy and some restraint on the proliferation of hire purchase' to check the position.[16] Accordingly, Butler decided to tighten monetary and credit policies, raising the Bank Rate, which had been at 3 per cent since May 1954, in two stages to 4.5 per cent and reintroducing hire-purchase restrictions which had been abolished the previous July.[17] With the government having allowed the Bank of England to support the rate for transferable sterling in February 1955 – widely viewed by the markets as a significant step towards convertibility – there was a general view that convertibility of sterling would be at a floating, rather than a fixed, rate. This tended towards a situation wherein a weak balance of payments position encouraged speculation against the pound, with a strong position tending to strengthen sterling. With the budget slack and the election won, the economy roared away; demand remained stubbornly unchecked, the balance of payments position, the reserves and sterling all deteriorated under various pressures.[18] By July, Butler had introduced restrictions on bank advances, cut the investment programmes of local authorities and nationalized industries and imposed new credit and hire-purchase restrictions.[19]

By September, however, the July measures were showing few signs of having had any impact and Sir Robert Hall was commenting that the economy was 'in a vicious circle which can only be broken by real deflationary action'.[20] With Butler having to reiterate at the Istanbul meeting of the International Monetary Fund (IMF) that convertibility of the pound would only be at a fixed rate, in an attempt to stem speculation against sterling, it became abundantly clear that an autumn budget could not be avoided. With senior officials, Butler worked out a series of measures designed to further dampen demand in the economy and relieve the strain on the balance of payments.[21] The Budget measures raised purchase tax by 20 per cent at all levels and extended the range of the measure, increased profits tax by 5 per cent, and sharply reduced local authority building programmes. By this stage, however, Butler knew that he was to leave the Treasury and the internal debates on the economy over the summer, where Eden had canvassed the views of various Cabinet colleagues, had been marked by the tabling of a paper by Harold Macmillan, which Eden suggested should be circulated as a Cabinet paper. Entitled 'Dizzy with Success', Macmillan sought in two pages to deal with the problems which the Treasury machine had been grappling with for years. The solution was simple; 'to use a variety of methods (recognising that growth is healthy in itself) calculated to prevent rank and excessive expansion. All that is wrong today is that the pace is a bit too hot.' The methods, according to the Foreign Secretary, involved reducing the basis of credit and raising the Bank Rate; abolishing all subsidies on consumption and reducing all government financed or supported schemes of capital development; achieving a 'real economy of effort' in defence; reducing tax on incomes and purchases and considering 'all schemes for making savings more attractive'. Assuming that his prescription was followed, Macmillan concluded on convertibility that:

> we might as well take the plunge. At present, we are in the absurd position that no foreigner will buy sterling against his future commitments until he needs it, because of the fixed rate. Since he doubts whether we can maintain the $2.80 rate, he holds off. He can't lose by doing so, and he may gain. But do not devalue to a fixed rate. You won't be able to hold it. Get some flexibility.[22]

In common with much of Macmillan's political *oeuvre* this was a bravura performance, mixing as it did hard analysis with seemingly incontrovertible solutions, in a tone that suggested that things were nowhere near as bad as they seemed. Certainly the upbeat tone of the paper was in marked contrast to other contributions and to a somewhat crisis-ridden air surrounding the government. How far it played on Eden's mind in the re-shuffle is difficult to ascertain, it probably ranked below his desire to get Macmillan out of the Foreign Office, although moving both Butler and Macmillan at the same time doubtless had its appeal. It was not long before Macmillan would have the opportunity to put his economic ideas into practice.

The confidence of August, however, was not to carry over into the New Year. In his first statement to the Cabinet, Macmillan's mood was drear. Reviewing the course of events and policy since February 1955, his view was that the trade figures for November and December failed to indicate that the pressure was being relieved. Rather than the required surplus of £250–300 million, the forecast was for a deficit in 1955 of £100 million: figures which, in Macmillan's mind, supported 'the view that our position is getting worse'. With the gold and dollar reserves standing at $2,120 million, just above the critical level of $1,500–2,000 million, they were 'in danger of falling so low that confidence in our ability to maintain the value of sterling will be lost'. The new Chancellor's conclusion was that the government was 'faced with the necessity of taking immediate action over a wide field of a more drastic character than has hitherto seemed necessary. Time is running out.'[23] Throughout January, Macmillan kept up the pressure, commenting that the country had reached 'the same vulnerable position as a private business which persisted in trading beyond its means', calling in minister after minister and pressing for cuts in expenditure, and telling the Economic Policy Committee that failure of the policy would mean a siege economy and 'the final end of the attempt to run our economic affairs on more or less freely organised lines'.[24] By the end of the month, Macmillan was seeking Cabinet sanction for a wide ranging package of measures well in advance of the budget on the grounds that what was needed was 'to take a substantial block from the load now pressing on our resources'. The blend was much as Macmillan had previously outlined but with greater detail and vastly increased scope. The suggestions were *inter alia*: a severe curtailment in the investment programmes of the nationalized industries and local authorities; cuts in all programmes financed by central government, with the abolition of the bread and milk subsidies and a sustained brake on investment in the private sector.[25] The scale of this, however, gave Eden pause for thought. Commenting that there had been several economic statements and two budgets, the Prime Minister's view was that 'the more I feel that if it can possibly be avoided it would be a real advantage to hold over any further statement or action until the Budget'. The budget, Eden thought, should be 'a great occasion, and the only one'.[26]

Macmillan's view was that 'it would be nice if we could do everything in a single operation', but that this was impossible. Citing both the parliamentary timetable and that for setting the local authority expenditure programmes, Macmillan asked for a package of measures in mid-February, including the abolition of the bread and milk subsidies and an increase in the Bank Rate to 5.5 per cent and that the budget should 'give some stimulus to savings and to incentives for the middle classes'.[27] Despite the fact that this argument between Eden and Macmillan continued to rumble on, Macmillan conceded to his officials 'that a startling or revolutionary Budget is off'.

The failure to bring forward a Capital Gains Tax denied Macmillan his budget theme of 'Slash the Speculator' and, accordingly, Macmillan asked his officials to work on the theme of savings and incentives. However, the disagreement between Macmillan and Eden continued to dog efforts to prepare an economic package. In February, Macmillan returned to the attack, stating that a rise in Bank Rate alone would be interpreted as a sign of weakness, whereas a package of measures plus a rise in Bank Rate would be taken as a sign of strength. As Eden temporized on the issue of subsidies, Macmillan's reply was that in being asked 'to abandon the most significant item' he was being expected to 'take a responsibility which, with all my desire to help you, I cannot accept'.[28] Eden was finding that he had swapped a resolute and independent minded Foreign Secretary for a similar Chancellor. When the issue went to Cabinet on 13 February, the divide was clear, with Eden arguing that ending the subsidies would make any appeals on wage restraint impossible, whereas Macmillan continued to argue that the proposed action was necessary 'in order to check on the inflationary movement' with 'the national accounts . . . tending towards insolvency'.[29] Eden's suggestion was that he could accept the package, including raising the Bank Rate but without the removal of the subsidies, which should go into the budget.[30] Over the next two days the Cabinet continued to debate the issue, with Macmillan arguing that he would agree to a policy of phasing the subsidies out if his colleagues would agree to the suspension of tax allowances on investment. Not surprisingly, this infuriated the man who had introduced them, Butler, who commented that it was a 'retrograde step' and that he 'deplored the necessity for adopting this course'. But it was to be of no avail and the Cabinet accepted the new package with its announcement due on 17 February.[31]

By the end of March, however, although the Treasury was conceding that the measures were showing signs of working, Macmillan resumed his assault on the Prime Minister in the run up to the budget, by stating that the only way in which the economy could be restored 'is by really getting down to the defence problem'. Commenting that 'we get no defence from the defence expenditure', Macmillan alleged that 'we know that it is defence expenditure which has broken our backs'. Accordingly, the Chancellor pressed the Prime Minister for 'a new approach to the whole defence problem', otherwise, he would have to 'abandon all ideas of giving some reliefs in the Budget and content myself with a swingeing increase of taxation'.[32] This approach now crystallized into a debate on the shape and content of the budget with Eden's private secretary, Frederick Bishop, commenting that whilst a budget which cut government expenditure would please government supporters, he did not think that they 'would particularly like the cut to be on defence'. Bishop's advice to Eden was that the budget should be 'temporising' with 'some little encouragement and incentive to the middle classes'.[33] The Treasury, by contrast, as the Permanent Secretary, Sir Edward Bridges minuted to Macmillan, believed that 'the safe side of this Budget is the stiff side'.[34] Prodigiously armed with the Treasury's latest statistics, Macmillan confided in the Prime Minister that in the view of his advisers there would be an economic crisis between August and November. (In view of later events they could not have known how correct they would be.) 'On present form', as Macmillan put it, 'the betting is pretty heavy odds on compulsory devaluation', with the only solution being increased taxation or reductions in government expenditure to raise between £100 and £150 million. Declaring that everybody was looking to the budget to 'decide the issue', the Chancellor proposed a package which would raise £144 million, whilst handing out £41 million on the savings package and allowances.[35] Eden finally had to acquiesce and the result was a deflationary budget dressed in the language of growth; as one commentator has noted, 'the combination of an expansionist speech and a restrictant Budget . . . [was] . . . symptomatic of Macmillan's whole conduct of economic policy'.[36] But in the budget which had introduced Premium Bonds, Macmillan had not been able to do anything about defence, although he was to return to this issue only a few weeks later.

In the immediate wake of the budget, Macmillan had Eden agree to a saving of £100 million in the Estimates for 1956–7. By early May, Macmillan was chiding the Minister of Defence, Walter Monckton, that his department was £20 million short of the £45 million which he was expected to contribute to the overall total.[37] When the issue went to a small group of ministers later in the month, Macmillan pressed the case that without major reductions in defence expenditure, cuts would have to fall on the social side, including increasing charges for school meals, milk and prescriptions, a proposal which the Lord Privy Seal, Butler, termed 'of doubtful social wisdom'. With Eden agreeing that it was 'highly desirable' to avoid further reductions in social expenditure, the hapless Monckton was told to press for what cuts he could and report to the full Cabinet in June.[38] By the time of the June meeting, Macmillan had only been able to secure £72 million of his £100 million package and as the Chief Whip, Ted Heath, commented, 'Government supporters would be disappointed that better results had not been achieved', and that 'a difficult political situation might therefore arise in the House of Commons'. The Prime Minister, this time with no prompting from Macmillan, took the view that 'the right course was to look again at the possibility of some effective cut in defence production', and accordingly, Monckton was sent off to try again.[39]

With the Suez Crisis about to intervene and come increasingly to dominate all other issues, Macmillan could have drawn some comfort from the Report of the Committee on Balance of Payments Prospects, which predicted a current surplus of £135 million for the first six months of 1956, during which period the reserves had risen by £95 million. On the basis that current deflationary policies were not relaxed, the Committee felt able to forecast an overall surplus for 1956, although it concluded that

> Even if we secure the better outrun for which we hope this year, we still have a long way to go before we have re-established our economy to the point at which exports are expanding fast enough to meet the demand for imports and provide a margin for building up the reserves.[40]

There could be no let up in the deflationary pressure and despite the increasing strain caused by Suez, Macmillan returned to the issue of defence savings. As he reported to Monckton, he was still £24 million short of his £100 million target and that whilst there was 'no intention ... of trying to find the £24 million and enough to cover the extra Defence expenditure on the Suez affair', he was still expecting defence to yield the £24 million.[41] By October, Macmillan had managed to close the gap to £5 million, with defence, health, agriculture and education all realizing further savings.[42] Thus, on the eve of the major strains of Suez falling on the economy, Macmillan with considerable insouciance, returned to the issue of defence with the new Minister of Defence, Anthony Head.

As Macmillan put it at the end of November, 'we face the most difficult economic situation in our history'. The Chancellor forecast drains on the gold and dollar reserves and an oil shortage, with 'the impact of these events' being 'felt in our economy for a long time to come'. Commenting that the circumstances made the need for economies more pressing than ever, Macmillan's view was that it was 'inevitable' that he 'should look to the Defence Budget for substantial savings'. Macmillan argued that he now needed greater savings than had been contemplated in August, and he suggested that the order of priorities which had been established in defence policy in October 1955 now needed to be radically overhauled. Macmillan's view was that the V-bomber force should be limited 'in more conservative terms' and a sustained attempt should be made to convince the Americans to contribute a greater share to the development of ground to ground ballistic missiles. Furthermore, the Suez experience had convinced Macmillan that there was now no point in even considering fighting 'local wars'. Accordingly, there should be 'major reductions in our forces in the Middle East and Far East', as the 'budgetary saving should . . . be very large – to say nothing of the effect on our balance of payments'. On the issue of global warfare, Macmillan's view was that even while this was at the bottom on defence priorities, the country could not afford to 'carry too many insurance policies'. As the Chancellor put it, the country could not 'hope to emerge from a global war except in ruins' and, accordingly, Macmillan suggested that this programme should be cut to an extent that did not diminish Britain's ability to influence world affairs and did not alienate essential allies. As Macmillan concluded: 'there is an urgent need to make real economies and to show that the Government are making them. I hope therefore that I shall very soon be able too to discuss with you the "ceiling" for the 1957–58 Defence Budget.'[43] It was an intriguing position. To be fair to Macmillan he had had the scale of defence budget in his sights for some time; but the Chancellor had been the leading cheerleader of the Suez operation and despite his protestations about the need for economies, he as much as anyone had taken the lead in imperilling the economy in the Suez Crisis.

On the eve of the Suez crisis, therefore, the condition of the economy could hardly be described as robust. Action by the Treasury followed immediately upon the nationalization of the Suez Canal on 26 July 1956. Two days later the Suez Canal Company's assets in the UK and France were frozen, Egyptian sterling balances were blocked and Egypt was expelled from the transferable account area. Only one week later, however, the Treasury was arguing that economic sanctions would take a long time to have any impact and that the key to their success was American support and action. The Treasury had not, as yet, given its full consideration to the likely economic impact of any protracted crisis, but the Chancellor's position was already fixed as the American diplomat, Robert Murphy, reported:

> I have had private separate and lengthy talks with Eden and Macmillan. . . . They said British Government has decided to drive Nasser out of Egypt. The decision they declared is firm. They expressed simple conviction military action is necessary and inevitable. . . . Macmillan indulged in much graphic discussion on British past history and stressed that if they had to go down now the Government and he believed British people would rather do so on this issue and become perhaps another Netherlands. To do another Munich leading to progressive deterioration of ME position and in end the inevitable disaster is he said something he Eden and his colleagues in Government are simply not prepared to do.

This telegram from Murphy to the American Secretary of State, Dulles, somewhat belies the accounts which have stressed the supposed confusions over US support for British military action. Indeed, despite the fact that Murphy had 'advanced all of the considerations' which Dulles and President Eisenhower had 'raised':

> Eden, Macmillan and Lloyd showed throughout unexpected calm and no hysteria. They act as though they really have taken a decision after profound reflection. They are flexible on procedures leading up to showdown but insist over and over again that whatever conferences, arrangements, public postures and manoeuvres might be necessary, at the end they are determined to use force.[44]

This message from Murphy to Dulles, drew from Eisenhower to Eden, the President's 'personal conviction' of the 'unwisdom even of contemplating the use of military force', believing 'that the American reaction would be severe and that great areas of the world would share that reaction'.[45] Thus, as early as the last day of July, positions had been struck which would remain pretty consistent throughout the crisis; certainly Macmillan's position would remain relatively unaffected by the impact of the crisis on the economy.

By 8 August, the Joint Permanent Secretary at the Treasury, Sir Edward Bridges, warned Macmillan that the Suez situation was already putting the balance of payments and gold and dollar reserves under considerable strain, and he warned that even if the London Conference were successful this was likely to remain the case. The more protracted the crisis became the more the proportionate strain on the economy was likely to be. To Bridges:

> The action to be taken is almost totally different according to the situation which we are faced with – a limited war, or a not so limited war – a war in which we go it alone, or a war in which we have the Americans with us from the onset. Frankly, I doubt whether anything much can be done under this head until we can know more clearly the assumptions which should be made . . . it may be that there are one or two essential matters that should be looked at to avoid our being caught short.[46]

It was a prescient view: Macmillan knew the assumptions but did not inform his officials, and he knew the Treasury advice but did not inform the Cabinet. Macmillan did ask the Treasury to work on a package of contingency measures, which included a 6*d*. rise in the rate of income tax, an increase of between 6*d*. and 1*s*. in petrol duty, increases in tobacco duty and perhaps on purchase and profit taxes. Given that any military venture would be bound to raise government expenditure, the Treasury was gloomy as to the efficacy of monetary policy and they also considered raw material import and exchange controls, along with the possible recourse to a fully floating exchange rate and 'a really big step backwards from convertibility'. The Treasury concluded that 'we are not in at all a happy position to bear any great degree of extra strain on our resources. Our resources are still dangerously low, and are certain to fall pretty sharply this month'.[47] This was a dire portent, representing as it did the utter ruin of the economic policy which the government had followed since 1951. Given the centrality of trying to edge sterling towards convertibility, its strength or otherwise was widely taken as a crude measure of the country's economic strength; therefore, anything which tended to actively encourage speculation against sterling had been anathema to previous Chancellors. There is little doubt that had the Treasury's view gone to Cabinet then there may well have been rather more reluctance to support military action against Egypt.

By early September, the Treasury had become thoroughly alarmed at the prospect of unilateral British action. Bridges outlined two alternative scenarios: the first envisaged Britain acting in accordance with United Nations wishes and overt support from the USA, Commonwealth and other countries; the second, rather prophetically, foresaw Britain, France and one or two other countries acting in opposition to the UN, USA, Commonwealth and other countries. As Bridges saw the situation:

> It seems to us that unless we can secure at least US support and a fairly unified Commonwealth then it is not possible to predict either the exact timing or the magnitude of the strains that are likely to come on our currency. At the worst, however, the strains might be so great that, whatever precautionary measures were taken we should be unable to maintain the value of the currency. . . . What this points to therefore is the vital necessity from the point of view of the currency and our economy of ensuring that we do not go it alone, and that we have the maximum US support.

This memorandum, with its trenchant warnings, is annotated by Macmillan with a laconic 'Yes: this is just the trouble the US are being very difficult.'[48] Remarkably enough, having had copious advice from the Treasury over the last six weeks and armed with this latest gloomy prediction, Macmillan went to Cabinet on 11 September, four days after receiving the Treasury's memo and one day after annotating it, and urged the Cabinet towards a military solution. Macmillan argued that:

> This was of great importance from the point of view of the national economy. If we could achieve a quick and satisfactory settlement of this issue, confidence in sterling would be restored; but if a settlement was long delayed the cost and the uncertainty would undermine our financial position.

This was an intriguing reformulation of the advice tendered by Bridges, which omitted the *sine qua non* of the Treasury mandarin's memorandum, the absolute necessity of having American support.

By the end of September, the Treasury was contemplating what action it could take if the drain on reserves continued. Among the possible options which they and the Bank of England considered were: the breaking up of the transferable account area and a reversion to a bilateral system of payments; the depreciation of sterling, either through devaluation or letting the rate float; and the possibility of approaching the International Monetary Fund for a fund drawing and claiming the Waiver on interest payments under the US Loan Agreement. Most of these options were considered to be as problematic as the problem they were attempting to solve. Contributing to this discussion the Chief Economic Advisor, Sir Robert Hall, remarked that 'sterling could hardly remain a currency in which people would hold substantial balances if we had another devaluation so soon after 1949' and there was general agreement that parity should be held as long as it was possible.[49] Throughout October, as the military situation developed, the Treasury continued to report somewhat bleakly to Macmillan that at least tacit American sympathy was essential if Britain's position were not to become catastrophic. Sir Leslie Rowan, the Second Secretary at the Treasury, estimated a loss of $80 million for October, and calculated that the reserves would fall below $2,000 million by the end of the year, what he termed 'a rather crucial dividing line'. The Treasury and the Bank of England were split over whether an approach should be made to the IMF, with the Treasury favouring an early approach on the grounds that it would not appear as if the country had been forced into such action, whereas the Governor of the Bank argued that an approach would, in and of itself, be construed as a sign of weakness. Both, however, were united in the view that without reasonable Anglo-American relations, either an approach to the IMF or a potential claim on the Waiver, would be more difficult than otherwise.[50] On 30 October, the day after Israel had attacked Egypt, and the day on which the Anglo-French ultimatums had been issued, Macmillan chaired a meeting of senior Treasury and Bank of England officials and declared that the policy was 'to remain firm and see the issue through'.[51]

Before the British and French landings on 5 November, it was becoming very difficult to remain firm and see the issue through.

By 2 November, the Treasury estimated that $50 million had been lost in two days, and reasoned that if the Canal were closed and the pipelines cut, the country would face a shortage of oil amounting to 25 per cent of total supplies, with the likely cost of obtaining alternative supplies costing between $500 and $700 million per year. Contemplating 'emergency action', the Treasury again rehearsed a familiar set of options, including approaching the IMF, imposition of a range of physical controls and exchange rate policy. Despite intensive analysis, the officials believed that they had reached 'a somewhat negative set of conclusions', in that the only way in which the capital outflow could be stemmed was by going to the IMF, whilst addressing the balance of payments problem through fiscal and monetary measures. The first intimation that the Cabinet had of how precarious the economic situation had become, occurred in the midst of a discussion of the ultimatums to be issued to Israel and Egypt, and the likelihood of this causing 'offence to American public opinion'. Macmillan had observed, with the absolute minimum of detail that 'Our reserves of gold and dollars were still falling at a dangerously rapid rate; and, in view of the extent to which we might have to rely on American economic assistance, we could not afford to alienate the US Government more than was absolutely necessary.'[52] Given the view of his officials and his own knowledge, Macmillan's use of the word 'might' is coy in the extreme. By the night of 5 November, however, Macmillan was telephoning the US, in advance of a Cabinet meeting in London on the morning of 6 November, in an attempt to arrange support for sterling, only to be told that no such support would be forthcoming without a cease-fire. With $85 million having been lost from the reserves in the first week of November, Macmillan was facing what his officials had been predicting for months. One commentator has remarked on the absence of 'stark' memoranda from Treasury officials for the days 5–6 November, but given that the officials had been telling their political master exactly what was likely to happen, with increasing force since 8 August, the absence seems of little note.[53] Before entering Cabinet on 6 November, Macmillan told the Foreign Secretary, Selwyn Lloyd, that 'in view of the financial and economic pressures, we must stop'.[54] According to Butler, Macmillan had 'switched overnight from being the foremost protagonist of intervention to being the leading influence for disengagement'.[55]

With a cease-fire arranged for midnight GMT on 6 November, worse was to come for the Chancellor, in that he was shortly to learn that a cease-fire, of itself, would not be enough to satisfy the Americans, but that the price of economic assistance would be withdrawal from Egypt. The Treasury, via the British Ambassador in the US, Sir Harold Caccia, sought the likely American response to a request for standby arrangements with the IMF of $236 million on the gold tranche, $325 million on the first credit tranche and an approach to the Export–Import Bank in New York. Caccia's reply was that 'there is at present no possibility of aid, which in any event would not be available until after further Congressional action and I think we must take it that there is at present no possibility of an EXIM bank loan'.[56] The stumbling block for the British Cabinet was that in an effort to retain some dignity and some control over the situation, they insisted on British troops being allowed to take part in the United Nations Emergency Force, then being assembled to oversee the Israeli–Egyptian cease-fire. Try as they might, however, with Selwyn Lloyd dispatched to New York to argue the case, British participation would not be countenanced by the UN or the USA. The situation in London, moreover, was continuing to deteriorate with the new Permanent Secretary at the Treasury, Sir Roger Makins, informing Macmillan, that in the view of the Governor of the Bank of England, sterling was 'a major casualty of recent events and that radical treatment . . . [would] . . . be required to save it', with the most important ameliorative measure 'an improvement in our relations with the Americans'.[57] Treasury and Bank officials were gloomy as to the prospects, noting that:

> We cannot continue to lose reserves at the present rate, and continue at the same time to hold sterling at its present value . . . the cohesion of the Commonwealth would be severely tested and there might be dangerous consequences to the structure of NATO arising from our inability to meet its commitments.

The officials, moreover, were in no doubt, as they had consistently been, as to the necessary steps: 'the most important and adequate measure which might be taken involves an approach to the United States and would require a friendly and compliant attitude on their part'.[58] A view that was reinforced the following day, when Rowan informed Makins that 'we should take every practicable step in other spheres of policy, eg withdrawal of troops from Egypt, to ensure the opening at the earliest possible date of general conversations with the United States and preferably at the highest level'.[59] Still the Cabinet tried to cling to participation in the UNEF as a face-saving device.

Macmillan now began to act in a manner which suggests that if he had not engineered 'the opportunity' he certainly perceived it. He and the Tory grandee Lord Salisbury called on the American Ambassador, Winthrop Aldrich, at his official residence in London. With Eden having announced that he was to go to Jamaica to 'rest', Lloyd in New York and Butler acting as Prime Minister, Macmillan now acted sedulously to cultivate American opinion. In the course of a long conversation with Aldrich, much of which was political window dressing, Macmillan revealed the economic figures to the ambassador, in advance of telling the Cabinet and indicated that a change of policy was imminent. Aldrich drew the conclusion 'that the British Cabinet is prepared to withdraw from Egypt now and leave to the UN the settlement of the problems involved in the relations between Israel and the Arab world and the problems relating to the operation of the Canal'.[60] This was remarkable in that it was not the policy which was being followed, and indeed, foretold a change in that policy. But, the same evening, 18 November, Macmillan was back in Ambassador's residence, although this time alone. If the earlier conversation had left Aldrich 'wondering whether... some sort of movement is on foot in the Cabinet to replace Eden', the second could have left him in no doubt. As he telegraphed to Washington:

Macmillan came to residence tonight at his request.... Eden has had physical breakdown and will have to go on vacation immediately, first for one week and then for another, and this will lead to his retirement. Government will be run by triumvirate of Butler, Macmillan and Salisbury. While Macmillan did not say so specifically, I gather that eventual set up will be Butler Prime Minister, Macmillan Foreign Secretary, Lloyd Chancellor of the Exchequer, with Salisbury remaining Lord President of Council. Possibly Macmillan might be Prime Minister. First action after Eden's departure for reasons of health will be on withdrawal of British troops from Egypt. Macmillan said, 'if you can give us a fig leaf to cover our nakedness I believe we can get a majority of the Cabinet to vote for such withdrawal without requiring conditions in connection with location of United Nations forces and methods of re-opening and operating Canal although younger members of the Cabinet will be strongly opposed'.[61]

As yet, however, there was no Cabinet agreement on unconditional withdrawal.

It was not to be long, however, before there was, and a Cabinet which had seen nothing from the Treasury for months, began to have papers tabled with each one prophesying ever more dire consequences as a result of continued American alienation. On 20 November, Macmillan revealed to the Cabinet, for the first time, the enormity of the situation which confronted them:

> The Chancellor of the Exchequer said that the Cabinet might shortly face the grave choice of deciding whether to mobilise all our financial resources in order to maintain the sterling/dollar rate at its present level, or to let the rate find its own level with the possible consequences that sterling might cease to be an international currency.

The Cabinet was doubtless shocked to learn of the grave choice confronting them and may well have felt inclined to question what the Chancellor had been doing for months had they known the substance of earlier Treasury advice. As it was, Macmillan began the process of softening the Cabinet up to change the policy, as he had already intimated to Aldrich, stating that 'we could not look for any assistance from the US in this course until the situation in the Middle East had been sufficiently clarified to enable us to re-establish our normal political relations with the US government'.[62] Memoranda from officials, which had previously been met by profound apathy, were now assiduously produced to keep up the pressure on the Cabinet. Accordingly, a very sharp memo from Rowan to Makins and Macmillan, which declared that:

> if we are to have any real chance of succeeding in our crash action, or better still of avoiding the necessity for it the first essential is the re-establishment of relations with the United States. It is quite clear that there is a conflict between economic and political considerations, and that the longer political considerations are allowed to prevail the greater danger there is to the whole fabric of our currency[63]

served to bring the Cabinet, meeting the same day, to a position of authorizing a 'token' withdrawal of British forces. However, the Cabinet remained convinced that full withdrawal should remain contingent upon clearance of the Canal and negotiations on the future status and operation of the Canal.

But this was not enough to convince the sceptics within the State Department and the Treasury; Hoover, the Secretary of State, and Humphrey, the Economic Secretary, continually informed Caccia and Lloyd that a resumption of relations along with the provision of financial aid was contingent upon 'full compliance with UN resolutions', and that the 'introduction of UN force and phased withdrawal of UK–French force should take place without delay and . . . once this is well under way we can enter into consultation with the British on basic issues'.[64] Humphrey, however, was somewhat disingenuous in stating that he was 'profoundly shocked' by the losses in Britain and that the Americans were prepared to act as soon as 'HMG has shown in a way which the world could accept that we were conforming to rather than defying the UN'.[65] Once the political situation allowed, the US would support drawing on the gold and first credit tranches, and a loan from the EXIM bank.[66] Although an increasingly cordial relationship between Macmillan and the US administration was being built up, through the channel of Aldrich, a frosty atmosphere continued to mar Anglo-American contacts in New York and Washington. As Selwyn Lloyd reported to R. A. Butler, acting in Eden's stead,

> the hard core of policy-makers some of whom have been strongly pro-British in the past are now against us . . . if we are going to have difficulty with the Party over announcing withdrawal I think we may have to tell certain selected individuals that the Americans have no intention of lifting a finger to help preserve us from financial disaster until they are certain that we are removing ourselves from Port Said quickly.[67]

This brought to an end a week of Cabinet meetings which had fruitlessly sought some face-saving compromise allowing as dignified a withdrawal as possible. The economic pressures had, in the end, however, proved to be too strong. As Macmillan informed the Cabinet on 28 November, the situation was so bad that an approach would have to be made to the IMF, but:

> For this purpose the goodwill of the United States Government was necessary; and it was evident that this goodwill could not be obtained without an immediate and unconditional undertaking to withdraw the Anglo-French force from Port Said.[68]

Having led the *volte face*, Macmillan was now speeding it along. At the Cabinet the following day he reiterated the point, claiming that the likely loss for November would be around $270 million, with $100 million lost in the third week of the month alone.[69] Two days later, the Chancellor, by now thoroughly warmed to his theme, told the Cabinet that the reserves had fallen below the benchmark figure of $2,000 million, and that by the year end, would not be far from the lowest post-war level of $1,340 million in September 1949, the outcome of which had been devaluation. In Macmillan's view 'no fundamental improvement in the situation could be expected unless we succeeded in re-establishing normal political relations with the United States'.[70] The Cabinet acquiesced and the formal announcement was made in the House of Commons on 3 December.

There was to be further political and economic fall-out before the end of the affair. With Eden not returning to London until 14 December, Macmillan in the United States for meetings with Treasury officials could only have been delighted to learn that his cultivation of Aldrich had paid off. As Macmillan informed R. A. Butler:

> In the course of a most private conversation with Mr Humphrey, he undertook to give us all possible assistance.
>
> He said it was like a business deal. They were putting a lot of money into the re-organisation of Britain and they would hope very much that the business would be successful. But, of course, when you were reconstructing a business that was in difficulties, the personal problems could not be ruled out.
>
> I said: 'Don't you trust the board?' and he said: 'Well, since you ask me, I think it would be as well if we could deal as much as possible with the directors.' This rather cryptic observation he enlarged on to say that he would like to feel that he could always be on terms of private, and, where necessary, telephonic, communication with you and me.[71]

Explicit evidence that the American administration had at least tacitly approved of the replacement of Eden. But the ultimate prize was still some weeks away and Macmillan had to shepherd the economy through the economic crisis. By 8 December, Washington was reporting to London that 'we now look certain of getting $1,300 million from the International Monetary Fund', and commented that 'another $700 million would give us the formidable total of $2 billion'.[72] But it was to be 21 December before Macmillan was able to report, to the recently returned Eden, that the EXIM Bank had authorized a line of credit of $500 million to Britain.[73] The Governor of the Bank of England, however, drew very firm conclusions from the Suez affair, claiming that it had exposed to public view weaknesses in the economy of which the Bank and Treasury had been long aware. The economy had been moved to uneasy equilibrium, but the basic problems had been left unsolved and confidence in sterling had been maintained by only a slender margin. To Cobbold, it was time to mount 'a radical attack on some of the fundamentals' and he argued that 'the fundamental trouble is that the economy and the public purse have been over-extended for many years'. He concluded that, 'dramatic far-reaching and convincing measures were needed and that there was no point in trying to "keep up with the Jones"' in relation to political and military affairs which would destroy the country's economic strength.[74] Eden's view was that 'Mr Governor rather likes making our blood run cold', and although he did concede that one of the main lessons of Suez was that economically Britain was no longer strong enough to 'go it alone', given that Cobbold's suggestions could only be met by checking public expenditure, he saw this as raising 'acute political difficulties'.[75] Eden then asked his Chancellor if there were any way of easing the burden on sterling, to which Macmillan replied that:

> There is no way of avoiding the dangers which come from our being bankers to the sterling area. We have inherited an old family business which used to be very profitable and sound. The trouble is that the liabilities are four times the assets. In the old days a business of this kind, like Coutt's or Cox's bank would have been sold to one of the big five. The trouble is I do not know who is to buy the sterling area banking system. I tried it out on Humphrey but he was not taking it. So we must either carry on the business with all its risks, or wind it up and pay 5s in the £.[76]

Stated with typical insouciance, Macmillan was arguing that the issues of confidence and the strain on sterling would simply have to be borne.

This was to be almost the last exchange between Eden as Prime Minister and the man who was to supplant him, but not quite. Only two days before his resignation as Prime Minister, Eden could not resist annotating a memorandum by Macmillan on the 'State of the Economy' with his view that 'I do not think that the events of

Suez can be reckoned as a tactical defeat'.[77] But for some time, the state of the economy had been taking second place to a bigger prize, that of replacing Eden as Prime Minister. The manoeuvring had began even before Eden had left for his 'rest' in Jamaica, and it had continued thereafter, and it was to rebound to Butler's disadvantage. To the casual, and indeed, to the informed observer, if the press reports following Eden's resignation are anything to go by, it appeared that Butler was the natural successor to Eden in the same way that the latter had been to Churchill. The end of his spell at the Treasury, however, had been marked by firstly overheating the economy and then having to take strong deflationary measures to correct it and this undoubtedly tarnished his reputation. Still, as the man who had 'acted' as Prime Minister in the absence of both Churchill and Eden, and then of Eden alone, it was widely assumed that Butler would inherit. This view, however, took no account of views in the Conservative Party on Butler's performance in the absence of Eden. He had, at best, been a lukewarm supporter of the Suez operation, although loyal to Eden, and it had fallen to Butler to chair a Cabinet and defend a policy in the House of Commons, unconditional withdrawal, which was deeply unpopular in the wider party.[78] Following an announcement in the Commons on 22 November, which began softening the Party up for full withdrawal, Butler and Macmillan were due to address the backbench 1922 Committee the same evening. It was to be, according to Butler's biographer, 'a highly expensive mistake', with Butler speaking 'briefly, sombrely and somewhat flatly', whereas Macmillan produced 'a veritable political organ voluntary lasting thirty-five minutes – pulling out every stop and striking every majestic chord', and it certainly had its impact. In the view of the then backbench MP Enoch Powell:

> One of the most horrible things that I remember in politics was seeing the two of them at that 1922 Committee Meeting – seeing the way in which Harold Macmillan, with all the skill of the old actor manager, succeeded in false-footing Rab. The sheer devilry of it verged upon the disgusting.[79]

It may not have been exactly a defining moment, but Macmillan had taken another step towards the Premiership. Unlike Butler, no taint of ambivalence over Suez attached to Macmillan, he had been amongst the strongest advocates of force. His apostasy could be disguised as a simple recognition of the facts and, even so, it was Butler, not Macmillan, who had been acting head of the administration when unconditional withdrawal was announced.

The denouement, when it came, was brusque. As Eden's biographer has commented on the Prime Minster's first appearance in the House of Commons: 'at that moment one knew it was all over'.[80] The Christmas recess then intervened and although the Chief Whip and the Chairman of the Party both thought that Eden could get through to the summer recess, Macmillan had told Butler that younger members of the Cabinet 'did not think Eden could or would go on'. A fact which in Butler's mind became linked with 'frequent talks and reunions . . . in the study at No 11' and 'a secret meeting of four Cabinet Ministers . . . on the very day the public drama of Eden's resignation began to unfold'.[81] Ostensibly, Eden had been told, on the basis of a number of medical opinions, that if he did not resign then he would die. Eden told his last Cabinet that he was to resign that evening, 9 January, and left the Cabinet Room with Butler and Macmillan. The rest of the Cabinet was then asked by Lord Salisbury, in the presence of the Lord Chancellor, Lord Kilmuir, as to their preference for the succession. The result produced an eleven to three majority for Macmillan. He saw the Queen the next day, 10 January, and the deed was done; Macmillan was Prime Minister.

It is impossible to separate Macmillan's tenure at the Treasury from his own breathtaking rise through the Cabinet ranks; rising from junior minister in 1951 to be the incumbent of two of the highest offices of state by 1955–6. Furthermore, assessing Macmillan's record as Chancellor, just over a year in office and with only one budget, is rendered all the more problematic in that it is inextricably linked with the political dynamics of both his rise and the opportunity represented by Suez. It is certain that Macmillan could do very little else than continue the policies inherited from Butler, but there are strong indications that he wanted to stamp his own authority on the office and, as the Sandy's Defence Review of 1957 betokens, the defence budget would have been early in the firing line. Additionally, a more pro-active line on Europe may have been forthcoming, although the later pursuit of this and Macmillan's involvement in Suez and cultivation of the US, probably doomed him and the pursuit of the policy, in General de Gaulle's eyes. The early indications of how a Macmillan Chancellorship would develop are, however, obscured by Suez. It should be noted, nevertheless, that Macmillan, on taking the job, had wrung a range of concessions and already perceived himself as being in a position to mount a challenge to Butler. It is perhaps too much to see Suez as a concerted effort by Macmillan to unseat Eden, but then it is also very difficult to account for the absence of any Treasury memoranda on the likely outcome, until almost the very end of the affair when they came thick and fast. There is also the testimony of Sir Guy Millard, Eden's Downing Street private secretary, who handled the paperwork concerning Suez, that: 'I'm not sure Eden saw the Treasury warnings. I didn't see them. Macmillan saw them, but he was a hawk.'[82]

There can, however, be no doubt that by 18 November, when Macmillan opened lines of communication to the US administration through Aldrich, that the Chancellor had the clear ambition of gaining the Prime Ministership and little else subsequently gives cause for much doubt. Once presented with 'the opportunity', Macmillan seized it with, depending on one's point of view, either an élan or ruthlessness, which, in either case, was quite breathtaking. His own biographer has noted that during the Suez Crisis one of the books which Macmillan read was Villari's biography of Machiavelli.[83] It is fair to conclude that Macmillan was well acquainted with the works of the subject.

NOTES

1. A. Howard, *RAB: The Life of R. A. Butler* (London: Jonathan Cape, 1987), p. 180.
2. A. Horne, *Macmillan, 1894–1956* (London: Macmillan, 1988), p. 332.
3. R. Lamb, *Macmillan: The Emerging Truth* (London: John Murray, 1995), p. 15.
4. J. Turner, *Macmillan* (London: Longman, 1994), pp. 95–126.
5. See, for example, H. Macmillan, *Riding the Storm, 1956–1959* (London: Macmillan, 1971), pp. 692–3; R. A. Butler, *The Art of the Possible* (London, 1971), pp. 178–82.
6. R. Rhodes James, *Anthony Eden* (London: Weidenfeld & Nicolson, 1987 edn) pp. 404–5.
7. A. Howard, op. cit., p. 15. See also J. Turner, op. cit., p. 106.
8. R. Rhodes James, op. cit., p. 410. Given the amount of material relating to the establishment of both the Common Market and the European Free Trade Association, no attempt has been made to discuss these

issues here. For the most recent analysis, cf. J. R. V. Ellison, 'Perfidious Albion? Britain, Plan G and European Integration, 1955–1956', *Contemporary British History*, vol. 10, no. 4 (1996), pp. 1–34. The relevant Treasury papers are at PRO T234/181 to 236.

9. Howard, op. cit., pp. 215–20.
10. Quoted, Turner, op. cit., p. 106.
11. Butler, op. cit., pp. 180–1.
12. Turner, op. cit., p. 106; Howard, op. cit., p. 217 and H. Macmillan, *Tides of Fortune 1945–1955* (London, 1969), pp. 692–3.
13. Quoted in Howard, op. cit., p. 221.
14. On the general performance of the economy in the 1950s cf. S. Brittan, *The Treasury under the Tories, 1951–1964* (Harmondsworth: Penguin, 1964); J. C. R. Dow, *The Management of the British Economy, 1945–1960* (Cambridge: Cambridge University Press, 1964); A. Shonfield, *British Economic Policy since the War* (Harmondsworth, 1959) and G. D. N. Worsnick and P. Ady (eds), *The British Economy in the 1950s* (Oxford: Oxford University Press, 1962).
15. Brittan, op. cit., p. 177.
16. PRO T172/2126, Chancellor's Personal Secret and Top Secret Carbons. Minute from R. A. Butler to Sir Anthony Eden, 17 February 1955.
17. For the debate on the issue cf. ibid., 'Economic Situation', Memorandum by Sir Robert Hall, 6 April 1955.
18. See PRO T171/450 to 468, 1955 Budget.
19. PRO T172/2126, op. cit., The Economic Situation and Government Expenditure. Letter from the Chancellor of the Exchequer to Ministers in Charge of Civil Spending Departments, 3 August 1955.
20. PRO PREM 11/887, memorandum from Sir Robert Hall to the Chancellor of the Exchequer, 1 September 1955.
21. PRO T234/266, Balance of Payments Prospects. Report of Committee on Balance of Payments Prospects, 14 October 1955 and 10th Meeting of Economic Policy Committee, 19 October 1955.
22. PRO CAB 129/77 CP (55) 111, The Economic Situation. Memorandum by the Secretary of State for Foreign Affairs, 30 August 1955.
23. PRO CAB 129/77 CP(56) 7, The Economic Situation. Memorandum by the Chancellor of the Exchequer, 5 January 1956.
24. PRO PREM 11/1324, UK Economic Situation, 1956.
25. PRO CAB 129/70 CP(56) 17, The Economic Situation. Memorandum by the Chancellor of the Exchequer, 21 January 1956.
26. PRO PREM 11/1324, UK Economic Situation, 1956. Letter from the Prime Minister to the Chancellor of the Exchequer, 29 January 1956.
27. PRO T172/2127, Chancellor's Personal Secret and Top Secret Carbons. Letter from the Chancellor of the Exchequer to the Prime Minister, 3 February 1956.
28. Ibid. Letters from the Chancellor of the Exchequer to the Prime Minister, 11 and 13 February 1956.
29. PRO PREM11/1324, op. cit., Cabinet, Confidential Annex CM(56)12 Minute 2, 13 February 1956.
30. Ibid. Note for the Record, 13 February 1956.

31. Ibid. Cabinet, Confidential Annex CM(56) 14 Conclusions, 15 February 1956.
32. PRO PREM 11/1326, Budget 1956. Letter from the Chancellor of the Exchequer to the Prime Minister, 23 March 1956.
33. Ibid. Memorandum from F. A. Bishop to the Prime Minister, 26 March 1956.
34. PRO T171/473, 1956 Budget. Minute from Sir Edward Bridges to the Chancellor of the Exchequer, 26 March 1956.
35. PRO PREM 11/1326, op. cit. Budget. Memorandum from the Chancellor of the Exchequer to the Prime Minister, 5 April 1956.
36. Brittan, op. cit., p. 183.
37. PRO T172/2127, op. cit. Letter from the Chancellor of the Exchequer to the Minister of Defence, 9 May 1956.
38. PRO PREM11/1327, Government Expenditure, Estimates for 1956. Government Expenditure: Economies. Cabinet Gen 527/1st Meeting, 16 May 1956.
39. Ibid. Cabinet CP(56) 43rd Conclusions, 14 June 1956.
40. PRO T234/266, Balance of Payments Prospects, 1955–1958. Committee on Balance of Payments Prospects, Report on Balance of Payments Prospects for 1956, 4 July 1956.
41. PRO T172/2127, op. cit. Letter from the Chancellor of the Exchequer to the Minister of Defence, 20 September 1956.
42. PRO PREM 11/1327, Government Expenditure. Estimates for 1956. Cabinet CM(56) 71st Conclusions. Minute 1, 18 October 1956.
43. PRO T172/2127, op. cit. Letter from the Chancellor of the Exchequer to the Minister of Defence, 14 November 1956.
44. Quoted in A. Gorst and L. Johnman, *The Suez Crisis* (London: Routledge, 1996), p. 63.
45. Quoted, ibid., p. 66.
46. Quoted, ibid., p. 128.
47. Quoted, ibid., p. 129.
48. Quoted, ibid., p. 129.
49. PRO T236/4188, Measures to Protect Sterling. Memorandum by Sir R. Hall, 2 October 1956.
50. Ibid., The Reserves. Memorandum from Sir L. Rowan to Sir R. Makins, 26 October 1956.
51. Ibid., Note for the Record by Sir L. Rowan, 31 October 1956.
52. Quoted in K. Kyle, *Suez* (London: Weidenfeld & Nicolson, 1991), p. 357.
53. See Kyle, ibid., p. 464.
54. Selwyn Lloyd, *Suez 1956* (London, 1978), p. 209.
55. Quoted in Turner, op. cit., p. 118.
56. PRO T236/4189, Measures to Protect Sterling. Telegram, Washington to the Foreign Office, 9 November 1956.
57. Ibid., Memorandum from Sir R. Makins to the Chancellor of the Exchequer 9 November 1956.
58. Ibid., Note of a Meeting held in Sir Leslie Rowan's room, 12 November 1956.
59. Ibid., Memorandum from Sir L. Rowan to Sir R. Makins, 13 November 1956.

60. Quoted in Gorst and Johnman, op. cit., p. 139.
61. Quoted, ibid., pp. 147–8.
62. Quoted, ibid., pp. 139–40.
63. Quoted, ibid., p. 141.
64. Quoted, ibid., p. 141.
65. PRO FO371/120816, UK Financial Situation Resulting from the Suez Crisis, Telegram from Washington to the Foreign Office, 26 November 1956.
66. Ibid., Telegram from Washington to the Foreign Office, 27 November 1956.
67. PRO PREM 11/1106, Memorandum from Selwyn Lloyd to R. A. Butler, 27 November 1956.
68. PRO CAB 128/30 Pt ll, CM(56)90, 28 November 1956.
69. PRO CAB 128/30 Pt ll, CM(56)91, 29 November 1956.
70. Quoted, Gorst and Johnman, op. cit., p. 144.
71. PRO T172/2127, Chancellor's Personal, Secret and Top Secret Carbons. Macmillan to Butler, 13 December 1956.
72. PRO PREM 11/1826, Washington to Foreign Office, 8 December 1956.
73. PRO PREM 11/1818, Financial Policy. Letter from the Chancellor of the Exchequer to the Prime Minister, 21 December 1956.
74. PRO PREM 11/1826, Letter from the Governor of the Bank of England to the Chancellor of the Exchequer, 20 December 1956.
75. Ibid., Letter from the Prime Minister to the Chancellor of the Exchequer, 28 December 1956.
76. Ibid., Letter from the Chancellor of the Exchequer to the Prime Minister, 31 December 1956.
77. Ibid., Note by the Prime Minister, circulated to Cabinet, 7 January 1957.
78. See, for example, Howard op. cit., pp. 229–48.
79. Ibid., p. 241.
80. Rhodes James, op. cit., p. 592.
81. Turner, op. cit., p. 123 and Howard, op. cit., p. 245.
82. Quoted, *Contemporary Record*, vol. no. 1 (Spring 1987), p. 5.
83. Horne, op. cit., p. 402.

5 Much Ado about Nothing: Macmillan and Appeasement

N. J. Crowson

During an interview in November 1958 Harold Macmillan told his interlocutor that in his opinion it did not matter if a Conservative MP rebelled against the party line provided the individual concerned had justified the behaviour with the local constituency party chairman.[1] Such a statement suggesting that the national party structure is powerless to discipline a rebel is not unique, but it is surprising that it should be so publicly stated by a Conservative Prime Minister. However, it was an observation based upon personal experience from the 1930s. During this time Macmillan was drawn into conflict with the leaderships of Stanley Baldwin and Neville Chamberlain over the conduct of British foreign policy towards the European dictators. The purpose of this study is to examine the attitude to appeasement adopted by Macmillan and to evaluate the implications of his behaviour in relation to the Conservative party.

Macmillan had entered Parliament in 1924 as MP for the northern industrial seat of Stockton. He continued to represent the constituency (with the exception of the years 1929–31) until defeat in the general election of 1945. During this time he established a reputation amongst the parliamentary party for being something of an eccentric.[2] As the decade of the 1930s drew to a close he appeared isolated and on the periphery. The Macmillan of the interwar years was seen as a radical, to the left of the party, who by his own admission in 1939 was close to ending his association with it.[3] Only the resignation of Chamberlain in May 1940 revived his political fortunes when his former political mentor, Winston Churchill, secured the premiership.

II

Little has been written explicitly about Macmillan's attitude to the national government's foreign policy. His official biographer devotes only a few pages, as does the most recently published biography; whilst for the most part the historian has been reliant upon Macmillan's own testimony as outlined in his memoirs.[4] Of course, these are recognized for what they are – Macmillan's projection and justification of his actions. The sole scholarly work has been Adrian Smith's review of Macmillan and Munich, which although based upon only published primary sources, highlighted the role the young MP played in facilitating contacts between the Conservative 'rebels' and Labour foreign policy specialists during the summer/autumn of 1938.[5] The analysis of Conservative foreign policy critics has a tendency to be skewed towards the events of 1938–9. Further it has been focused towards the activities of the Edenites and Churchill Group (something of which this author has also been guilty). With the gradual opening up of the Macmillan archives at the Bodleian Library, one is left wondering whether perhaps the emphasis has been wrong? There is increased evidence that the period 1935–6 was more significant for the evolution of foreign policy criticism than has been previously supposed. With the emphasis upon those around Eden and Churchill (to the mutual exclusion of all others), historians have been missing the point that the era was a time of turmoil, when backbenchers played an influential role in defining the parameters in which Britain's foreign policy was conducted. It was in these environs that Macmillan operated.

III

The outright opposition of the Stockton MP to foreign policy first became apparent in the immediate aftermath of the 1935 general election. The foreign secretary, Samuel Hoare, had secretly sought to reach a diplomatic compromise to the Italo-Abyssinian war. When news of the Hoare–Laval plan leaked in Britain a political outcry from the Conservative backbenches obliged Baldwin to insist upon Hoare's resignation.[6] Macmillan had been vocal in his demands for the removal of Hoare. Having been a passionate supporter of the League of Nations and collective security, Macmillan believed the

Hoare–Laval plan signed the death warrant for the League. Writing to *The Times* he welcomed the prospect of Hoare's removal and noted the irony that the Prime Minister was being supported in his foreign policy by those right-wing Conservatives who had been agitating for his removal since the beginning of the decade:

> It must indeed be galling for the Prime Minister to reflect on the character of the limited support which his new foreign policy is receiving. In the House of Commons many members on the government side are in open revolt; many more anxious and distressed.

Concluding, he drew an analogy with a funeral for a murdered man believing 'that at such a ceremony some distinction is made between the mourners and the assassins'.[7] The appointment of Anthony Eden to the Foreign Office as Hoare's successor was welcomed by Macmillan based upon an assumption that the new foreign secretary would continue to strive for collective security and ensure that British policy would thereafter 'be characterised by consistent support for the League Covenant'.[8] To Macmillan's mind support for the League was 'the cardinal and basic element' necessary to successfully maintain peace.[9]

The Hoare–Laval fiasco was the impetus for a number of Conservatives, encouraged by Edward Spears (Carlisle's MP), to form a dining club. The original conception was that the Club would convene on alternate months 'for the purposes of meeting distinguished British and foreign statesmen whose views it might be of interest . . . to hear'. But furthermore it was conceived that 'it might also be called together at any time the political situation warranted it . . . and could, if deemed desirable, place its views before the government'. Macmillan was one of those national government supporters initially approached; the criteria for selection being based upon the ability of the individual concerned to be

> perfectly prepared in a real emergency to take independent action of the Whips . . . and who . . . realise the enormous interest taken by the country in the League of Nations and in foreign affairs.[10]

Macmillan's response was positive, although once the December Club began meeting his attendance was somewhat erratic.[11] His limited involvement most likely explains why the dining club receives no mention in Macmillan's memoirs. The lack of active participation may have stemmed from Macmillan's belief in his own superiority which led to an inability to accept the role of subordinate and team player. This had already been highlighted with regard to his involvement in the Next Five Years Group and the Northern Group of MPs.[12] At the same time, ill health and personal tragedy did beset the Macmillan family during 1936, providing ample distraction from political affairs.

Within a few months of Hoare–Laval, with British attentions still distracted to the Mediterranean and Africa, Hitler remilitarized the Rhineland zone in March 1936. It was an event that destroyed the 1925 Locarno treaty and broke another clause of the 1919 Versailles peace treaty. The episode raised questions about the viability of sanctions and the League, and also placed the new British defence programme into perspective. Whereas Macmillan had found himself expressing the views of the majority of the parliamentary party over Hoare–Laval, with the Rhineland crisis he was very much out of line with the prevailing assumptions. With the backbench foreign affairs committee providing the forum for the party's debate it was quickly evident that the crisis was obliging many Conservatives to begin a rapid re-evaluation of their expectations. Although many condemned Hitler's behaviour, it was generally accepted that there was a legitimacy to the event. Furthermore, a sizeable number were concerned that French intransigence might drag Britain unwillingly into a conflict with Germany. The conclusion reached by the committee shortly before the Parliamentary debate on the incident was that energies should be directed to diplomatically resisting Germany. This could be achieved by detaching Italy from Germany. This would only happen if the government admitted sanctions had failed and recognized the conquest of Abyssinia. Italy would then be able to return to the negotiating table. This was a position Macmillan could not accept. For him, Britain had possessed two options: either resist Mussolini; or ignore Abyssinia with the aim of keeping Italy out of the Nazi camp. Baldwin's attempt to steer a middle path meant Britain had lost on both accounts.[13]

From the beginning of the Abyssinian crisis a major debate had been occurring amongst the backbenchers about the suitability of imposing economic sanctions upon the Italians. It was a debate that closely involved Macmillan and one which ultimately brought him into direct conflict with his leaders. Once the Baldwin administration had decided to resist Mussolini by economic sanctions Macmillan favoured their rigid imposition. He feared that

> unless the League can effectively prevent her [Italy] from 'getting away with it' (to use a common phrase), I think it will be the end of the League. Moreover, from the English point of view, I think it immensely increases the danger of German aggression.[14]

When Hitler re-took the Rhineland, Macmillan's doomsday scenario appeared prophetic. It intensified the need to continue the sanctions and for bolstering the League of Nations.[15] Yet Macmillan found himself increasingly isolated amongst Conservatives; only Vyvyan Adams, Conservative MP for Leeds West, appeared to earnestly favour their maintenance. From March 1936 the imperialist right wing of the party, who had argued that continued British action increased the risks of war and inevitably threatened universal peace, began winning the argument. Amongst the wider party a consensus began to emerge recognizing that to continue sanctions effectively drew Germany and Italy closer together – the very effect British foreign policy had been trying to prevent. Conversely Macmillan, although having no wish to see this scenario, felt that having adopted sanctions they had to be fulfilled with resolution. To drop them now would show weakness to the dictators and encourage further aggression. He felt that since Hoare–Laval, British foreign policy

> had fallen between two stools so that our prestige had been lowered in every part of the world, and the international situation rendered more dangerous by the failure of the League to preserve the peace even between two of its own members.[16]

Keen to add resolve to the Cabinet's deliberations on the maintenance of sanctions, Macmillan added his name to a Early Day Motion tabled on 11 May stating approval for the policy. It drew support from only 27 Conservatives.[17] However, Neville Chamberlain, the Chancellor of the Exchequer, sealed the fate of sanctions when during a speech in early June 1936 he condemned their retention as 'the very midsummer of madness'. When the matter was debated in the Commons, Macmillan joined Vyvyan Adams in condemning the government's behaviour. At the calling of the division both men voted against the government. From some of the material being released amongst the Macmillan archive it is evident that the Stockton MP's actions were being encouraged by others from outside the party. Filed amongst his papers is literature from the Friends of Abyssinia organization, highlighting the plight of the Abyssinian nation since the Italian invasion. Included was a picture postcard showing an aeroplane bombing/gassing a village with a native woman and child in the foreground weeping.[18] In addition, Macmillan was invited by Norman Angell, Walter Layton, Wickham Steed and Eleanor Rathbone to attend an 'informal and strictly private' conference on Abyssinia that included representatives from the League of Nations Union, the trades unions, Press, academia, women's organizations and opposition parties. The conference's agenda was to decide:

> What action should be taken in respect of:
>   (i) any remaining means of [putting] pressure on Italy, e.g. through refusal of financial aid;
> (ii) protection of native rights and welfare in Abyssinia;
> (iii) protection of European and British interests;
> (iv) the future of the Stresa front;
>   (v) the future of the coercive provisions of the covenant?[19]

Such a gathering was very much in keeping with Macmillan's ideal of a new central political coalition. No doubt it encouraged his decision to go a stage further and resign the National government whip – a deed which 'received a frigid note from Mr Baldwin'.[20]

To Macmillan's mind, the options before the British government with the ending of sanctions were clear. Strong leadership was required in order to prevent any further misunderstanding of Britain's position. Furthermore, the opportunity should be seized to take the initiative in reconstructing the League. In addition, Germany should be invited to participate in a conference

> in which this country should announce its readiness to give a fair deal in an effort to negotiate a completely new world peace settlement. If Germany refused to do so or the conference broke down, the only course open to us would be protective alliances with our neighbours in western Europe, it being made clear to Germany that she could always come into this circle whenever she desired.[21]

The lineage for this support of the League and collective security can be traced back at least as far as Macmillan signing the 1934 Liberty and Democratic Leadership manifesto which evolved into the Next Five Years Group.[22]

When Neville Chamberlain succeeded Baldwin in May 1937, Macmillan, in common with many Conservatives, welcomed the new leader believing that he would provide the necessary lead in foreign affairs. To show his approval he reapplied for the national whip. On a different level it was an admission that 'independents' could achieve little influence without the necessary party coupon. The concession was eased by the virtue of Eden remaining as foreign secretary, and to Macmillan's mind Eden was still committed to the League of Nations. As a consequence, Macmillan was quickly drawn into conflict with the leadership when Eden resigned in February 1938. Macmillan's name was added, along with other members of the December Club, to a parliamentary motion which deplored the circumstances obliging the foreign secretary's resignation.[23] He followed this 'rebellion' by abstaining in the censure vote on Eden's departure. However, the impact of his abstention is less clear. Macmillan admitted in his memoirs that 'to "abstain" is not perhaps a very courageous Parliamentary gesture'.[24] Furthermore it appears that he was soon expressing remorse to his Stockton Association. Whilst he 'regretted' Eden's resignation, 'he felt that the difference of opinion was merely one of method rather than objective'. He then sought to score party political points by noting the irony that the opposition were now championing Eden whereas six months before he had been an object of vilification.[25]

For Macmillan the March 1938 *Anschluss* was further evidence of the dangers presented by the dictators. Certainly, many Conservatives were left feeling uncomfortable with the yields of Chamberlain's foreign policy. Nevertheless, in public the Stockton Member maintained a conciliatory tone. He felt able to tell the ladies of his local Conservative Association that the German breaches of Versailles thus far 'were not, in principle, of a kind to which real objections could be made'. Indeed, he felt 'there was a good deal of reason' behind the reoccupation of the Rhineland, rearmament and the *Anschluss*. He did qualify this by adding that in Austria's case 'it was not the actual union which provoked resentment, but the brutality and persecution which would inevitably follow'.[26] Furthermore, contrary to the impression Macmillan gave in his memoirs, he felt sufficiently reassured by the Prime Minister's response to the crisis with his 24 March statement to the House of Commons to be able to support the government in the division lobbies against a Labour vote of censure.[27] It was an action accorded by a number of the other normally sceptical backbenchers.[28]

As the Czech crisis deteriorated during the summer and autumn of 1938, Macmillan continued to be disturbed by the direction of Chamberlain's foreign policy. When the Prime Minister began his shuttle diplomacy to Germany in September, Macmillan became involved in the discussions amongst a small band of backbenchers centred around Anthony Eden. He also discussed the diplomatic and international situation with the small number of acolytes who courted Churchill. The significance of Macmillan's involvement in these two groupings of foreign policy sceptics was that he acted, along with Edward Spears, as a intermediary between Churchill and Eden.[29] This culminated in both factions meeting on the morning of the Munich parliamentary divisions and agreeing to co-ordinate their voting strategies and abstain *en bloc*.[30] However, Macmillan was seeking to do more than unify the various Conservative opponents to Chamberlain. He was also in close contact with senior Labour figures, particularly the Shadow Foreign Secretary, Hugh Dalton, seeking to draw together the various strands of parliamentary opposition into a centre/popular front grouping. Ultimately nothing came of these approaches, but it illustrated Macmillan's continued flirtation with the idea of creating a new centre party, between the best elements (to his mind) of the Labour and Conservative parties.[31] It also suggested an ugly duckling syndrome offering an indication of his isolation from his fellow Conservatives, his having not been admitted to the very inner sanctums of the foreign policy sceptics. This desire to support a new third party, combined with his opposition to appeasement, meant that Macmillan felt able to publicly support the Master of Balliol, A. R. Lindsay, when he stood as an independent against the official Conservative candidate, Quintin Hogg, in the October 1938 Oxford by-election. This by-election was taken as a referendum on the Munich agreement. As it stood, Macmillan felt, the Munich agreement represented 'a complete capitulation to the racial principles of Nazi philosophy'.[32] The young undergraduate Edward Heath, later to be Macmillan's chief whip, also supported the Lindsay campaign.[33] However, the Lindsay campaign failed to attract support from other leading Conservative sceptics and Hogg managed to retain the seat for the Conservatives, whilst Macmillan was faced with expulsion from the Carlton Club and the possibility of party disciplinary action.[34]

In common with a number of other foreign policy sceptics during this period Macmillan had begun championing rearmament. Given Macmillan's interest in both foreign affairs and economics this was not surprising. His book *The Middle Way* linked his views on foreign policy with the need for planned capitalism – a half-way house between the free market and socialism that allowed a mixed economy in which there was both central co-ordination and ample scope for free enterprise. In the aftermath of Munich he privately published a short pamphlet in which he argued that economic planning was necessary to ensure that rearmament did not disrupt the civilian economy,[25] arguments that were articulated further in his 1939 publication *Economic Aspects of Defence*.[36] As a result of his favour for planning, Macmillan was an advocate for the creation of a Ministry of Supply, a cause espoused also by Churchill. Unsurprisingly, the idea for such a ministry found little favour with the Chamberlain administration and it was only in mid-1939 that one was created, albeit with limited powers. Furthermore, the idea of a Ministry of Supply had only restricted support amongst Conservatives. This Macmillan discovered in November 1938 when he defied a three-line whip and supported a Liberal call for such a ministry. He found only Churchill and Brendan Bracken from the Conservative side in the 'Aye' lobby. His support for the cause most likely explains Churchill appointing Macmillan as parliamentary secretary at the Ministry of Supply in May 1940.[37] With the belief that a strongly defended Britain would deter the dictators from further acts of aggression, Macmillan also became a convert to the cause of national service. By April 1939 with the international situation continuing to deteriorate and it being evident that the government's voluntary scheme of national service was failing to attract enough recruits, Macmillan sought to put pressure on the government by writing to *The Times* announcing his conversion to conscription.[38] On a more practical level, Macmillan's support for rearmament was influenced by the nature of his Stockton constituency. Its experiences with the Depression and the likelihood that any expanded rearmament programme would lead to economic benefits for distressed areas such as the North East of England made rearmament an attractive cause to espouse.[39]

IV

This study began with Macmillan's observation that to be a successful rebel in the Conservative party required keeping the local association on side. He was speaking with the wisdom of action. Whilst representing Stockton between 1924 and 1945 he was never once subject to a motion of censure from the Association, despite regularly failing to support his government and in 1936 resigning the whip in protest at the abandonment of sanctions. This level of flexibility granted to Macmillan by his Association made his role as a foreign policy critic considerably easier. This was something that was unusual for the era. From reading the Association's minute books it is apparent that Macmillan heeded his own advice, always taking consummate care to ensure that the local executive was briefed on his actions. For example, in September 1935 he specifically requested a meeting to explain his economic policies as outlined in *The Next Five Years*. Likewise, the following year on resigning the whip he sought to explain his opposition to the Baldwin government's Abyssinian policy and in return received a vote of confidence.[40] It should be observed that other local Associations during this period were not so tolerant of 'rebel' Members, as the Duchess of Atholl in Kinross and Vyvyan Adams in Leeds West discovered to their cost.[41] As with these other foreign policy dissidents, Macmillan sought to justify his action upon the grounds that he had

> made it abundantly clear that he reserved to himself a considerable degree of latitude as to how he should exercise his vote on any particular question, and asked for a free hand from the electors.[42]

Yet Macmillan was faced with only limited grumbling from sections of his Association – why? A number of factors can be identified to explain this phenomenon. These illustrate Macmillan's skills as a politician, but also the extent to which he was not a 'natural' Conservative, and maybe if he had been representing any seat other than a marginal one he would have felt obliged to leave the party. The first point is that Macmillan always adopted a conciliatory tone when addressing the Association. Although from his memoirs the impression is given that when speaking to his activists he clearly laid out his criticisms, the reader is actually being treated to selective quotation, as the speech to the Stockton women after the *Anschluss* referred to earlier illustrates.[43] Second, to a considerable extent his 'independence' was bought. The survival of the Association throughout the inter-war years relied upon Macmillan's financial generosity. Financial assistance in itself was not an unusual feature, but the extent of Macmillan's was. For example, in 1928 he found £2,000 to help buy new premises, the following month he gave £67 to clear the Association's overdraft. In 1935 he arranged and paid for the re-decoration of the Association's meeting hall. The following year he, alongside the Association's chairman, Leonard Ropner, paid off the Association's £332 overdraft. By 1938 he was paying the salaries of the Agent and the Women's Organizer. As the new chairman remarked the following year, 'if it were not for the generosity of Mr Macmillan, it would be impossible for the Organisation to carry on'.[44] The third factor links in with the financial position of the Association, namely, the marginal nature of the Stockton constituency located in the industrial north. It granted Macmillan that extra degree of independence. This was borne out when, having lost in Stockton in 1929, Macmillan considered contesting the safe seat of Hitchin in the Home Counties in a by-election. Despite having the support of Lord Beaverbrook, the Press magnate, it is apparent that the Hitchin Association began to have second thoughts about Macmillan's suitability. They were aware of his radical views, but had initially seen these as still compatible with mainstream Conservatism. However, Macmillan had written a letter to *The Times* in May 1930 commending Oswald Mosley for his unemployment pledges and for having resigned from MacDonald's government. An article in the right-wing journal *Patriot* later that year attacked Macmillan for being a free-trader and for threatening to vote against Baldwin. This caused Macmillan to inform the local chairman that he had no intention of yielding his radical beliefs to right-wing threats. In due course his nomination floundered when the sitting member was persuaded to reconsidered his decision to step down.[45] The marginal nature of Stockton had a further benefit for Macmillan. The level of activism was minor and characterized by abominable laziness and indifference, which meant that in occasions of strife he had fewer people to convince of the legitimacy of his actions.[46]

V

In the post-war years as Macmillan steadily rose through the political ranks, it became apparent to many observers that he was both a very ambitious individual and a very calculating politician. His actions, especially once Prime Minister, were conceived and acted out for maximum political effect, as with his 'little local difficulties' aside prior to his departure on the Commonwealth tour in 1958. The fact remains that the same was true of the Macmillan of the inter-war years. His bursting into a discordant rendition of *Rule Britannia* on hearing the results of the Norway division in May 1940 being one of the few occasion when genuine spontaneity took over.[47] His decision to become a Conservative was driven by opportunism rather than political conviction. As a young man he had been influenced by three very distinct political traditions: the old radicalism of the Christian Socialist Movement; orthodox Liberalism (pre-Home Rule split); and Unionism.[48] During his days at Oxford he had been inspired by Lloyd George and even into the 1930s the 'Welsh Wizard' continued to influence the Conservative backbencher. His marriage to Dorothy in 1920 meant him marrying into a Whig family and there is evidence that serious consideration was given to standing as a Liberal MP. However, the Macmillans were ambitious and from 1922 with the Carlton Club revolt and the continued divisions amongst the Liberal party it was evident that the Conservatives offered the best political career opportunities. Joining Labour was not a consideration. He had 'to remember that I am a very rich man'.[49] Once a Conservative, a persistent theme for Macmillan became the need for the Party to occupy the centre ground of British politics. In 1924 he had stated that the Party stood for 'a temperate and moderate policy of progress'.[50] It was a theme he returned to in his speech accepting adoption as party leader in 1957, when he drew the analogy that the Conservative Party was a 'broad stream' which 'was fed by many tributaries which we must not allow to dissolve into a shapeless delta'.[51] When, during the 1930s, he became disillusioned with what he perceived as the Conservative's self-interest, he gave consideration to the formation of a British popular front, or 'Centre Party', comprising the left of the Conservatives and the right of the Labour under the possible leadership of Herbert Morrison. Not untypically, the matter is underplayed in his memoirs, but the episode was symptomatic of his desire to take the 'Middle Way' and continue along the route trodden by Disraeli and other Tory Democrats. At the same time, Macmillan sought to manipulate the system to his advantage. His resignation of the whip in 1936 happened to be purely for the 'national' and not the 'Conservative' whip. As a consequence he had not gone beyond the pale. It guaranteed him national attention and added to his notoriety amongst colleagues, but, as the executive committee of the National Union of Conservative Associations decided, because he retained the party whip he could still be treated as a Conservative MP.[52] Furthermore, his ability to both charm and bankroll the local constituency Association was politically shrewd. The autonomy of local associations meant that they held the ultimate decision over selection and deselection. So long as a rebel retained the sanction of the local party, Central Office would have found it next to impossible to run an 'official' candidate against them.[53] Overall, Macmillan's experiences in the inter-war years were important lessons for the ambitious career politician and were a solid apprenticeship for the future leader. It is questionable whether Macmillan's alternative vision of 1930s foreign policy would have been viable. The League of Nations as it was constituted lacked the necessary international clout to effectively intervene, either diplomatically or militarily. Most Conservatives recognized that with many of the leading nations either absent from Geneva or having never joined, there was little point in giving it new duties which it had no hope of carrying out. It would be highly speculative to suggest that any revision of the League's Covenant would have secured the necessary international unanimity. As with much of Macmillan's political thinking in the 1930s, his response to appeasement placed too great an emphasis upon an idealism that accorded little reality to the situation. It is likely that behind the need to challenge the orthodoxies of party policy lay an element of political frustration which stemmed from his own failure to secure political advancement. Overall, Macmillan's views on appeasement made him an isolated figure on the Conservative backbenches. Equally, as this study has shown, Macmillan's own carefully crafted version of the 1930s bears only a limited resemblance to the actualities and the heroism of his stance against party and constituency pressure is fatally weakened.

NOTES

1. R. Jackson, *Rebels and Whips* (London: Macmillan, 1968), p. 254n.
2. R. R. James (ed.), *Chips: The Diaries of Sir Henry Channon* (London: Weidenfeld & Nicolson, 1968), 8 July 1936, 16 November 1939, pp. 69, 225; S. Ball (ed.), *Parliament and Politics in the Age of Baldwin and MacDonald: The Diaries of Sir Cuthbert Headlam Diaries, 1924–35* (London: The Historian's Press, 1992), 13 October 1934, 13 December 1934, pp. 311–12, 317.
3. Headlam Mss: unpublished diaries, 10 June 1939, D/He/34, Durham Record Office.
4. A. Horne, *Macmillan, 1894–1956*, vol. I (London: Macmillan, 1986), pp. 112–21; J. Turner, *Macmillan* (London: Longman, 1994), pp. 44–6; H. Macmillan *Winds of Change, 1914–1939* (London: Macmillan, 1956).
5. A. Smith, 'Macmillan and Munich: The Open Conspirator', *Dalhousie Review*, vol. 68, no. 3 (1988), pp. 235–47.
6. N. J. Crowson, *Facing Fascism: The Conservative Party and the European Dictators, 1935–40* (London: Routledge, 1997), pp. 58–65.
7. *The Times*, 18 December 1935.
8. Macmillan Mss: Macmillan to Raymond Buell, 26 December 1935, MS. Macmillan dep. c. 99 f. 34, Bodleian Library.
9. Stockton C[onservative] A[ssociation], special general meeting 23 July 1936, DX332/5, Durham Record Office.
10. Macmillan Mss: Edward Spears to Macmillan, n.d., MS. Macmillan dep. c. 99 ff. 358–9. The following national government supporters had agreed to attend: W. H. Carver; R. Bower; H. Nicolson; Marquess of Hartington; V. Cazalet; A. Crossley; R. Boothby; J. Mellor; H. Macmillan; A. Herbert; B. Cruddas; J. W. Hills; G. Bower; E. Makins, R. Tree; E. Spears; H. P. Latham. See Macmillan Mss: E. Spears to Macmillan, 12 February 1936, MS. Macmillan dep. c. 100 ff. 307–8.
11. Macmillan Mss: Macmillan to Edward Spears, 2 January 1936, MS. Macmillan dep. c. 99 f. 357. I am grateful to Paul Short (an MA student at LSE, who was working on aspects of the December Club) for our discussions on the December Club and for the information about Macmillan's attendance.
12. Ball (ed.), *Headlam Diaries*, 24 July 1935, p. 338.
13. Horne, *Macmillan*, vol. I, pp. 112–3.
14. Macmillan Mss: Macmillan to Ernest Imeson, 15 January 1936, MS. Macmillan dep. c. 99 f. 174.
15. Macmillan Mss: 'draft' letter to *The Times* from the executive committee of the Next Five Years Group, 28 March 1936, MS. Macmillan dep. c. 101 f. 36.
16. Stockton CA, special general meeting 23 July 1936, D/X332/5.
17. *Notice of Motions*, 11 May 1936.
18. Macmillan Mss: MS. Macmillan dep c. 104 f. 104.
19. Macmillan Mss: 'The Question of Continued Sanctions against Italy', 12 June 1936; 'The Abyssinian situation and its results', agenda, MS. Macmillan dep. c. 104 ff. 1–2, 314.

20. Macmillan, *Winds of Change*, pp. 458–9; James (ed.), *Chips*, 8 July 1936, p. 69.
21. Stockton CA, special general meeting, 23 July 1936, D/X332/5.
22. Turner, *Macmillan*, p. 45.
23. *The Times*, 23 February 1938. Compare these names with those listed in Macmillan Mss: MS. Macmillan dep. c. 99 ff. 358–9.
24. Macmillan, *Winds of Change*, pp. 538–9.
25. Stockton CA: men's branch AGM 10 March 1938, D/X322/8.
26. Stockton CA, women's AGM 19 March 1938, D/X322/11.
27. *Hansard* vote of confidence 4 April 1938.
28. See N. J. Crowson, 'Conservative Parliamentary Dissent over Foreign Policy during the Premiership of Neville Chamberlain: Myth or Reality?', *Parliamentary History*, vol. 14, no. 3 (1995) p. 325.
29. Smith, 'Macmillan', pp. 240–5.
30. See editorial in J. Barnes and D. Nicholson (eds), *The Empire at Bay: The Diaries of Leo Amery* (London: Hutchinson, 1988), pp. 483–90.
31. Macmillan, *Winds of Change*, pp. 568–9, 589.
32. H. Macmillan, *The Price of Peace: Notes on the World Crisis* (London: Heron, 1938), p. 9.
33. J. Campbell, *Edward Heath: A Biography* (London: Pimlico, 1993), pp. 33–4.
34. Macmillan, *Winds of Change*, p. 584.
35. Macmillan, *Price of Peace*, pp. 17–19.
36. Macmillan, *Winds of Change*, pp. 645–51.
37. Although this was only a very junior position, Macmillan threw himself into his job to the amusement of Westminster observers. James (ed.), *Chips*, 29 May 1940, p. 255.
38. *The Times*, 23 March 1939.
39. Horne, *Macmillan*, vol. I, p. 113.
40. Stockton CA, special executive 26 September 1935 and special general meeting 23 July 1936 D/X322/5.
41. For further examination see Crowson, *Facing Fascism*, pp. 85–7.
42. Stockton CA, special general meeting 23 July 1936, DX332/5
43. Compare this with the part of the speech quoted in Macmillan, *Winds of Change*, p. 542, which puts an entirely different gloss on affairs.
44. Stockton CA: finance committee 27 April 1928, 22 May 1928, 7 October 1935, 23 November 1938, executive 27 February 1939, D/X322/4, D/X 322/5; Macmillan MSS: Leonard Ropner to Macmillan, 17 January 1936, MS Macmillan dep. c. 99 ff. 322–3.
45. Horne, *Macmillan*, vol. I, pp. 90–2.
46. Macmillan MSS: Leonard Ropner to Macmillan, 17 January 1936, MS Macmillan dep. c. 99 f. 323.
47. James (ed.), *Chips*, 8 May 1940, p. 247.
48. H. Macmillan, *Past Masters: Politics and Politicans, 1906–1939* (London: Macmillan, 1975), p. 20.
49. Horne, *Macmillan*, vol. I, p. 127.
50. Stockton CA, newsclipping *Darlington and Stockton Times*, 26 January 1924, D/X322/4.

51. N. Nicolson (ed.), *Harold Nicolson: Diaries and Letters, 1945–62* (London: Collins, 1968), Nigel Nicolson to Harold and Vita Sackville-West, 22 January 1957, p. 330.
52. Conservative Party Archive: Micro Fiche Archive, National Union Executive 16 July 1936, card 54.
53. As acknowledged by party chairman, Douglas Hacking, Collin Brooks MSS: journals 5 October 1938.

6 Macmillan and Europe[1]
Richard Lamb

Alistair Horne has written that in 1949 Harold Macmillan had boundless, almost excessive, enthusiasm for Europe. This is correct, but between 1949 and 1961 he was not consistent and at one period did his best to sabotage the EEC in order to preserve the interests of the Commonwealth.[2]

Winston Churchill as leader of the Conservative Party in the immediate post-war years displayed great enthusiasm for the Council of Europe, which he envisaged as a European parliamentary authority, and at the first Congress of Europe at The Hague in 1948 he had launched the European Movement which brought together the various groups in Britain and Western Europe working for European unity. Then he called for unity in high-faluting although imprecise terms, playing down his reservation that Britain while working closely with Europe would never became integrated.

The first positive move towards the Common Market came in May 1950 when Robert Schuman, the French Foreign Secretary, unexpectedly launched dramatic proposals for pooling the coal, iron and steel resources of France and Germany and of any other European country willing to join them under the control of an independent high authority. This was followed in October by a proposal to place each of Nato's armed forces under a supranational authority to create an European army. The Attlee government spurned both proposals, with the Prime Minister telling the French Ambassador that they could not hand over the key coal and steel industries 'to irresponsible persons' while the Foreign Secretary, Ernest Bevin, commented 'We cannot buy a pig in a poke.'[3]

In a Commons debate at the end of June 1950, during what amounted to a vote of censure on the Government for refusing to negotiate over the Schuman Plan, Churchill said 'We are prepared to consider and if convinced to accept the abrogation of sovereignty provided we are satisfied with the conditions and safeguards . . . national sovereignty is not inviolable.' Eden in the same debate said he would be prepared to enter discussions to set up a high authority whose decisions would be binding upon the nations who were parties to the agreement.

Macmillan agreed enthusiastically with Churchill and Eden. However, the high hopes aroused with pro-Europeans in Britain were soon dashed. Once in office in 1951 the Conservative government under Churchill, like their Labour predecessor, refused to consider yielding power to the supranational institutions proposed, and they ate the words they had uttered in opposition.

On 28 November Eden, now Foreign Secretary, announced in Rome that Britain would not participate in an European army, and a fortnight later Eden and Churchill in Paris told Schuman that they could not join in the Schuman Plan.[4]

Macmillan, like other Europhile Conservatives, was dismayed and wrote to Eden in January 1952 that Britain should give a lead to Europe in the creation of a confederation organized on the same lines as the Commonwealth, with a common currency and a European customs preferential area interlocking with Imperial Preference. Eden was negative when Macmillan raised the issue in Cabinet, replying that Macmillan ignored that 'much of Europe wants to federate'. This was true. Unhappy with the Cabinet discussion Macmillan wrote to Churchill stating that the government's continued opposition to the movement for European unity was inconsistent with the pronouncements, while in opposition, by Churchill and Eden on the Schuman Plan and the European army, and with the conduct of the Conservative delegates to the Council of Europe at Strasbourg.

At this stage, Churchill was enjoying being Prime Minister. Eden, who was adamantly opposed to Britain being part of Europe, was his popular heir-apparent and Churchill was not going to make life difficult for himself by having a brush with his Foreign Secretary. He snubbed Macmillan saying nothing more than what Eden was doing was practical.[5] Churchill had become ambivalent and had probably created his plan for an united Europe with a view to establishing political ascendancy over Attlee by re-evoking his role as the great wartime saviour of Europe. Perhaps Churchill was guilty of muddled thinking, but as leader of the opposition he was definitely inspired by both the vision of a European parliamentary authority and of a European army. Out of touch with civil servants, he probably became carried away by his own oratory. Yet as Prime Minister, in deference to Eden from 1951 to 1955 he consistently rejected any suggestions of European union which involved supranational institutions.

Without Britain, the high authority of the European Coal and

Steel Community assumed office in August 1952, and Jean Monnet, their first President, became the driving force behind an ever-strengthening move towards a united Europe which was to become the Common Market of the Six (EEC). Monnet extended European co-operation to atomic energy (Euratom) and prepared plans for a customs union. Britain was ready to join a free trade area but not a customs union, because the government was determined not to erode or abolish Commonwealth preference which would be inescapable in a customs union. When the Faure government, which included several convinced federalists, took office in France in February 1955, the drive for a European customs union gathered pace.

When Eden succeeded Churchill as Prime Minister in April 1955, Macmillan became Foreign Secretary. The enthusiasm for a united Europe he had displayed a few years before had disappeared. When the Foreign Ministers of the Six (France, Germany, Italy, Belgium, the Netherlands and Luxemburg) met at Messina at the beginning of June 1955 and laid down realistic plans for a Common Market Treaty, Eden and Macmillan made the fatal mistake of not even sending a representative. Churchill would never have made this mistake.[6]

At Messina the Six wanted Britain to participate from the start, and a great opportunity to join with the EEC tailor-made for British requirements was thrown away. Eden as Prime Minister dominated foreign policy, but both he and Macmillan had the gut feeling that there were three great powers – Britain, the USA and the Soviet Union – and they would not contemplate Britain abandoning Imperial Preference and accepting equal status within the Six by pooling national sovereignty and entering a customs union. Macmillan has made it clear in his memoirs that in 1955 he did not want a Six-power Europe with a customs union.

At Messina Paul-Henri Spaak, the Belgian Foreign Minister, was made Chairman of a Committee of the Six in Brussels to prepare a formal treaty, and he drove ahead at great speed. Although Britain had no intention of joining the Six, the Cabinet appointed a senior civil servant, Russell Bretherton, to joint the committee mainly to find out what was happening. Bretherton, who favoured the EEC ideal, told the author that he found himself in great difficulties because he could not guide the propositions into shape without giving the impression that Britain would be committed to the result, while on the other hand if he sat back and said nothing, unpleasant things would get into the report from the UK point of view whether we took part in the Common Market or not.[7] Bretherton hoped the British government would change their minds and join the EEC, but the Cabinet Economic Policy Committee firmly rejected the idea. After Bretherton had reported that it was certain the Six would succeed in finalizing a treaty, the Cabinet tried to divert the discussion into the Organization for European Economic Cooperation (OEEC) in Paris. This was abortive and led Macmillan as Foreign Secretary into making a hostile statement in Paris in December 1955 which enraged the Ministers of the Six. Impervious to British objections, at Venice at the end of May 1956 the Six agreed their terms for the Treaty.[8]

Overtures to Britain were made by the Six; these were rejected, but as it became clear the Six were about to sign a treaty to establish economic integration, the Cabinet decided an alternative must be found. Macmillan, now Chancellor of the Exchequer, much concerned at British exports being disadvantaged by high tariffs in the Common Market, pushed the civil servants, and on 27 July, the day on which the Suez crisis erupted, he circulated a note prepared by the Foreign Office, Treasury and Board of Trade, with help from the Ministries of Agriculture, the Colonial Office, the Board of Customs and Excise and the Bank of England. This became the report entitled *UK Initiatives in Europe: Plan G*.

Plan G was a milestone because it envisaged Britain changing from having her industry protected by high tariffs to being part of a free trade area. This meant abolishing the high level of protection for British industries which had been cushioned against competition from imports by the 1932 Import Duties Act together with other out-of-date tariffs such as the 33 per cent Key Industries Duties dating back to the First World War. However, Plan G envisaged allowing into Britain duty free Commonwealth food imports and low tariffs on Commonwealth industrial goods. This was anathema to the Six, and they correctly recognized the plan as a tactic designed to wreck the Common Market with its customs union and supranational institutions. A free trade area as a substitute had no attractions for them. However, Macmillan held high but unwarranted hopes for the success of Plan G and wrote to Spaak on 3 October entreating him:

to keep things as fluid as possible at the meeting of the Foreign Ministers of the Six on 20 October so as to permit us and other countries to associate with the Customs Union in a wider Free Trade if you can do so. Binding decisions at this stage might be difficult.[9]

At the end of September Macmillan discussed Plan G in general terms with the Commonwealth Finance Ministers at their meeting in Washington. According to Macmillan, 'the younger Ministers seemed favourable; some of the older ones doubtful or hostile'. On his return to London Macmillan told the Cabinet:

We must be satisfied before we would contemplate entering a Free Trade Area in Europe that agricultural products were excluded and we preserved both the interests of Commonwealth agriculture in the United European market and of the system of Commonwealth preferences.[10]

This meant Plan G was doomed because the Six had now decided to include agriculture in their treaty.

An important ministerial meeting of the Six Messina powers in October went badly. Both the Germans and the French made reservations and it was the first real setback Spaak had experienced. For a short time British hopes were raised that the EEC Treaty might not come off and instead the French and Germans might be tempted by Plan G. However, just as it seemed French intransigence might provide a successful opening for Free Trade Area negotiations on the lines of Plan G, Spaak gave France all the concessions she wanted and the fleeting opportunity disappeared.[11]

Faced with a *fait accompli* by the Six, the Cabinet at their meeting on 13 November during the Suez crisis decided to announce in Parliament that Britain would negotiate with the Six for a Free Trade Area.[12]

In the Commons on 16 November Macmillan argued strongly for Plan G, and the Labour Party, influenced by Harold Wilson, concurred. The government spokesmen emphasized that agriculture would be completely excluded. This led Roy Jenkins to say the Six would not 'swallow' this. Indeed Plan G was so ill-received by the Six that it led them to press on even faster with their treaty.

On 7 January 1957, two days after Eden resigned and Macmillan became Prime Minister, Spaak came to London. Macmillan told Spaak that agriculture must be excluded from any agreement and that was 'non-negotiable'. Alas, it was also the sticking point for

Spaak, and the visit was a failure with Spaak insisting if there was agreement on a Free Trade Area all British food imports must pay the EEC common external tariff; he objected strongly to Britain continuing to keep the price of food low by deficiency payments to farmers because this cheap food gave Britain considerable economic advantages.[13]

The European Economic Community came into being despite the Macmillan government doing everything in their power to thwart the Messina powers by importuning with them for a Free Trade Area. The European Press was full of reports that Britain was trying to sabotage the EEC and, spurred on by fears of British proposals bringing negotiations to a halt, the Six signed the Treaty of Rome on 27 March 1957 with internal tariff reductions beginning on 1 January 1958, much to Britain's disadvantage.

After the signing of the Treaty of Rome the Macmillan government strove hard to create an EFTA of Seventeen which would include the Six and Britain and the other ten OEEC countries with tariffs harmonized from 1 January 1959. Two years of negotiations ending in success had given the Six a sense of cohesion; they feared that a larger Free Trade Area would prejudice the evolution of the Common Market.

In October 1957 important OEEC meetings in Paris boded well for Britain. The Council declared its determination 'to secure the establishment of a European Free Trade Area (of Seventeen) which would associate on a multilateral basis with the EEC and other member countries'. An intergovernmental Committee of Ministers was set up, and Reginald Maudling, President of the Board of Trade, was elected Chairman. (Macmillan had put him in charge of European negotiations.) Significantly, at the first meeting of the Maudling Committee the French delegate Edgar Faure declared baldly that unless the Treaty of Association of EFTA was roughly similar to the Treaty of Rome the French would not accept it. This was the writing on the wall.[14] Gladwyn Jebb, the British Ambassador in Paris, reported growing French opposition to Commonwealth food being imported duty free by Britain; this, as should have been foreseen, became the main stumbling block. On 17 March Maudling had a long conversation with Macmillan which made it clear a breakdown was probable. However a ray of light appeared when Guido Carli, the Italian Foreign Minister, put forward proposals by which the goods of the Eleven, who had widely varying external tariffs, should circulate freely throughout EFTA except when the country's import tariffs were above a 'norm'. If the country's import tariffs were above the norm compensatory tariffs would be levied upon them.[15] Here was the germ of a solution, but the snag was that producing certificates of origin by customs authorities was too complicated, and least of all were Carli's own Italian customs capable of operating such a system. The Carli Plan was examined exhaustively by OEEC committees and there was more optimism about the successful outcome of the negotiations for the Seventeen than at any other point. It was eventually rejected because of the mammoth customs complications.

While the Carli Plan was under debate the French produced their own Faure Plan. This stipulated that British Commonwealth countries must accept at preferential rates a quota of European goods which would pay only the standing Imperial Preference duty. Faure complained that the British would not open their markets to the Six's farm produce, and because of this there must be substantial compensation in other fields. However, the rest of the Six would not accept the Faure Plan and when the French government fell in April 1958 it was abandoned.[16]

With France without a government, the visit to London of Adenauer, the German Chancellor, was important. Maudling briefed the Prime Minister that the French had been working hard on him recently and had told Adenauer:

(1) That the British never liked the Common Market, and the Free Trade Area is merely a plan to sabotage it.
(2) That the British were trying to put pressure on France to fall in with a scheme designed to meet British interests.
(3) That the British are trying hard to have it both ways particularly in maintaining Commonwealth Preference while claiming access to the Common Market.

At this stage both the French and Germans hoped they might obtain advantages out of Commonwealth Preference. Christopher Steel, Ambassador to Germany, reported 'The Germans have an idea of using the Free Trade Area as a means of getting a cut out of imperial preference.' Maudling's reaction was that 'We should firmly resist the suggestion that we owe the Six some form of compensation for Commonwealth entry.'[17]

The Macmillan–Adenauer talk in which Maudling and Ludwig Erhard, the pro-British German Finance Minister, also took part went well, with the Germans promising to pressurize the French towards a satisfactory settlement.

On 1 June 1958 de Gaulle became Prime Minister of France and Britain faced a tougher struggle. Faure while Prime Minister had genuinely tried for an agreement between the Six and the Eleven, but now he was outside the government. The Maudling Committee made no progress in the autumn of 1958. Macmillan became frustrated and on 24 June even sent a memorandum to the Foreign Secretary toying with withdrawing British troops from NATO if de Gaullist France stayed intransigent. He was out to wreck the EEC if the Six would not give way.[18]

On 10 October de Gaulle announced that France would not consider any arrangements which excluded agriculture and because of France's many concessions it was up to the United Kingdom to make some. On 6 November the French Foreign Minister, Couve de Murville, came to London and finally dashed Britain's hopes by saying the Free Trade Area was 'unacceptable' to the French, and the Six must have a special position between themselves. Macmillan told Couve that it depressed him that 'Sparta and Athens must quarrel; the Russians were getting stronger and stronger all the time and here was the free world voluntarily weakening and dividing itself. History will regard this as a tragic decision and the crowning folly of the twentieth century in Europe.' In a letter he begged de Gaulle to do something to prevent the erection of barriers 'between two halves of Europe'.

De Gaulle paid no attention, and a week later (13 November) on de Gaulle's orders the French Minister of Information, Jacques Soustelle, announced 'It was not possible to form a Free Trade Area as had been wished by the British to result in free trade between the Six and the Eleven other OEEC countries unless there was a common external tariff and harmonisation in the economic and social spheres.' With the Soustelle veto the Free Trade Area of Seventeen was dead.[19]

After the Soustelle veto, Macmillan more than any other member of the Cabinet strove for an agreement with the Six and still hoped for a *modus vivendi* until February 1959 when Walter Hallstein, President of the EEC Commission, met Maudling in London and stated categorically that it would be 'useless' to bring the Seventeen together again. Macmillan then gave up hope of negotiating a *modus vivendi* with the Six and in retaliation decided to try for a Free Trade Area of Seven to bargain with the Six.[20] The countries were to be Britain, Norway, Sweden, Denmark, Austria, Portugal and Switzerland, and the project was christened Uniscan.[21]

The first important Foreign Office minute about it stated: 'A Uniscan FTA has many drawbacks. It will serve to divide Europe even more deeply and our initiative in producing it will provoke US displeasure.' This was correct. America was keen on France drawing Germany out of Soviet influence and disliked the Uniscan initiative. At first Macmillan saw Uniscan as a strong bargaining counter from which to make a bridge with the Six. Later he blew cold on the Seven, and sought a British settlement with the Six regardless of the rest of the Seven.

The member countries of the Seven at Stockholm on 21 July 1959 signed an agreement to remove all import tariffs between them. Macmillan's hopes that this might improve the chances of an agreement with the Six came to nothing, and in fact EFTA of Seven became an added complication in Britain's tortuous relations with the EEC; it also angered America. So vehement was Douglas Dillon, US Under Secretary of State, when he came to London that Macmillan sent a minute to the Foreign Secretary querying whether the Special Relationship still existed.[22]

Initially there had been enthusiasm in Britain for the Uniscan Plan as a reaction to the humiliation suffered at the hands of France by their veto on the proposed linking of the Six with the Eleven. By the time the Stockholm convention was ratified on 20 November 1959 this had largely vanished mainly because trade figures showed that despite the tariff barrier British exports to the Six were increasing far faster than to the Seven.

At the end of November 1959 the Six accelerated their internal tariff reductions, and despite Macmillan appealing to de Gaulle to halt the acceleration these came into operation on 1 July 1960. This convinced Macmillan that he was backing the wrong horse, and he persuaded the Cabinet to appoint Sir Frank Lee, Joint Head of the Treasury, to examine all possible solutions to the European problem and to report on how the Six could join the Seven as a unit and how Britain could be part of a Customs Union while retaining the advantages of Imperial Preference and excluding agriculture completely.

This shows Macmillan as accepting the inevitability of Britain joining the EEC, although he was unrealistic in believing that farming could be excluded because by now the Six had embarked on their agricultural policy and wanted uniform food prices throughout the

Community, which was incompatible with Britain enjoying cheap Commonwealth food.

Sir Frank Lee's report became the watershed; and after digesting it Macmillan started in earnest to try and convince his colleagues that Britain's future definitely lay with the Six. In his report Lee wrote 'our exports becoming increasingly disadvantaged in the growing markets of the EEC would be a serious matter for Britain' and the creation of a 'bridge between the Six and Seven was improbable'. His conclusion was:

> We must maintain our broad objective of having the UK form part of a single European market . . . we shall not get the solution we want on the cheap . . . we shall have to be prepared for the sort of settlement we want – in political terms of inconvenience for or damage to some of our cherished interests – the Commonwealth domestic agriculture, our tariff policy, perhaps indeed our political pride and sense of self reliance.

The Lee Report was discussed at an important Cabinet meeting on 13 July 1960. Heathcoat Amory, Chancellor of the Exchequer, was ready to join the EEC 'provided it did not impair our relations with the Commonwealth'; Maudling disagreed, saying to join would be 'disastrous', while Duncan Sandys, Minister of Aviation, a strong European, disagreed strongly with Maudling and wanted Britain to join 'where she might hope eventually to achieve leadership'. Although a majority of the Cabinet were against joining, Macmillan had broken the ice, although in the Commons on 25 July the government attitude was that there were 'insuperable difficulties' in the way of joining. After a Cabinet reshuffle Macmillan made the European enthusiast Edward Heath Lord Privy Seal and entrusted him with exploring the possibility of Britain applying to join.[23]

Heath, with Macmillan's backing, got the upper hand over the Eurosceptic Maudling in Cabinet, and began to make informal approaches through the Ambassadors to the Six. These were followed by a visit by Macmillan to de Gaulle at Rambouillet in January 1961. Particularly discouraging was de Gaulle's remark to Macmillan that he did not see how it was 'possible for the Commonwealth and the Six to make an economic community without destroying one or the other'. The official account of the talks shows that de Gaulle was off-putting, but Macmillan recorded 'Broadly speaking

I think we made good progress.' Sir Pierson Dixon, the newly appointed Ambassador in Paris, who was present was doubtful of a successful outcome to any negotiations. Dixon's view was confirmed when Frank Lee met Oliver Wormser, the chief French negotiator. Wormser stated abruptly that if Britain decided to join the EEC she must abandon her cheap food policy, although he assured Lee that if Britain did decide to join then the response would be one 'of unreserved welcome'. As Wormser had just told Lee that if Britain joined she would have to apply the common external tariff to all Commonwealth imports including food, it was unpromising.[24]

In meetings held on 20 and 21 April 1961 Macmillan pressed his Cabinet to agree to apply to join. Macmillan said that for some time after the war Europe had been dependent on American aid and content to accept Anglo-Saxon leadership, but she had now regained her strength and there was now a new situation in which the economic state of Britain might be 'undermined'. Therefore it was in our interest to join the Six if we could gain admission on terms which would be tolerable. De Gaulle did not want us in since he wanted to hold the reins in Europe, but his attitude might change if he saw that the West 'could not prevail against the Communists unless its leading countries worked together'. The Cabinet conclusion was that there was no reason of principle why the United Kingdom should not accede to the Treaty of Rome subject to the interests of the Commonwealth and the other EFTA countries.

Macmillan had cleverly swung his colleagues round. However, he had not dared to suggest that Commonwealth Preference and cheap food must be abandoned.[25]

Talks in Paris on 22 and 23 June between Sir Roderick Barclay of the Foreign Office and Sir Eric Roll of the Ministry of Agriculture with Wormser were the red light. They should have made it clear to Macmillan and Heath that only minor concessions over the Commonwealth would be wrung out of the French, and in effect Britain had to accept the Rome Treaty hook, line and sinker or stay out. Maudling saw it that way and wrote to Macmillan that the French had rejected in advance 'any proposals on the points of vital interest to us'.[26]

Macmillan, although he had a high regard for Maudling, ignored Maudling's letter, and at a weekend conference at Chequers on the weekend of 17–18 June 1961 a majority of ministers were in favour of making a formal application to join the EEC provided that special terms were given for the Commonwealth. The Cabinet approved the Chequers decision and after ministers had been sent on a fruitless round of visits to soften up Commonwealth Prime Ministers, the Cabinet decided that Macmillan should announce in the Commons on 31 July 1961 that Britain was applying to join the EEC.[27] In the debate there were only twenty-two Conservative abstentions and the Conservative Party Conference also gave overwhelming support. This near consensus in favour of Europe by a former generation of Conservatives is a marked contrast with the way in which Eurosceptics wreck the Conservative Party today.

Macmillan's main problem was to persuade the Six to allow preferential treatment for the Commonwealth and to prevail upon the Conservative pro-Empire lobby to accept some watering down of Commonwealth preference. Also he had to convince the Six that Britain would co-operate with the ideals and principles of the Six as expressed in the Treaty of Rome despite there being few signs of British enthusiasm for federalism or supranational institutions.

The Cabinet hoped that the Six would make slashing concessions over Commonwealth food, but to do so ran counter to the whole thrust of the EEC common agricultural policy which was already outlined in the Mansholt report. A thorn in Macmillan's flesh was Lord Beaverbrook. Passionately devoted to the Empire, his influential newspapers backed to the hilt British opponents of EEC entry.

Heath put his finger on the main problem in his 'introductory statement' to the EEC Council of Ministers in October 1961, saying that Britain could not join the EEC under conditions in which the Commonwealth trade connection was cut with grave loss and 'even ruin for some of the Commonwealth countries'. Heath also pointed out that under the Treaty of Rome generous treatment had been given to the former French African colonies and Tunisia.[28] Unfortunately Britain was too late. The Six were not prepared at this stage of their evolution to water down their common agricultural policy by agreeing to the continuing entry to Britain of cheap Commonwealth food, nor would they accept tariff free competition for industrial goods from the Commonwealth. In December, without consulting Britain, the Six as part of their agricultural policy agreed to put levies on all imports of food and to use these levies both to subsidize farm food production and dump surplus food production abroad. This made Heath's negotiating position difficult.

As 1962 opened, the British tried to speed up negotiations in the hope of becoming a full member by January 1963. There was a reluctance on both sides for tough negotiations over the Commonwealth problem for fear of a breakdown. Five out of the Six wanted Britain in, but de Gaulle was rigidly opposed, although he did not want France to be seen as the obstructionist.

From his post at Geneva as Secretary General of EFTA Sir Frank Figures of the Treasury had a ringside view. He was pessimistic on 28 February, writing:

> he doubted whether our present tactics would solve the Six/Seven problem and were causing real distress not only to our friends amongst the Six but also to some countries within the Seven ... the only hope was the acceptance of the Treaty of Rome subject not only to special arrangements for the Commonwealth and adoption of their agricultural policy would be necessary. We should not underestimate the feeling of hatred against the UK being put out at all levels by both the European Commission and the French administration.

Figures was correct in diagnosing 'the feeling of hatred' towards Britain in France. However, this was due not to the attempt to adjust the Treaty of Rome to accommodate the Commonwealth but to the refusal of Britain to help France to become a nuclear power on which aim de Gaulle had set his heart. Dixon from Paris told Heath in March that the reaction of the French to the British application 'would depend to a great extent on whether France is now considered to be a nuclear power'.[29]

A minute from Heath shows that he saw this nuclear policy as the key factor in securing French agreement to British entry into the EEC. Heath minuted:

> What alarms me more than anything else is that, at the same time as we are trying to negotiate our entry into the EEC – in which we have all too few cards to play – we are giving every indication of wishing to carry out political policies which are anathema to the two most important members of the Community.... What they see here is our apparent determination with the United States to prevent the French from developing their atomic and nuclear defence.[30]

At the time the Americans insisted on strict interpretation of the rule that there should be no dissemination of nuclear secrets to the French. In Cabinet it was never questioned whether Britain should, in order to placate de Gaulle, try to break this US ruling. Dixon and Heath were correct; if Britain had aided de Gaulle in his efforts to make France an independent nuclear power he might have yielded over EEC entry.

Dixon, who was both Ambassador in Paris and head of the British negotiating team in Brussels, continued to send gloomy reports from Paris pointing out that de Gaulle did not want the negotiations to succeed and was hoping that we would abandon our attempt to join. Within the Paris Embassy there was a cold sense of realism, but in London unjustifiable optimism existed, and a disregard that Dixon was better placed than anyone else to gauge the chances of success.[31]

Heath and his team of civil servants ponderously negotiated in Brussels; Commonwealth imports and British farm policy were tough problems, but solutions to them were in sight when in July there came increasing indications that France would say 'No'; these were heavily signposted from the British Embassy in Paris. In May the British had insisted that part or all of the levies (financial contributions) collected on imported food should be returned to the country collecting them and would not be part of the community's budget income. Then in August the French demanded that no monies from levies should be returned to the collecting country. As the biggest food-importing country this would hit Britain hard.

Feeling against the financial contribution was strong both in Britain and the Commonwealth. John McEwan, the Australian Deputy Prime Minister, had made a devastating statement in London on 16 July:

A price basis as you suggested would mean that Britain would be paying for Australian wheat substantially less than would be paid from a supplier in the community. She would be collecting on Australian wheat levies at least part of which could very well be used to subsidize community wheat to our disadvantage in other markets. This is a situation to which we would have strong objections.[32]

In his memoirs Macmillan wrote that 'we' were encouraged by Mr McEwan's general attitude to the Common Market. This cannot be true.

At a marathon session on the night of 5/6 August the French prepared a trap for the British on de Gaulle's orders, undoubtedly with a view to causing a breakdown. At 3 a.m. in the morning of 6 August Couve de Murville for the French produced a paper which meant that no levies would be returned so that the levies on Commonwealth food could be used to subsidize EEC food exports and the British liability would be sky high with no refunds allowed.

Heath, taken unawares, refused to discuss the French paper. Pierson Dixon wrote in his diary that the night of 5/6 August was 'the end of the Brussels negotiations'.[33] He was correct; he did not mean that the levy problem was insoluble but that de Gaulle was determined to find some pretext to keep Britain out.[34]

The Deputy Prime Minister of New Zealand, John Marshall, said hopefully 'The death sentence has been pronounced.' Arnold France, a Treasury representative at the British Brussels delegation, wrote that the French had tried to bounce Heath by highly discreditable means into a formal agreement that the levies on food imports from the Commonwealth could be used for the community budget, and France with a high proportion of their own food would pay only small levies while Britain would pay large levies.[35]

Neither Heath nor Macmillan accepted that all was lost. De Gaulle was hoping that the Commonwealth Prime Ministers at their London Conference starting on 10 September would be so opposed that Britain would be forced to abandon the application. He was disappointed.

Adroitly, Macmillan prevailed on the Commonwealth Prime Ministers to agree to an anodyne press statement:

The Prime Ministers took note that the negotiations in Brussels were still incomplete, and that a number of important questions have still to be negotiated. Only when the full terms were known would it be possible to form a final judgement.

Macmillan's next hurdle was the Conservative Party Conference in October. Here all went swimmingly. An anti-Common Market amendment moved by the Conservative former ministers Robin Turton and Derek Walker Smith was defeated with only fifty out of 4,000 voting for it. So enthusiastic were the delegates after Macmillan's winding up speech that Heath feared it would give the Six the impression that Britain would join at any price and thus weaken his bargaining position at Brussels.

Meanwhile, France had a political crisis. On 5 October the Pompidou government was unexpectedly defeated; Parliament was dissolved, with 25 November scheduled for a General Election; simultaneously de Gaulle called for a referendum on his presidency. It is possible that while the outcome of the French elections was uncertain British pressure for urgent agreement to accession might have succeeded. The fleeting moment, if it existed, was lost in unrewarding discussions on how long it should take to align British farm policy with the Community's, the financial regulations, and what preferences should be given to the Commonwealth. The Gaullist parties convincingly won the General Election, and de Gaulle triumphed in the referendum so that his political authority was absolute.

At this period Macmillan had doubts about whether de Gaulle would allow British entry. In his speech to the Conservative Party Conference he insisted that arrangements must be made to safeguard the Commonwealth, home agriculture and fellow members of EFTA – a repetition of his message to the Commons in the July 1961 debate. Iain Macleod, Chairman of the Conservative Party, said Britain must not pay too high a price for entry, while Fred Erroll, President of the Board of Trade, declared 'it would be no disaster' if Britain stayed outside. These statements, obviously co-ordinated, may have been a ploy to convince the Six that Britain would not join unless the terms were satisfactory; more probably they were to prepare the British public for failure.

A revealing circular was sent to all British Ambassadors on 26 November stating that it was out of the question for us, as the Six have suggested, to abandon our whole (farm) deficiency payments 'immediately upon entry'; it was essential to 'secure reasonable arrangements to safeguard Commonwealth interests and the successful outcome of the Commonwealth Conference should not be allowed to obscure the very serious misgivings which exist and which we must strive to meet'.[36]

On 12 December in a Commons debate Harold Wilson (Leader of the Opposition) said that an enormous revenue would go to the European Fund partly to subsidize European agriculture and partly to subsidize exports of high-costing European produce to the Third World countries, and it would 'have the effect of penalizing further Commonwealth producers who have already been pushed off our market'. 'We cannot', he declared, 'accept the agricultural programme if it is based on this penal levy.'

At the same time, a Gallup Poll showed that the percentage in favour of joining 'on the facts as you know them at present' had declined from 40 per cent in October to 29 per cent, while the figure for those who opposed had risen from 28 to 37 per cent.

Thus there were dark clouds over the negotiations when de Gaulle and Macmillan met at Rambouillet on 15 and 16 December 1962. Long discussions according to Macmillan's memoirs became a 'wrangle'. De Gaulle told the British Prime Minister bluntly that 'it was not possible for Britain to enter tomorrow', and the arrangements inside the Six 'might be too rigid for Britain'. Macmillan replied that he was 'astonished and deeply wounded'. De Gaulle's last point was that France at the moment could say 'No' to any policies of the Six with which she disagreed, but once Great Britain and Scandinavia joined then it would be different. Macmillan's final words to him were 'If this was really the French views it should have been put forward at the very start.'

Macmillan had run up against a brick wall. Sir Michael Butler told me the Prime Minister was very distressed, and in the library at the Paris Embassy was almost in tears when he related to the Embassy staff that de Gaulle intended to block Britain's entry, and thus all the negotiations had been in vain.[37]

False hopes then sprang up in Macmillan's breast. On the first day of talks at Rambouillet, de Gaulle indicated that he had no real interest in nuclear weapons, which he knew France could not manufacture, but for the prestige of France he wanted a token *force de frappe*. Macmillan misunderstood and believed that if he could persuade President Kennedy to allow France nuclear weapons de Gaulle might soften his attitude to British entry. At Nassau on 19 December 1962, Macmillan, with considerable difficulty, prevailed upon Kennedy to supply both France and Britain with launchers for Polaris atomic missiles.[38] He hoped this would be the quid pro quo which would induce de Gaulle to change his mind about British entry. He could not have been more wrong. It only strengthened de Gaulle's resolve to veto British entry.[39]

De Gaulle looked on the offer of Polaris by America as evidence that Britain rejected all co-operation between France and Britain over atomic weapons. Heath told me his firm view is that de Gaulle was intensely annoyed at the patronizing way in which Kennedy and Macmillan at Nassau offered France a share in a NATO nuclear deterrent subject to American strings, and that without this provocation he might still have been able to overcome the difficulties and successfully negotiated entry at marathon meetings in January 1963.[40]

Heath's view that the Nassau offer was the deciding factor in de Gaulle denying British membership is not shared by survivors of his negotiating team or the Paris Embassy. The truth must be that unless Britain pooled her nuclear secrets with France de Gaulle would not allow us in, and the Americans rigidly refused to allow the British to disseminate nuclear knowledge. De Gaulle was intent on a nuclear weapon independent of America.[41]

Despite the gloom shed by Rambouillet, the Cabinet still hoped that agreement on entry would be reached at the meetings of Ministers in mid-January 1963. On 20 December 1962 Heath told the Cabinet:

> My expectation is, and certainly my hope is, that we shall be able to achieve satisfactory arrangements. Beginning on 14 January there will be a series of Ministerial meetings in Brussels as a result of which I hope to bring the negotiations to a successful conclusion.

On the controversial financial levy, Heath explained that he had reason to hope that Britain's share would be agreed 'as equal to that of France and Germany' at about 22 per cent. The Cabinet gave him a mandate to settle the outstanding issues on the basis of a Cabinet paper which he had submitted to the meeting.[42]

No more negotiations took place. Instead, de Gaulle imposed a veto. At a press conference on 14 January he declared Britain 'unfit for membership'. With his hopes for co-operation in nuclear know-how shattered by Nassau, the French President was not prepared to share leadership of the Common Market with Britain.

Although Macmillan had throughout been reluctant to face up to the implications of full membership, he was convinced there was no other acceptable course. His comment was 'All our policies at home and abroad are in ruins.'[43] The negotiations had caused friction with the Commonwealth; in return there was nothing to show except that Britain might never have become a member after de Gaulle's downfall if it had not been for this first try.

NOTES

Richard Lamb's *The Macmillan Years: The Emerging Truth* (London: John Murray, 1995) pp. 102–203 covers the negotiations for EFTA of Seventeen, EFTA of Seven and the application for entry to the EEC with numerous quotations from official documents.

Jacqueline Tratt's *The Macmillan Government and Europe* (Basingstoke: Macmillan, 1996) is an in-depth survey of relations with Europe from 1956 to 1961.

Miriam Camps' *Britain and the European Community* (Princeton, N.J.: Princeton University Press, 1964) covers the whole period, but was written before the official documents were available in the Public Record Office.

1. Based on a paper given to the Centre of International Studies at Christ's College, Cambridge, on 5 September 1996.
2. Alistair Horne, *Macmillan: 1957–1986*, vol. 1 (London: Macmillan, 1989), p. 314.
3. Richard Lamb, *The Failure of the Eden Government* (London: Sidgwick and Jackson, 1987), p. 61.
4. FO 953/1207.
5. Cab 129/50; Prem 11/153; Cab 128/24.
6. A myth has arisen that a Board of Trade official attended. This is incorrect.
7. Conversation with Russell Bretherton, 1986.
8. Ibid.; BT 11/5402; FO 371/122023; FO 371/122024; T 234183; Lamb, op. cit., pp. 60–92.
9. FO 371/122035.
10. Lamb, op. cit., p. 97; Cab 129/82.
11. FO 371/134520; Prem 11/2826.
12. Cab 129/82; FO 371/122046.
13. FO 371/122035; FO 371/134488; FO 371/134886; Prem 11/2133; Lamb, *The Macmillan Years*, pp. 109–10.
14. Prem 11/2531.
15. Maudling in his memoirs described Carli as 'one of the most able men I have had the good fortune to encounter'. Maudling, *Memoirs* (London: Sidgwick and Jackson, 1968), p. 70.
16. FO 371/134450; FO 371/134498.
17. FO 371/134450; FO 371/134504.
18. Prem 11/2532.
19. FO 371/134510; FO 371/134511; FO 371/134513.
20. The original suggestion for this had come from Bretherton who from his observation post in Brussels had realized no agreement would be reached between the Six and the Seven. FO 371/134450.
21. Prem 11/2827; Prem 11/2826; FO 371/134450.
22. FO 371/134514; FO 371/142504; Prem 11/3132.
23. Cab 128/34; Prem 11/3133.
24. FO 371/158264; FO 371/158171; Macmillan, *Pointing the Way* (London: Macmillan, 1972) p. 327.
25. Cab 128/35.

26. FO 371/157178; FO 371/158177.
27. Prem 11/3557; Prem 11/3558; Cab 128/35.
28. Lamb, op. cit., pp. 158–61.
29. FO 371/164778; FO 371/171149.
30. FO 371/171149.
31. FO 371/164835; FO 371/164780; FO 371/164781.
32. Cab 134/1537.
33. FO 371/837; FO 371/164802; Piers Dixon, *Double Diploma* (London: Hamish Hamilton, 1968), p. 292.
34. Letters to author from Sir Patrick Reilly and Lord Roll.
35. Cab 134/1536.
36. Cab 134/1539.
37. Prem 11/4230; interview with Sir Michael Butler.
38. De Gaulle would have to rely on US nuclear warheads.
39. Ian Clark, *Nuclear Diplomacy and the British Relationship* (Oxford: Oxford University Press, 1994). p. 481, quoting from papers in the Kennedy Centre.
40. FO 371/173308; interview with Sir Edward Heath.
41. Interviews with Sir Patrick Reilly and Sir Michael Butler. Reilly who was in charge at the Foreign Office much admires Heath for the way in which he conducted the negotiations. Butler, who worked with Dixon in Paris is highly critical believing Heath should have signed on the dotted line and renegotiated afterwards.
42. Cab 128/36.
43. Horne, op. cit., vol. 2, p. 447.

7 'Ne pleurez pas, Milord':[1] Macmillan and France from Algiers to Rambouillet

N. Piers Ludlow[2]

France was much less central to Macmillan's thought than the United States. There are long tracts of his memoirs, and lengthy sections of his two most recent biographies, in which no reference to the French can be found.[3] Yet dealings with France contributed significantly to the start and the end of Harold Macmillan's ministerial career. His war-time success in handling the Free French in Algiers represented Macmillan's first, significant achievement as a minister; his failure to manage the French during Britain's unsuccessful bid to enter the European Community in 1961–3 was, by contrast, his last great failure. An examination of Macmillan's handling and mishandling of France thus forms an important part of any audit of his career. This article will look briefly at Macmillan's North African interlude, before assessing in rather more detail the disappointments of the 1950s and 1960s. Particular attention will be given to the 1961–3 membership application and to the vision of Anglo-French leadership in Europe with which Macmillan hoped to win over President de Gaulle.

Macmillan's activities in North Africa in 1943 were important for two reasons.[4] First, Macmillan's success in handling the French in general, and Charles de Gaulle in particular, was a major feather in his cap. He had arrived, as Roosevelt's envoy in North Africa put it, without 'any exceptional knowledge of French or African affairs'.[5] He left having played an important role in managing the tense internal politics of the Free French and, in particular, having contributed to General de Gaulle's triumph over his American-sponsored rival General Giraud. Both his reputation and his self-confidence grew significantly as a result. Second, Macmillan had acquired in the process a wide range of contacts with what was to become the post-war French élite. While in Algiers he had the opportunity to encounter three future French Prime Ministers, Henri Queuille, Pierre Mendès-France and Maurice Couve de Murville; two subsequent IVième République cabinet ministers, Daniel Mayer and Jacques Soustelle; René Massigli, Henri Bonnet and Hervé Alphand, three of the most influential post-war French diplomats; and Jean Monnet, the architect of both French post-war economic recovery and of the early stages of European integration. And, of course, he had had extensive dealings with de Gaulle himself. These had not been easy. Nevertheless, both men appear to have developed a wary respect for each other and an awareness of each other's strengths. Furthermore, Macmillan had been able to develop an insight into the difficulties of dealing with the future French leader that few of his British counterparts could have matched. His war-time assessment of de Gaulle was uncannily prescient:

> General de Gaulle is one of those horses which either refuses to come to the starting-gate at all, or insists on careering down the course before the signal is given, or suddenly elects to run on a race-course different from the one appointed by the Stewards of the Jockey Club.[6]

Given this early opportunity to gain experience of de Gaulle, it is all the more remarkable that of all post-war British politicians it should have been Macmillan who suffered most at the General's hands.

It was over European integration that Macmillan's next serious dealings with the French occurred. Throughout the 1950s, Macmillan distinguished himself as one of the few senior British politicians who took at all seriously the process of integration underway between France, Germany, Italy and the Benelux nations. This did not always mean that he was supportive of their efforts. Indeed, in 1950 a joint plan by Macmillan and David Eccles to create a non-supranational body to control the European coal industry was angrily dismissed by Jean Monnet as an attempt to sabotage the much more ambitious European Coal and Steel Community, while in 1955 Macmillan as Foreign Secretary bore at least partial responsibility for a British *démarche* which was seen by many on the continent as an effort to nip in the bud the negotiations that eventually led to the EEC's formation.[7] But even unsuccessful policy ventures such as these highlighted the extent to which Macmillan felt that Britain could not stand idly by as its continental neighbours strove to develop both economic and political unity. They are therefore consistent with Macmillan's more positive moves, such as his 1952 memo to Anthony Eden in which he called for a new British policy towards Europe or his 1955 insistence that Britain send a high-level representative to the Spaak committee discussions about a possible European common market.[8] In total contrast to his long-standing rivals 'Rab' Butler and Eden, Macmillan was never bored by European integration.[9]

Equally distinctive was Macmillan's awareness that the process underway among the Six was about more than simple economic co-operation. In a period when responsibility for following developments in the integration process tended to be left to the economic sections of the Whitehall machinery, and when, tellingly, Britain's representative on the Spaak committee had been a relatively junior Board of Trade official rather than the senior foreign ministry delegates sent by the Six, Macmillan was already conscious that a successful outcome of the Messina process might pose a serious political danger to Britain. In February 1956, for instance, he had written in alarmist fashion about the possibility of Germany becoming the dominant power in Europe through the integration process, and he concluded: 'I do not like the prospect of a world divided into the Russian sphere, the American sphere and a united Europe of which we are not a member.'[10]

Despite this anxiety about the prospect of German dominance in the long term, Macmillan was convinced that in the immediate future the key player among the Six was France. It was the French who had made the original decision in 1950 to press ahead without Britain, it was the French who were the principal determinants of the pace of the Treaty of Rome negotiations and it was the French who would need most persuading if Britain was to be allowed either to join or in some way to associate itself with the EEC project. In the late 1950s, just as was to be the case during the 1961–3 application, Paris, not Bonn or Brussels, was the focal point for Macmillan's attention. At times, indeed, Macmillan's reflections about how to redefine Britain's position *vis-à-vis* the Continent convey the impression that Germany, Italy and the Benelux countries mattered only in so far as they could coax, cajole or pressurize France into agreement with the UK. But for all his interest in what was happening on the Continent, for all his sensitivity to the political as well as economic dimension of integration, and for all his awareness of the centrality of France to the whole process, Macmillan, first as Foreign Secretary, then as Chancellor of the Exchequer and finally as Prime Minister, endorsed and promoted a policy response to the Messina process which was hamstrung from the outset by its failure to take into account the needs, hopes and anxieties of the French.[11]

Plan G was an ingenious policy. In essence it was a proposal to create a free trade area for industrial goods encompassing all eighteen members of the Organization for European Economic Cooperation (OEEC).[12] It represented a major development in UK commercial policy, but one which, because of the exclusion of agriculture and the absence of any requirement to harmonize tariff levels towards the rest of the world, would leave Britain's trade links with the Commonwealth largely unaffected. Furthermore, it could be seen as compatible with the parallel arrangements being devised among the Six. If the Six succeeded in their attempt to create a closely knit economic community, complete with a common external tariff, strong institutions and a common agricultural policy, they would constitute the inner kernel of a wider European free trade zone, but their co-operation would not harm economically those Western European countries which chose to remain outside of the EEC. If, by contrast, the Six failed, a scenario which the Foreign Office deemed likely until 1957 at least, an OEEC free trade area would ensure that their set-back did not undermine the wider process of trade liberalization within Europe. The plan thus seemed to reconcile both Britain's European and Commonwealth ties and to cater for either completion or collapse in the Treaty of Rome negotiations.

The proposal, moreover, appeared likely to reconcile a number of apparently incompatible interests. Thus the advocacy of Macmillan and Peter Thorneycroft, the President of the Board of Trade, was sufficient to win the backing of the British Cabinet in September 1956, while at a specially convened conference of Commonwealth representatives in July 1957, the acquiescence, albeit grudging, of Britain's former empire was obtained.[13] Several European governments also seemed enthusiastic. In West Germany and in the Benelux countries there were many who had expressed anxiety that the Six constituted too narrow and too restrictive an outlet for trade. The prospect of tariffs being removed throughout Western Europe was therefore warmly welcomed. In Germany, the Minister for Economics, Ludwig Erhard, tried in October 1956 to persuade the Cabinet to abandon the deadlocked negotiations about the EEC in favour of the British plan.[14] He was defeated, but his personal support for the British scheme survived and was shared by much of the German political and industrial élite. Others, such as the Belgian Christian Democrat Baron Snoy, saw the scheme as a useful supplement to, rather than replacement of, the EEC.[15]

Unfortunately for Macmillan, however, there was little such support for the scheme in France. This was not due to Anglophobia. On the contrary, many amongst the French élites had regretted the 1950 decision to start building European institutions without Britain, had welcomed the brief flurry of Anglo-French co-operation which had culminated in the joint operation in Suez, and were keen to see close cross-channel co-operation reestablished.[16] But the free trade area was ill-designed to bring about such a *rapprochement*. Indeed, the whole scheme constituted a major threat to the French government's plans to win public and parliamentary approval for the EEC. It was therefore essential for France that the project be postponed for as long as possible, if not abandoned altogether.

The French government's approach to the Treaty of Rome negotiations had been extremely cautious. The Prime Minister, Guy Mollet, and his closest collaborators were acutely aware that the proposed common market would provoke strong opposition both from those such as the Gaullists who were politically hostile to supranational integration and from the economic interests who had successfully thwarted several planned customs unions in the late 1940s. Public and parliamentary opinion was thus encouraged to concentrate on the proposals for European co-operation in the field of nuclear energy – a project which enjoyed widespread support in France – while French negotiators in Brussels were instructed to win a wide variety of concessions designed to make the common market scheme more palatable. Foremost amongst these was a pledge that the EEC would incorporate a common agricultural policy, thereby opening up the prospect of lucrative foreign trade for French farmers, and special provisions for the soon-to-be-independent French territories in Africa. Equally important to France were a series of measures designed to ensure that the liberalization brought about by the EEC would not give too severe a shock to the fragile French economy. Paris had thus insisted that the level of the common external tariff be set at a point substantially above the average German or Benelux tariffs and that internal tariff disarmament be accompanied by steps to harmonize social security costs across the Community. A further goal dear to the French was the inclusion

of safeguard clauses, intended to allow the French to delay imple-
mentation of certain aspects of the Treaty of Rome should the French
economy encounter difficulties. The French government thus hoped
that the EEC would bring about a controlled and partial abandonment of traditional French protectionism, inside a Community which
would also enable the French to obtain certain long-cherished aims.[17]

The free trade area plan offered no such guarantees. It specifically excluded both agricultural trade and commerce between European states and their imperial or former imperial territories. It
provided for no common external tariff barrier nor any timetable
for the harmonization of social security provisions across all eighteen participating countries. It made no mention of safeguard clauses.
And of course it would confront the French economy with unhin-
dered competition from all seventeen other members of the OEEC
rather than just her five European Coal and Steel Community (ECSC)
partners. It also lacked the long-term political aim of the EEC:
the yearning for a stronger Europe, less dependent on the US,
which had reached new heights in France in the aftermath of the
Suez crisis, would not be satisfied by a mere free trade arrangement.[18] None of the features of the European Community that were
central to the French government's plans to win parliamentary support
were thus shared by the free trade area. Furthermore, the French
saw a real danger that the British proposal might undermine all
that they were trying to achieve in the Treaty of Rome negotiations.
Germany, they feared, would be much less likely to acquiesce in
an expensive agricultural policy, a set of measures designed to assist
Francophone Africa, and provisions for the harmonization of social
costs – all aspects of the Treaty of Rome that had been highly
controversial within the Federal Republic – if the British were offering
the prospect of industrial free trade without any of the associated
costs. The free trade area was thus not only unappealing *per se*,
but it also threatened to destroy all that the French hoped to obtain
from their involvement in the Treaty of Rome process.[19]

The French thus mounted a determined effort to delay and obstruct
the British plan. It could not be rejected outright – it enjoyed too
much support elsewhere in the Community, and Britain was too
close an ally to be summarily rejected.[20] But it could both be delayed
– an objective which was attained in the spring of 1957 when the
French received a promise from London not to press ahead with
the free trade area scheme until the ratification of the Treaty of
Rome was complete – and, through careful diplomacy, transformed

into something much more akin to the Treaty of Rome. The OEEC committee which was to examine the proposal was inundated with French requests designed to transform the British project into something more substantial than a simple free trade area. With the Six divided and the British unwilling to allow their scheme to be totally altered, deadlock was the inevitable result.

Macmillan's response was ineffective. He had placed too much faith in the French fear of Germany, calculating wrongly that France would be ready to pay a high economic price in order to secure close British involvement in European cooperation.[21] When France proved to prefer more economically advantageous co-operation with Germany and without Britain, he had little to fall back upon. He did try briefly to put together a series of limited British concessions on agriculture. He also successfully persuaded the cabinet to endorse the idea that the free trade area should have strong common institutions.[22] But neither of these steps proved enough to satisfy the French; indeed, the token nature of such concessions only underlined the extent to which Macmillan had allowed his policy proposal to become so hemmed about with promises to the Commonwealth or pledges to British interest groups that substantial movement away from the UK's starting position proved impossible. Nor did Macmillan, by now Prime Minister, use his increased personal clout to launch a bilateral diplomatic offensive in support of his scheme. He did travel once to Paris for talks with Felix Gaillard. He also went to Bonn and urged Adenauer to intervene on Britain's behalf with the French. But on neither occasion did the Prime Minister have much to offer and little was accomplished as a result.[23] Furthermore, both Continental visits were totally overshadowed by Macmillan's much more evident diplomatic effort to mend fences with the Americans after the strains of the Suez affair. As James Ellison has argued, there was little in the overall thrust of British diplomacy at this time to convince either the French or their allies amongst the other five that Britain was serious in its intent to transform its relationship with Europe.[24]

De Gaulle's return to power in June 1958 briefly seemed to renew the prospects of the free trade area. An outspoken critic of supranational integration, the General would not necessarily abide by the Treaty of Rome and might, some predicted, opt instead for looser and wider co-operation within a free trade area without supranational powers. Macmillan indulged briefly in such speculation.[25] But as quickly became apparent, de Gaulle was also a pragmatist, well aware that his hopes of modernizing the French economy and of forging close ties with the Germans in particular – both essential prerequisites of his longer-term plans – would not be furthered by reneging on his predecessors' promises. France thus implemented the Treaty of Rome on time and in full.[26] The free trade area by contrast was brushed aside. On 11 November 1958, de Gaulle's spokesman announced that France was no longer ready to consider the British scheme. A week later the President travelled to Germany and persuaded Adenauer to accept that the free trade area plan was dead.[27] Taken together, these two events publicly underlined the impossibility of Macmillan's hopes. In reality, the failure to address French needs had ensured that the prospects of the free trade area plan had never been good, and by mid-1958 the scheme was clearly moribund. What has sometimes been described as de Gaulle's first veto was, in fact, an act of euthanasia.

Macmillan was angered and shaken by the French rejection of the free trade area. In bilateral discussions with the Americans he is widely reported to have compared the formation of the EEC without an accompanying free trade area to Napoleon's planned economic integration of Europe, and suggested that Britain's response should as vigorous in the twentieth century as it had been in the nineteenth.[28] But to his credit, the Prime Minister soon channelled this anger and frustration into the search for a new constructive approach to the Six. Thus, little more than a year after the collapse of the free trade area scheme, Macmillan seems to have privately decided that Britain's future lay inside the newly formed European Community. It would not be easy, however, either to win round his cabinet and party colleagues or to persuade public opinion that so significant a policy change was required.

The story of Macmillan's efforts to coax his government to a point where a membership application became possible has been well told elsewhere.[29] What is relevant to this essay is that by mid-1961 the Prime Minister had secured the consent of his cabinet, the Conservative Party and the Commonwealth to a new approach to Europe, this time based upon a conditional membership bid. Furthermore, Britain's new policy had been enthusiastically received by five of the six Community member states. The exception, repeating the pattern of 1957–8, was France.[30]

French qualms about British membership had a wide variety of explanations. At an economic level, the French government feared that the UK, both during the membership negotiations themselves and once inside the Community, would damage or destroy the fledgling CAP, lower the level of Community tariffs on a range of sensitive products, and alter the advantageous system of EEC support for former French colonies in Africa and the Caribbean. Politically, moreover, British membership threatened to disrupt Franco-German *rapprochement*, lessen the ability of the French to assume the political leadership of the grouping, and bolster American influence within the EEC. With Britain inside the Community, de Gaulle's hopes of transforming the EEC into a unified political grouping, able, under French leadership, to play a role on the world stage which was increasingly autonomous from the United States would be seriously compromised. That de Gaulle's response to the British diplomat who delivered the news that the UK had decided to apply was stiffly polite and totally lacking in the enthusiasm so noticeable in other European capitals was not at all surprising.[31]

In 1961, however, Macmillan had anticipated French opposition. Over the preceding years the Premier had toyed with a variety of ideas designed to give France a political incentive to resolve the division of Western Europe between the EEC and EFTA. These had included the suggestion that Britain might intervene in Washington in favour of de Gaulle's quest for greater tripartite consultation and, more radically, the possibility that the UK might in some way assist the French in their lengthy and time-consuming struggle to develop an independent nuclear deterrent.[32] By December 1960 these varied strands had come together in a document which Macmillan was to describe as his Grand Design.

The Grand Design quite deliberately set out to place British membership of the EEC in the wider context of Western unity. The Free World, it argued, risked losing ground to the Soviet bloc unless it could come to terms with the reappearance of a dynamic and strong Western Europe. Britain and America's priority aims should therefore be the resolution of the Six/Seven divide – an economic split which, according to Macmillan, risked hardening into a harmful political fracture – reform of the Atlantic Alliance, and the incorporation of French efforts to develop a nuclear deterrent of its own into a safe Alliance framework. De Gaulle and France were central to all three projects. As a result Britain and America would have to make an effort to satisfy de Gaulle's aspirations in the latter two fields in exchange for French acquiescence to the entry of Britain into the European Community. The Grand Design was thus in essence the sketch of a complex transatlantic bargain between Britain, America and France.[33]

Unfortunately for Macmillan, the American consent so central to his plans did not prove forthcoming. Neither a series of letters setting out his vision to Kennedy, nor Macmillan's April 1961 visit to Washington, were sufficient to convince the new US administration that so much had to be done to win over de Gaulle. Kennedy was loud in his praise of the British decision to apply for EEC membership, and Dean Rusk, his Secretary of State, declared his country's willingness to help British accession, but neither were prepared to promise nuclear assistance to France so as to bribe de Gaulle into allowing Britain in. To do so, Kennedy made clear, would violate the US stance on non-proliferation, invite demands from the Federal Republic for similar assistance, and incur the wrath of the US Congress.[34]

Macmillan was deeply disappointed by this American reply. In May he wrote in his diary that the European problem was 'obviously insoluble'; a month later he confessed that 'my great plan has failed'.[35] But despite his momentary depression, Macmillan did not abandon all hope. Neither the American veto of spring 1961, nor a second American prohibition on nuclear deals with the French that was delivered almost exactly a year later, destroyed the Prime Minister's belief that an arrangement could be reached with de Gaulle. Instead he pressed on, using the three summit meetings with de Gaulle that took place between Britain's application to the EEC and the collapse of the negotiations in January 1963, to set out a far-reaching vision of European co-operation centred on an Anglo-French core.[36] So radical was some of the rhetoric about Anglo-French co-operation employed by Macmillan in his encounters with the French leader that it deserves to be looked at in detail.[37]

The Prime Minister deliberately tailored his vision to fit in with de Gaulle's plans for political union among the Six. Indeed, one of the most remarkable tactics used by Macmillan in his attempts to win over the French leader was the repeated affirmation of Britain's belief in, and support for, an intergovernmental political grouping organized along the lines set out by the French President. At Birch Grove in November 1961 Macmillan declared himself to be in favour of a 'union des patries' – a label for European political union normally associated with de Gaulle; in May 1962 the Prime Minister informed de Gaulle that he was fully in agreement with the views

on political union which the General had set out in his May 15
press conference; at Champs, the British statesman ridiculed the
obstinacy which Belgium and the Netherlands were showing towards
de Gaulle's plans; and at Rambouillet in December 1962 the premier predicted that political union would actually be agreed more
easily once Britain was inside the Community than while she remained without.[38] The French President was thus left in no doubt
as to the harmony that existed between British views of political
union among the EEC member states and his own attitudes.

Macmillan also went out of his way to emphasize the importance of European political unity in general and Anglo-French co-
operation in particular. At the Birch Grove meeting in November
1961 Macmillan, as so often, used an historical analogy to under-
line the dangers of a persistent split between the Six and the Seven
and the necessity of political union, warning 'that if the solution
[to the question of British membership] was not found in 1962 the
idea of the restoration of Europe would fail. History would regard
it as a repetition of the story of the city states of Greece which
could not unite or could only unite occasionally as at Marathon.
The dream of French and British leadership of Europe would be
gone for ever as would all hope of giving Europe a strong and
individual personality which would enable it to survive as an independent force in the world.'[39] Six months later at Champs the Prime
Minister made use of rather more recent history. This time he
emphasized the importance of cross-channel co-operation by suggesting that both World Wars might have been averted had harmony existed between Paris and London. Russia had now replaced
Germany as the principal threat, but the need for a strong Anglo-
French entente remained as pressing as ever.[40]

Even more striking were the Prime Minister's references to the
need for Anglo-French co-operation in the field of defence. These
could be traced back as far as the January 1961 summit at Rambouillet, in the course of which Macmillan had first floated the
idea of the United States, Britain and France together acting as
'trustees of nuclear weapons' for all of the Free World, but they
became more radical as Macmillan's determination to succeed in
the membership application grew.[41] In the wake of Kennedy's refusal
to sanction Anglo-French nuclear co-operation, Macmillan's comments also began to contain pointed references to the need for a
European defence mechanism which was not totally dependent on
the United States. In November 1961, the premier suggested that

'Europe could be organised in concentric circles. There could be a political and military core around which there would be an economic organisation' – the implication clearly being that Britain and France would constitute this inner core.[42] Then, in the run-up to the Champs summit Macmillan had two very confidential meetings with Jean Chauvel, the outgoing French Ambassador in London, and Geoffroy de Courcel, his replacement. The Prime Minister explained to both men his belief that, in the light of Russia's newly acquired parity with the US in the nuclear field, Europe could no longer rely on the American nuclear guarantee. Britain and France should thus take the lead in transforming Europe into a credible nuclear power in its own right. To this end, technical co-operation between the two countries was desirable. No specific details were provided on either occasion, but in the meeting with de Courcel Macmillan again spoke of Britain and France holding their nuclear weapons as 'trustees for Europe'.[43]

At the Champs meeting itself, Macmillan was somewhat more circumspect. Contrary to press speculation at the time, and much academic discussion since, no nuclear deal was struck between the two leaders. Nevertheless, the way in which the British Prime Minister claimed to envisage the future of the Western Alliance and of Franco-British co-operation continued to be extremely radical. NATO, he argued, should become 'a double-headed alliance' – in fifty years time, he explained, it would be much better for Europe as a whole to be putting its views to the Americans, rather than individual states doing so. Indeed, as he explained the next day, the inclusion of Britain in the evolving Europe would open up a wide range of possibilities: 'There might be a European organisation allied to the United States. There would be a plan for the defence of Europe. The nuclear power of European countries would be held as part of this European defence.' Once again, the premier remained vague both about the details of any such European defence co-operation, and about the time-frame within which such an arrangement could emerge. But for a British leader to talk to his French counterpart in such terms, albeit without specifying when and how any European defence co-operation would occur, was all but unprecedented.[44]

Taken together, Macmillan's comments to de Gaulle and to the two French Ambassadors constituted a remarkable declaration of Britain's newly found European credentials. The UK, the Prime Minister appeared to suggest, was not only ready to contemplate European co-operation in the political as well as economic field, but was also ready to see transatlantic relations alter accordingly. The special relationship would not necessarily disappear, but it would be complemented by an equally close rapport between Paris and London. Macmillan, in other words, seemed to be ready to accept both de Gaulle's 1958 call for tripartite consultation between France, Britain and America and the General's subsequent schemes for European political union. Furthermore, as part of its joint effort with France to develop a credible European defence policy, Britain, it seemed, would be willing to co-operate in the technical development of atomic weapons. The nuclear assistance for EEC membership deal, about which so much speculation has raged, was not mentioned overtly, but Macmillan did imply that nuclear co-operation was a likely component of any new, closer, London–Paris axis.

Unfortunately for Macmillan, however, the vision he described was ill-suited to persuade de Gaulle. From a French point of view there were three major flaws. The first was simply that Macmillan's suggestions lacked credibility. Talk of extensive Anglo-French co-operation in the defence field, or of a British commitment to a European defence scheme, was far removed from Britain's traditional policies, from the discourse of other British politicians during the 1961–3 period, and from the disappointing realities of ongoing Anglo-French co-operative projects.[45] It was therefore difficult to treat Macmillan's ideas as anything more than airy mirages, designed to lure the French from their intended course. Furthermore, the British proposals were highly dependent on American consent. As a result, even if Macmillan was in earnest, and even if the Premier succeeded in converting the British Cabinet and Parliament to his radical new approach, there was still a strong probability that the US would quash any talk of Anglo-French co-operation in the nuclear field. The gift offered by Macmillan was not entirely in his control.

Second, the Prime Minister's vision remained too Atlanticist for de Gaulle. For all his talk of close Anglo-French co-operation, Macmillan had not promised to abandon either the special relationship or the Atlantic Alliance. Indeed in both of his conversations with the French Ambassadors, Macmillan had specifically acknowledged that Britain could only proceed in the direction outlined with US consent. Somewhat implausibly, he had suggested to Chauvel that this might not prove particularly difficult to obtain. The US, after all, was keen to share the tremendous burden of Western leadership with responsible partners. But, as de Gaulle was well aware, no partnership that the US would agree to was likely to provide Europe with the degree of independence to which he aspired. A *Europe européenne* was unlikely to be sanctioned by Washington.

Third, Macmillan's vision, although described as an Anglo-French partnership, would have given Britain too many advantages, and France too few. The UK would have represented the central player in the new Atlantic arrangements, the most established voice on the world stage, and the senior partner in any Anglo-French nuclear co-operation; France, by contrast, would be weakened economically by the likely effects of Community enlargement, and overshadowed by Britain in all international fora. These disadvantages were particularly striking if the arrangements suggested by Macmillan were contrasted with de Gaulle's own plans for European unity centred on a Franco-German core. Within a Franco-German pairing, the General was confident that France would assume and retain the leadership role. Of the two powers, France alone would be a nuclear power, France alone would be a permanent member of the United Nations security council, France alone would retain strong world-wide links with its former colonies. Germany, moreover, had strong reasons to avoid being assertive on the international stage, and had shown in Community negotiations a recurrent tendency to sacrifice much in order to preserve French goodwill. Paired with Britain, by contrast, France would see most of its assets matched and would, moreover, have to deal with a country accustomed to making its views known internationally and unlikely to give much away in negotiation. It was not in de Gaulle's interest to give up so much in return for so questionable a gain. Macmillan's political strategy for overcoming the French was thus deeply flawed.

Macmillan's greatest mistake *vis-à-vis* France, however, lay not in the shape of the political offer with which he tried to woo de Gaulle, but in his belief that France needed to be wooed at all. Had the Premier examined the French position more carefully, he might have realized that de Gaulle's sullen response to the news of the impending British application concealed serious weaknesses on the part of the French. France and de Gaulle needed the Community. Without it French economic modernization would be seriously disrupted. Furthermore, they needed Franco-German *rapprochement*, since without harnessing West Germany's economic muscle French ambitions of becoming a major international player once more were unlikely to be fulfilled. Both the Community and Franco-German understanding would, however, have been severely shaken, if not destroyed, had de Gaulle tried summarily to reject a British membership application which all five of France's partners were eager to accept. And the international repercussions of an early move against Britain would have been mirrored by the consequences within France. Any rejection of British membership before the Parliamentary elections of November 1962, when the Gaullist Union pour la Nouvelle République (UNR) unexpectedly gained an absolute majority, would have prompted a rebellion by the Mouvement Républicain Populaire (MRP) and centrist deputies upon whom the coalition governments of Michel Debré and Georges Pompidou depended. The result would almost certainly have been an early general election, fought on the unfavourable terrain of European issues. As de Gaulle was told forcefully by his cabinet colleagues in July 1962, France could not bar Britain's road overtly. Its only hope was to use the technical discussions in Brussels to place as many obstacles as possible in Macmillan's route.[46]

Britain could thus have defied de Gaulle. His goodwill was not necessary for Community enlargement to go ahead, since he was in no position to veto British accession until late 1962. An early agreement in Brussels – bought at the price of British concessions on Commonwealth trade and British agriculture – would have thwarted the French. Unfortunately, Macmillan overestimated the power of the French leader and shied away from the sacrifices in Brussels which would have been necessary if the General were to be frustrated. He opted to speculate about a distant future of Anglo-French nuclear and security co-operation rather than to deliver immediate economic concessions which would have outflanked the French in the Brussels negotiations and clearly demonstrated Britain's new European credentials. A readiness to buy French wheat in place of Australian, or to oblige British farmers to accept CAP protection in place of the deficiency payments to which they had become accustomed, was the route to success in 1961–3. Instead, Macmillan tried to talk his way into the Community, over-confident of his ability to win the General round to his side and unaware that his vision of a Franco-British partnership was neither credible nor desirable for France. In 1943 much of Macmillan's success in Algiers had been attributable to his deft handling of de Gaulle. Two decades later, the greatest foreign policy failure of his years as Prime Minister, ironically, sprang precisely from his erroneous belief that personal intervention with de Gaulle would once again prove the most effective and painless route to success.

NOTES

1. The comment de Gaulle was supposedly tempted to make to Macmillan after he had made clear in the course of their December 1962 Rambouillet meeting that he would not allow Britain to join the European Community. See Alain Peyrefitte, *C'était de Gaulle* (Paris: Fayard, 1994), p. 333.
2. The author would like to thank James Ellison, Martin Schaad, Liz Kane and Constantine Pagedas for their help in preparing this piece – and Richard Aldous and Sabine Lee for persuading him to attend the Macmillan conference in the first place.
3. Alistair Horne, *Macmillan*, 2 vols (London: Macmillan, 1990, 1991); John Turner, *Macmillan* (London: Longman, 1994).
4. See Horne, *Macmillan*, vol. 1, pp. 153–90.
5. Robert Murphy, *Diplomat among Warriors* (London: Collins, 1964), p. 206.
6. Macmillan to Churchill, May 1943; cited in Horne, *Macmillan*, vol. 1, p. 181.
7. John W. Young, 'Churchill's "No" to Europe: the "Rejection" of European Union by Churchill's Postwar Government, 1951–2', *Historical Journal*, vol. 28, no. 4, p. 927; Young and Michael Dockrill (eds), *British Foreign Policy, 1945–56* (London: Macmillan, 1989), pp. 210–15; Paul-Henri Spaak, *Combats inachevés* (Paris: Fayard, 1969), vol. 2, p. 77.
8. Young, 'Churchill's "No" to Europe', p. 932; Simon Burgess and Geoffrey Edwards, 'The Six plus One: British Policy-making and the Question of European Economic Integration, 1955', *International Affairs*, no. 64 (1988), p. 399.
9. See Michael Charlton, *The Price of Victory* (London: BBC, 1983), p. 195.
10. Referred to in James Ellison, 'British Policy towards European Integration: The Proposal for a European Free Trade Area, June 1955–December 1958', PhD thesis, Christ Church College, Canterbury (1997).
11. The following section draws heavily upon Elizabeth Kane, 'Tilting to Europe? British Responses to Developments in European Integration 1955–1958', DPhil thesis, Oxford (1996) and James Ellison, 'British Policy towards European Integration'.
12. The Plan is reproduced as an appendix to Harold Macmillan, *Riding the Storm* (London: Macmillan, 1971), pp. 753–4.
13. Kane, 'Tilting to Europe?', pp. 106–11.
14. Hanns Jürgen Küsters, *Fondaments de la Communauté Economique Européenne* (Brussels: Editions Labor, 1990), p. 197.
15. Jean-Charles Snoy et d'Oppuers, *Rebâtir l'Europe* (Paris: Duculot, 1989), pp. 116–33.
16. For one outspoken critique of the 1950 break with Britain see René Massigli, *Une comédie des erreurs 1943–1956: Souvenirs et réflexions sur une étape de la construction européenne* (Paris: Plon, 1978), pp. 199ff.
17. Christian Pineau and Christiane Rimbaud, *Le Grand Pari: L'aventure du traité de Rome* (Paris: Fayard, 1991), pp. 151–218; Pierre Guillen, 'Europe a Cure for French Impotence? The Guy Mollet Government and the

Negotiation of the Treaties of Rome', in Ennio di Nolfo (ed.), *Power in Europe? Great Britain, France, Germany and Italy and the Origins of the EEC, 1952–1957* (Berlin: Walter de Gruyter, 1992), pp. 505–16.
18. Pineau and Rimbaud, *Le Grand Pari*, pp. 219–39.
19. Bernard Picot, 'La France et l'entrée de la Grande-Bretagne dans le Marché commun', PhD thesis, Lyon (1965) pp. 91–5.
20. For good examples of French equivocation see 'La Zone de Libre Echange devant l'Opinion Française', *Revue du Marché Commun*, vol. 1, no. 1 (1958), pp. 30–2.
21. Ellison, 'British Policy towards European Integration'.
22. Ibid.
23. Ibid.
24. James Ellison, 'Harold Macmillan's Fear of "Little Europe": Britain, the Six and the European Free Trade Area' (University of Leicester Discussion Papers on Britain and Europe, BE95/5), pp. 12–20.
25. Martin Schaad, 'Anglo-German Relations during the Formative Years of the European Community, 1955–1961', DPhil thesis, Oxford (1995) pp. 181–2.
26. Jean-Marc Boegner, '1958, le général de Gaulle et l'acceptation du traité de Rome', *Espoir*, no. 87 (1992), pp. 28–30.
27. Gérard Bossuat, 'The Choice of "La Petite Europe" by France, 1957–1963: An Ambition for France and for Europe', in Richard Griffiths and Stuart Ward (eds), *Courting the Common Market: The First Attempt to Enlarge the EEC, 1960–3* (London: Lothian Foundation Press, 1996), pp. 59–82.
28. PRO FO371 150269; Steel to FO, 31 March 1960.
29. Wolfram Kaiser, *Using Europe, Abusing the Europeans: Britain and European Integration, 1945–63* (London: Macmillan, 1996), pp. 120–67; Richard Lamb, *The Macmillan Years: The Emerging Truth* (London: John Murray, 1995), pp. 126–57; Miriam Camps, *Britain and the European Community, 1955–1963* (Oxford: Oxford University Press, 1964), pp. 274–376.
30. For more detail on this and most of the following points see N. Piers Ludlow, *Dealing with Britain: The Six and the First UK Application to the EEC* (Cambridge: Cambridge University Press, 1997).
31. PRO FO371 158179; M615/195; Sir A. Rumbold to FO, 28 July 1961.
32. See Kaiser, *Using Europe*, pp. 157–66; Constantine Pagedas, 'Troubled Partners: Anglo-American Diplomacy and the French Problem, 1960–3', PhD, King's College, London (1996), pp. 73–164.
33. Ibid.
34. PRO PREM 11 3311 contains details of both the visit and the correspondence.
35. Cited in Kaiser, *Using Europe, Abusing the Europeans*, p. 165 and p. 166.
36. For the second American refusal see PRO PREM 11 3712l, Ormsby-Gore to Macmillan, 17 May 962.
37. Many of the points that follow are discussed at greater length in N. Piers Ludlow, 'Le Paradoxe Anglais, Great Britain and Political Union', *Revue d'Allemagne*, vol. 29, no. 2 (April–June 1997), pp. 259–72.

38. The records of the three encounters are in PRO PREM 11 3561, 24–5 November 1961; PREM 11 3775, 2–3 June 1962; PREM 11 4230, 15–16 December 1962.
39. PRO PREM 11 3561, 25 November 1961.
40. PRO PREM 11 3775, 2 June 1962.
41. Pagedas, 'Troubled Partners', p. 160.
42. PRO PREM 11 3561, 25 November 1961.
43. The meeting with Chauvel is in PRO PREM 11 3792, 19 April 1962. That with de Courcel is in PREM 11 3775, 9 May 1962.
44. PRO PREM 11 3775, 2–3 June 1962.
45. For the halting reality of Anglo-French scientific co-operation, see the description of the ELDO project in Pagedas, 'Troubled Partners', pp. 119–45.
46. This argument is developed in more detail in Ludlow, *Dealing with Britain*, pp. 239–40.

8 Pragmatism versus Principle? Macmillan and Germany[1]

Sabine Lee

Anglo-German relations have never had the special quality that has been attributed at times to Anglo-American or Franco-German relations. The period of Harold Macmillan's premiership was no exception. He never saw in Germany a partner of similar significance to the United States, the Soviet Union or, indeed, France. However, his view of Germany changed over time and, partly as a function of this, the development of relations between Britain and Germany took a decisive turn for the worse while he held office in 10 Downing Street.

As with many of Macmillan's attitudes and policies, the key to his perception of Germany lies in his formative years and especially in his experiences during the two World Wars. Although his first-hand experience of fighting in the Great War was brief, he suffered two injuries which resulted in years of physical pain. Far worse and longer lasting were the mental pains of being one of a few survivors of a large group of university acquaintances and friends, a feeling of guilt which affected him for the rest of his life.[2] It is not surprising, therefore, that he should have had ambivalent feelings about the country with greatest responsibility for the outbreak of both World Wars. Germany was associated with militarism, manifested across Europe especially in its Prussian image. The strength of Macmillan's feelings about war and his recollections of the First World War in particular, made a certain reserve *vis-à-vis* Germany almost inevitable. He remained sensitive to anything resembling his recollections of Prussian militarism. This apprehension survived in Macmillan despite his experiences of decades of Germany as a democratic and explicitly non-militaristic state as part of the Western world after 1945.

As Harold Macmillan pointed out in a conversation with Alistair Horne, his impression on attending Konrad Adenauer's funeral in 1967 pointed in this direction: 'The guard of honour, all those coal-scuttle helmets . . . they haven't changed.'[3]

But this resentment was only one side of the coin. As a power politician with clear sight of political necessities, he was one of the first to advocate the integration of West Germany into the Western bloc. In this he followed Winston Churchill's policy of bringing the Germans into Europe. Against calls for harsh denazification, he demanded in the House of Commons to accommodate the Germans in order to avoid them becoming a menace to world peace again. He entirely agreed with Churchill's assessment that the immediate threat to peace had moved from Germany to the Soviet Union. Consequently Germany had to become an ally, the country had to enter the West 'as a free and equal member',[4] if it was to be won for the West. But the integration of the Federal Republic into Western Europe was at the same time part of Macmillan's grander concept for Europe, and it corresponded with the role he envisaged for the United Kingdom, first at the fringe and later at the heart of Europe.[5]

In these few examples we find traces of what at first sight appears to be an inconsistent attitude to the country across the Channel. But his views, rather than being inconsistent, reflected a multifaceted approach to a country which throughout Macmillan's political career could be found in the roles of enemy, alliance partner, economic rival, Cold War player and object, occupied and sovereign, dictatorship and democracy alike. Therefore, it is less surprising that we find a multitude of different and discrepant views about and a variety of policies *vis-à-vis* Germany. Anglo-German relations in the post-war period reflected these altering policies just as they were influenced by them.

Anglo-German relations never really took off after the war. They lacked the warm quality of the Franco-German axis that formed between Adenauer and de Gaulle, and certainly never reached a level of understanding as existed between the United Kingdom and the United States, however 'special' these relations may have been.[6] The reasons for this are manifold. The atrocities committed by the Germans during the war are only one, and probably not the primary, factor. Although the British associated (and probably still associate) Germany with aggression, militarism and nationalism, the nature of the bilateral relationship is less crude and the underlying reasons for the problems of both countries are more subtle. When the *News of the World*, in 1969, proclaimed: 'It is the simple truth that the British never liked the Germans and will never like them', many British people would have agreed. There was a strong sense of bitterness, because whereas Germany had by now experienced an economic miracle, Britain had failed to recover from the war in the same way. On the contrary, the British had lost their position as the centre of the Empire, and even the position as No. 1 partner of the United States in Europe was under threat not least from the increasingly strong Germany.[7] If the early post-war years had been characterized by a sense of responsibility for the defeated Germany which was in desperate need of food and fuel, attitudes changed with the changing fortunes or rather degrees of economic recovery.[8] On the other hand, the Germans were equally prejudiced against the British, seeing them as a nation of shopkeepers whose main characteristics were jealousy and scepticism. Hence, intellect and ability as well as commitment were often underestimated. Chancellor Adenauer spoke for many when he quoted an English friend of his saying: 'If the English worked six days a week, they would be a lot better off. But they finish work Friday lunch time and don't start again until Monday morning. They should not complain when they don't succeed.'[9]

But it was not prejudice alone which accounted for a difficulty in overcoming the effects of the war on the mutual relationship. There were differences in outlook which were the effect of what could be described as 'national character'. One former Federal President juxtaposed British pragmatism and German principle[10] – a comparison which sums up the difference in outlook well. It was felt in politics and international affairs: in particular it became a stumbling bloc for British–German relations in the field of East–West relations, where the German legalistic approach came face to face with British pragmatism.[11]

During the height of Macmillan's political power, the man firmly in charge of affairs in Germany was Chancellor Konrad Adenauer. Just as Macmillan had certain reservations about Germany, Adenauer had ambivalent feelings about Great Britain. These grew stronger as his commitment to Franco-German reconciliation became more pronounced. When he developed strong links with de Gaulle's France after late 1958 his appreciation of Britain's role in Europe and the world decreased.[12]

The relationship between the leaders of the two countries is a complex one, and the image of it always having been tainted by their respective prejudices is too simplistic. Even though their personal understanding never reached the level of cordiality of de Gaulle or Dulles and Adenauer, or Kennedy and Macmillan, in the early years of Macmillan's premiership the relationship between them was good.

It appears that until 1957/8, when relations between the United Kingdom and Germany were improving (especially after Eden's activities in the aftermath of the failure of the EDC), these neither prevented nor promoted mutual understanding on a private level. Conversely, it was hoped that private friendship between the two statesmen could influence inter-state relations and politics. When in 1958/9 more important conflicts arose, the inability to solve them hampered the personal relationship between Macmillan and Adenauer. At this point, it became clear that 'personal chemistry' did not transmit the positive influence that was being felt in the relations between, for example, France and Germany.

There is plenty of evidence for this assertion. Looking at the letters and messages between Chancellor and Prime Minister, one detects a clear change of atmosphere throughout Macmillan's Premiership. The early correspondence developed from a respectful to a friendly tone in the mid-1950s, and there appears to have been a distinct wish on both parts to come to a satisfactory working relationship. Macmillan, for instance, wrote to Adenauer before his first state visit to Bonn, in May 1957, in very forthcoming terms, keeping him informed about his recent communications with the Soviet leader, Bulganin: 'I look forward to discussing this with you at the end of next week. You can be sure that in any case I should not act on it without the closest consultation with my friends.'[13] During the visit itself, the impression of a generally friendly atmosphere was confirmed.[14] Macmillan himself was pleased with his own performance in Bonn and was convinced that his carefully pitched speeches left the Chancellor impressed.[15] In the regular exchange of notes and letters that followed the visit, Macmillan did not tire of stressing the importance which he personally attached to their relationship and he expressed particular interest in a return visit of the Chancellor.

In those early years, there is no indication that there were any serious difficulties in the mutual relationship, but here, already, another trait of Macmillan's policy *vis-à-vis* the Chancellor is obvious. He continually overstated his own influence on Adenauer, the Chancellor's fondness of him and his own ability of impress the German. Macmillan was aware, from their first encounter in 1954 onwards, but even more so after becoming Prime Minister, that the only way to achieve anything with regards to German foreign policy was to get Adenauer on his side.[16] Therefore, he rightly concentrated his efforts on the 'old man'. Harold Macmillan had been impressed by Adenauer in previous encounters. He had not yet experienced the repetitions of Adenauer's elaboration of the dangers of Soviet expansionism and communism and the history of Germany, which caused considerable boredom during many of their later encounters. Macmillan's generally positive impression of Chancellor Adenauer in the mid-1950s, however, gave rise to the assumption that it would be an achievable task to influence him. In particular, the Prime Minister expected that he would succeed in gaining Adenauer's support in the policy area closest to his interest, the negotiations of a free trade area with the nascent EEC.[17] An additional factor that came into play at that time was the political disarray in France which seemed to present a good chance of steering the Germans away from too close a political alliance with France and 'bending him [Adenauer] in the right direction'.[18]

The first half of the year 1958 saw a continuation of a friendly atmosphere between Bonn and London with a return visit of the German Chancellor to London, which again took place in a good and amicable climate.[19] In the latter half of the year, however, a new dimension to the bilateral relations between the UK and Germany (and at the same time between Adenauer and Macmillan) was felt for the first time: the influence of Franco-German understanding. Anglo-German relations were to become a function of Franco-German relations.

Triggered by a deep pessimism about future developments in the United Kingdom and the United States, the Chancellor – consciously or not – moved away from the Anglo-Saxons to find security with the French President de Gaulle. As the British Ambassador in Bonn put it, Germany, which 'should be one of the greatest forces of stability in Europe', had turned out to be an 'almost neutral factor'.[20]

This meant for Britain that German support over economic questions which they were hoping for, became highly questionable. As previously in phases of pressure, the Prime Minister, who firmly believed in the value of diplomacy at head-of-government level, chose to intervene personally. Assuring Adenauer of the UK's stability and stressing the insecurity in France's political situation, he tried to ensure the Chancellor's support in the free trade area negotiations. More personal messages and another visit to Bonn followed.[21] During this visit, again Macmillan grossly overestimated his own standing with Adenauer. The latter had just met General de Gaulle for the first time in their historic encounter in Colombey-les-deux-Eglises,[22] and this meeting had had an electrifying effect on the German. It was to be the beginning of a deep friendship between two elder statesmen who still had political power ambitions, and indeed their understanding was to have important repercussions for European affairs, and in particular Britain's standing with the Germans.

However, shortly after their first encounter President de Gaulle surprised the Western leaders with the proposal of a NATO-triumvirate, an idea which disturbed the Germans and above all Adenauer. This three-power directorate comprising the United States, the United Kingdom and France was not favourably received by the NATO partners, but Macmillan believed it to be a blessing in disguise for his own ambitions of convincing Adenauer of the strength and reliability of Britain. As he put it in his diary: 'The Chancellor is still very hurt and angry. I do not think he will ever trust de Gaulle again'.[23] And then: 'The Germans have up to now been very good, I think I can exploit his [Adenauer's] anger with the French over the de Gaulle memorandum to some extent.'[24] But Macmillan could not! The fact that de Gaulle's NATO triumvirate proposal did not have a lasting negative influence on Adenauer and on Franco-German relations, was symptomatic of the Chancellor's foreign policy during his final years in office. Unwelcome French moves would at worst overshadow the mutual relationship temporarily without seriously endangering the long-term relations. In contrast, any indication of misunderstandings with the United Kingdom, and increasingly also the United States, had a lasting negative impact on the Chancellor's attitude towards the Anglo-Saxons. This led to a decline in British and American influence on the Chancellor's decisions.

During the October state visit to Bonn, Macmillan clearly failed to recognize the limits of his influence on the Chancellor as he did not realize (and perhaps could not have done so) the significance of France's position in Adenauer's calculations. Ambassador Steel noted a few days after the visit that, contrary to Macmillan's own assessment, the Chancellor showed an 'unexpectedly pessimistic attitude' *vis-à-vis* Britain.[25]

A final attempt by Macmillan, in another letter to the German Chancellor warning him about the consequences of a failure of the free trade area negotiations, proved unsuccessful, since Adenauer did not intervene to secure a favourable outcome of the discussions, and less than two weeks after this final try, the negotiations broke down. What was not clear at the time was that this period between September 1958, the meeting at Colombey-les-deux-Eglises, and February 1959, Macmillan's visit to Moscow, was the turning point not only in the personal relationship between Adenauer and Macmillan, but also – if to a lesser extent – between Germany and Britain.

It was due to Macmillan's failure to handle the German Chancellor with sensitivity, caused by his desire to display superiority and independence – as evident for instance in this Moscow visit – that their personal relationship broke down. But it was clearly the attraction that de Gaulle had for Adenauer which enabled the German Chancellor to turn away from Macmillan and the British so decisively in the late 1950s. Adenauer's plea for trust in the 'new Germany' was answered by de Gaulle, and it was rewarded by the Chancellor's trust in French support in this critical time of the Berlin ultimatum crisis. Nikita Khrushchev had triggered a new crisis over Berlin, when in November 1958, he threatened that the Soviet Union would be prepared unilaterally, if the Western Allies were not willing to 'reach an adequate agreement' over the status of Berlin, which he envisaged to turn into a 'free demilitarised city'. Despite a steadfast official Western line, diplomatic activities at the end of 1958 showed that the willingness of, above all, the United Kingdom to defend Western rights in Berlin by force was diminishing.[26]

When Harold Macmillan, without prior consultation, informed his Western partners about his intentions to visit the Soviet Union (despite the continuing Soviet threat), this caused both consternation and disapproval in Germany, and it had a profound effect on the German Chancellor. He had been persuaded that British policy was 'unreliable and anti-German'.[27]

Adenauer's suspicions were only one side of the coin. Hand-in-hand with the new surge of anti-British feelings in the German Chancery went a phase of growing dissatisfaction with the Chancellor in the British Foreign Office. Although British and German diplomats tried to minimize the damage done by Adenauer and Macmillan in the course of the early months of 1959, their actions left a feeling of mistrust and decline in mutual relations.

During this time Adenauer – more than usually – lost his temper with the British in public,[28] and Macmillan got increasingly impatient with the Chancellor. The Prime Minister's disappointment was two-fold. On the one hand he deplored the fact that the Chancellor let himself be seduced by the French President; on the other hand he felt deceived by the German. In May 1959, he commented: 'Adenauer has become – like many old men – vain, suspicious, and grasping. . . . [He] had been carrying on a great campaign of vilification of HMG and especially of me.'[29] In June: 'Adenauer is now half crazy. . . . De Gaulle and Adenauer are just hopeless. Adenauer because he is a false and cankerous man.'[30]

But in addition to Macmillan's growing awareness of Adenauer's scepticism, he came to realize that in some issues of vital importance for both countries their interests diverged substantially and their policies were becoming more and more incompatible. The British programme of European co-operation ran counter to French interests, and German support of the British plans would potentially endanger Franco-German understanding. Consequently, in 1958, when Adenauer had discovered de Gaulle's terms of co-operation, Macmillan could not hope for Adenauer's help any more.

Conversely, British policies in East–West relations called into question the German hard-line position over the 'German Question' and Berlin. Up to the end of 1958, Macmillan could not risk taking a 'soft' line if he wanted to secure German support on European issues. This *do ut des* situation was no longer existent after Adenauer's acquiescence in the breakdown of the free trade area negotiations, because the Chancellor no longer seemed willing to give. Therefore, there was not much incentive for Macmillan and British officials to take into account German wishes to the same extent as in the previous two years.

The situation in 1959 differed significantly from that at the beginning of 1957 in another respect. When Macmillan succeeded Eden as Prime Minister, the Suez Crisis had dented British self-confidence and seriously shaken the Conservative Party and its leadership. By 1959, there was a new feeling of confidence among the people, the party and the political leadership. The economy had recovered, the Special Relationship had partially been restored, and the Conservative party had good prospects of winning the forthcoming general election.

For Adenauer, almost the opposite was true. In 1957 won the general election with an absolute majority of votes and mandates. His party and leadership were at the peak of their popularity. Economic as well as foreign policies had proved successful. Soon afterwards, the Chancellor's fortunes changed. His popularity began declining, and, when changing his mind again and again about standing for the Federal Presidency, his prestige inside and outside Germany suffered.[31]

In other words Macmillan, in 1957 the new and inexperienced head of government, impressed and fascinated by the Chancellor at previous meetings, had gained ground – by 1959 they were 'equal'.

In 1960, another attempt was made to restore the personal relationship between Adenauer and Macmillan. In August, when the low point in Anglo-German relations after a number of anti-semitic incidents in Germany and the 'Spain affair'[32] had been overcome, Adenauer – at short notice – invited Macmillan to Bonn. There were reservations and mutual suspicions on the part of the two policy-makers, and Harold Macmillan had to be persuaded to accept the invitation.[33] As he recalled in his diaries:

> I am not looking forward to our visit in Bonn. Dr Adenauer has deceived me before, over the great economic issue. . . . But – although many Germans are very sympathetic and secretly ashamed of Dr. Adenauer's trickiness . . . I fear I have never succeeded in getting anything tangible out of these talks.[34]

Given all this, the meeting was a remarkable success. The British Prime Minister went as far as calling it an 'historic' meeting.[35] Even if this was an exaggeration, the talks did improve strained relations. The *Auswärtiges Amt* spoke of a 'noticeable improvement of atmosphere',[36] and both press and public reacted positively to the visit.

There were clear signs that an Anglo-German rapprochement was being sought at least in official relations. Germany increased efforts at 'bridge-building' between the EEC and EFTA, which was a major concern of the British. In return, Macmillan in his speech at the United Nations on 29 September 1960 and Lord Home in his inaugural speech as foreign minister in the House of Lords on 2 November 1960 strongly supported Germany on issues of European security, the German Question and Berlin. This continued in 1961 when statesmen during their meeting in February again pledged mutual support.[37]

However, in the early 1960's, although relations were not under severe strain, there was a feeling of unease on both sides. The autumn and winter of 1959 had marked an irreparable turning point in the relations between Macmillan and Adenauer and with it a decline in the relations between the two countries they represented.

It is during the Berlin Crisis that we see most clearly the various characteristics of Macmillan's policies *vis-à-vis* Germany and difficulties in dealing with the Federal Republic. First, there was the problem of how to reconcile the position of Germany as an object of policy (namely in questions of Four-Power responsibility over Germany as a whole and Berlin) with that of Germany as a partner within an alliance (namely the now sovereign Federal Republic of Germany).

Second, with regards to the Berlin issue the British pragmatic approach clashed with the German more legalistic approach more directly and with graver consequences than in any other policy area.

Third, in the context of the German question, there was more at stake for the Federal Republic than in other foreign policy questions. Hence it was significantly more difficult to overcome Chancellor Adenauer's suspicions concerning British steadfastness.

Fourth, British policies appeared to by competing and contrasting with de Gaulle's rigid line *vis-à-vis* the Soviet Union more clearly.

And, finally, with view to the domestic front, it was over Berlin that the question arose as to how to relate to the former enemy which – in the context of the East–West conflict had become a partner. Would it be necessary to fight for Germany on the Continent; and if so would it be possible to rally the British polulation behind such a cause.

It is clear from the sources that Harold Macmillan shared the conventional wisdom of most British and Western politicians and officials that it was necessary to bind West Germany firmly into the Western alliance system, if the country was to be prevented from turning eastwards towards an understanding with the Soviets.[38] Similarly, it was understood that it was necessary to pacify the Germans by proclaiming the desire to reunify Germany.[39] There was a clear sense of 'Rapallo', the potential danger of German–Soviet understanding at the expense of the West.

At the same time, Macmillan was keen on improving East–West relations by creating a more meaningful dialogue with the Soviet leaders, primarily Khrushchev. Towards the end of 1958, when Khrushchev single-handedly tried to withdraw from the Four-Power agreements, the two conflicting interests openly clashed. On an abstract level, Macmillan had to choose between the British pragmatic approach of trying to improve the relationship with the Soviet Union without much concern for potential diplomatic upsets on the one hand, and the more legalistic and principled approach of not negotiating with the Soviets as long as the Berlin ultimatum stood.

Macmillan decided in favour of pragmatism. In the eyes of the Germans, and above all Chancellor Adenauer, Macmillan had to make a choice between Germany and the Soviet Union, and the Prime Minister opted for the Soviets over and above his German allies.

The first indication of this were the notorious telegrams 8112 and 8113. These were later turned into a memorandum which summed up British thoughts on the subject of Berlin immediately after Khrushchev's first speech on 10 November 1958. In a nutshell, the argument was that in the long term the only feasible option was some sort of recognition of the GDR, because Khrushchev was in control of the situation.[40] When the content of the telegrams became known to the Germans, their reaction was excited, disappointed and suspicious.[41] British views appeared to contrast sharply with American firmness and, even more so, with strong French expressions of support and rigidity *vis-à-vis* the Soviet Union. This impression of British weakness in the face of the Soviet threat and the perception of a certain willingness on the part of Macmillan to trade away German (and Western) rights in Berlin was reinforced after the ultimatum speech of 27 November, and it become almost insurmountable after Macmillan's announcement, in early 1959, that his way of dealing with the crisis was a direct encounter with Khrushchev in Russia.

After Macmillan had decided to take up the Soviet invitation (originally addressed to his predecessor Eden) to visit the Soviet Union, concrete negotiating tactics needed to be developed. To this end, the Prime Minister summoned back to London Gladwyn Jebb, at the time British Ambassador in Paris. He was to deal with the problems of Berlin and Germany by addressing five questions posed by Macmillan:

(1) Would the Soviet Union accept a reunified Germany which remained a member of NATO?
(2) Would a reunified Germany which remained a member of NATO be compatible with the general détente in Europe, including a considerable degree of disengagement by the West and the Soviet Union?
(3) What chance is there that after Adenauer's death, Germany would succumb to a Soviet offer to accept the reunification of German territory provided that a reunified Germany left NATO?
(4) Could NATO survive effectively without Germany?
(5) If NATO for all practical purposes disappeared, could we in conjunction with the United States and France maintain an adequate defence against the Soviet Union?[42]

This catalogue of questions shows on the one hand that Macmillan was interested in an assessment of the various Allied moves and their implications. But it also indicates that he was prepared to consider what for many other Western statesmen (above all the German Chancellor) would have been unthinkable: NATO was not sacred, and there were alternatives.[43]

Jebb's answers as elaborated in his memorandum are interesting in that they anticipated a number of ideas which, over the course of the next few years, would become part of Western policies on Berlin and Germany as a whole. Jebb argued for the preservation of the status quo, a strengthening of continental Europe culminating in Britain's joining the Common Market, an avoidance of a neutralization of Germany, but – if necessary – the sacrifice of Western rights in Berlin.

There is no doubt that Macmillan, during his visit to Moscow, did not show any willingness to make concessions on substantial questions, despite Lloyd's *tour d'horizon* with the Soviet deputy foreign minister, Kusnetzov.[44] But it is equally clear that Macmillan was prepared to listen to almost any suggestion that might end the East–West stalemate – with little concern for German interests. He oversaw the development of Foreign Office thought on the recognition of the GDR, the agency theory, the recognition of the Oder/Neiße line and the Berlin Question, and the more fed up he became with the increasingly stubborn and inflexible German Chancellor, the more he discounted a German voice in the security questions. There is little indication of any meaningful exchanges between Macmillan and the Germans on these issues from the time of the Khrushchev ultimatum until the erection of the Berlin Wall almost four years later.

At the same time as the Germans were preoccupied with the Berlin and German questions, the British government was in a process of reappraisal of the country's European policy. In July 1961, only weeks before the erection of the Berlin Wall, the Prime Minister announced that Britain would seek to enter the European Economic Community. The subsequent negotiations were to dominate Anglo-German relations for the final years of Macmillan's premiership. Although the Prime Minister knew that the key to success or failure of the negotiations lay with the French, he hoped that German support and pressure would help influence the French in favour of British EEC entry.

In contrast to the Berlin Question, where the Germans were looking to the United Kingdom for support, in EEC affairs it was the British who were both actor and object of policy and negotiations; and it was the British who were asking for political support from the Germans. The dilemmas in Britain's attempts at enlisting German help have been described elsewhere,[45] but some observations are of significance in our context. The previous years of tension between the heads of government of both countries had left their mark on Macmillan and Adenauer alike. Neither was in conciliatory mood throughout the various encounters between 1961 and 1963, and considerable distrust remained between them. It is evident that the decisive consideration in Chancellor Adenauer's 'Grand Design' was de Gaulle and not Macmillan. Therefore, Adenauer was prepared, as he had been in November 1958, to sacrifice the pawn Great Britain to save Franco-German rapprochement and European integration.

Unlike in 1958 however, when there was general German acquiescence in the face of de Gaulle's free trade area veto, the German reaction in January 1963 was much more ambivalent. Adenauer took the last big foreign political decision of his chancellorship when he decided to push through the politically sensitive Franco-German friendship treaty of January 1963, despite de Gaulle's veto of the British. He had not been given prior warning of the General's intentions of blocking British EEC entry, and German political, public and published opinon was clearly in favour of the British joining the Common Market. But Adenauer had no intentions of risking Franco-German rapprochement for the sake of the British. Reconciliation with France was his political legacy. He was heavily criticized for this, even by his own party colleagues, let alone the opposition and the press. There were even thoughts of jeopardizing the ratification of the treaty in the *Bundestag*. In the end, the only visible sign of disapproval by the *Bundestag* of Adenauer's and de Gaulle's policies was the addition of a preamble to the friendship treaty which emphasized the significance of transatlantic relations. This did nothing to reconcile the British![46]

Macmillan hoped that after Adenauer's departure from the political scene (the chancellor's mid-term resignation had been part of the coalition agreements after the 1961 general elections) he could set about rebuilding his trust in German politics. Adenauer's most likely successor was Ludwig Erhard whom he knew to be supportive of the British. Ironically, Harold Macmillan himself did not remain in power long enough to do just that – his own resignation virtually coincided with Adenauer's.

In his discussions with the Germans and in particular with Adenauer and his foreign ministers, Macmillan made a number of tactical errors. It has already been mentioned that he continually overstated his own role in bilateral and multilateral negotiations on the head of government level. He also miscalculated the negative effect his Moscow trip would have on the cohesion of the Western camp and in particular the extent to which it undermined his position in Germany (and not just with the Chancellor). He misread the mood of the time in late 1958 and early 1959, by attempting to play a 'tit for tat' game on economic and security issues. After the disappointing German acquiescence over de Gaulle's veto of the free trade area proposals in late 1958, which coincided with Khrushchev's reopening of the Berlin discussions, Macmillan threatened to 'retaliate' by not giving Germany support over Berlin.[47] This in turn made it more difficult to impress on the Germans the need to support the UK during the EEC accession negotiations a few years later.

Moreover, Macmillan failed to recognize the importance of the Berlin issue which touched the very existence of Germany as a free and democratic country and which had a great symbolic and emotional significance. Berlin was not a bargaining chip. By implying a willingness to 'desert' Germany in a (perceived) hour of great need, the British Prime Minister put at risk German confidence in British reliability and his own credibility.

Most of these tactical 'errors' occurred when the Prime Minister was preoccupied with establishing himself as a world political leader. In the vacuum created by John Foster Dulles' illness in early 1959 and his subsequent death, Macmillan saw the opportunity of assuming the role of the foreign political leader of the Western camp. If he had to alienate other heads of government, this had to be outweighed against the potential power position he would gain as the motor of the East–West dialogue and the inclusion of Britain in any great power summitry.

By late 1959, it became clear, however, that he had harvested the fruit of his labour only on the domestic front. His foreign political activities in the spring and summer of 1959 were rewarded by a convincing electoral victory in the autumn. But America had moved centre stage again in the international theatre, and Macmillan's role as a broker of international peace came virtually to a standstill. He had lost the confidence of both Germany and France, and the coming negotiations, the 1960 abortive summit and the discussions around the time of the Berlin Wall, saw him in the position of a supernumerary.

It can be argued that he played this role more successfully than that of the main actor, because he managed to make his influence felt in the United States without attracting German suspicions immediately. So rather than bringing up East–West questions directly with the Germans, Macmillan tried to channel them through the Americans.[48] It certainly helped that Adenauer mistrusted the newly elected Kennedy as much as Macmillan. Also, Kennedy was open to Macmillan's views which largely coincided with his own in terms of the necessity to establish a dialogue with the East. Kennedy's motto: 'Let us never negotiate out of fear, but let us never fear to negotiate' could easily have come from British Prime Minister himself.

By 1961, Macmillan, in agreement with large sections of his Foreign Office, had settled for a policy of 'accepting the stabilisation of

Germany's Eastern frontier and the Oder/Neiße line', and an abandonment in all but official policy of reunification.[49] But unlike in the late 1950s, he did not expose himself with statements to that effect, but he let the Americans under Kennedy and Rusk make the running. In late 1961, he urged the American President to convince Adenauer to adopt a more flexible policy leading among others to *de facto* recognition of the GDR, acceptance of the Oder/Neiße line' and a loosening of the links between Berlin and West Germany.[50] This approach, in conjunction with a change in government after the general elections of 1961 (which brought a larger number of so-called Atlanticists into the Federal Government) allowed relations between Britain and Germany to resume a better quality. But it was not until both Adenauer and Macmillan had left the scene as heads of government that any lasting improvement occured.

NOTES

1. I would like to thank Richard Aldous for his comments on the essay.
2. He was one of only two survivors of all the Balliol scholars and exhibitioners of 1912. For some details of his experiences during the Great War see Richard Davenport-Hines, *The Macmillans* (London: Mandarin, 1992) Ch. 6.
3. Alistair Horne, *Macmillan: Official Biography*, 2 vols (London: Macmillan, 1989), here, *Macmillan*, vol. 1, p. 48.
4. Horne, *Macmillan*, vol. 1, p. 316.
5. Sabine Lee, 'Coming into the Game? Staying in the Game? Harold Macmillan and European Integration', S. Lee and R. Aldous (eds), *Harold Macmillan and Britain's World Role* (Basingstoke: Macmillan, 1996), pp. 123–48.
6. For details see essays by Scott Lucas, Nigel Ashton and Sir Oliver Wright in this volume.
7. For more recent studies see, for instance, David Reynolds, *Britannia Overruled* (London: Longman, 1991), pp. 156ff; John W. Young, *Britain and the World in the Twentieth Century* (London: Edward Arnold, 1997), Ch. 6.
8. Hans Heinrich Herwarth, 'Anglo-German Relations: a German View', *International Affairs*, vol. 39 (1963), pp. 511–32. See also Report Becker (Auswärtiges Amt) for Königswinter Conference, 22.5.1959, Politische Abteilung (PA)/Auswärtiges Amt (AA): Länderabteilung (LA) 3/304/99.
9. Günther Buchstab, *Wir haben wirklich etwas geschaffen. Die Protokolle*

des CDU-Bundesvorstandes 1953–1957 (Düsseldorf: Droste, 1990), pp. 852–3.

10. Frank Giles, *Forty Years On: Four Decades of Königswinter Conferences* (Blackpool, 1989), p. 1.

11. For recent analysis see Thomas Kielinger, *Crossroads and Roundabouts* (Bonn: Bouvier, 1996).

12. Adenauer's attitudes towards Britain have frequently been simplified as those of a narrow-minded politician who, as a Catholic Rhinelander had a 'natural' disinclination concerning the UK. In the light of primary evidence this cannot be upheld. There is a clear development in the Chancellor's views throughout the late 1950s which is largely a function of his relationship with de Gaulle. See Sabine Lee, *An Uneasy Relationship: British–German Relations between 1955 and 1961* (Bochum: Brockmeyer, 1996), pp. 64–70. The following is based on chapter 3 of the book.

13. Macmillan, Harold, *Riding the Storm, 1955–1959* (London: Macmillan, 1971), p. 291.

14. Report Caspari, May 1957, PA/AA:LA 3/304/34. Macmillan, *Riding the Storm*, p. 206.

15. Horne, *Macmillan*, vol. 2, p. 33. There is little indication that Macmillan left as remarkable an impression as he assumed.

16. Ibid.

17. For a particularly opinionated account of this aspect see Wolfram Kaiser, *Using Europe, Abusing the Europeans: Britain and European Integration, 1945–1963* (London: Macmillan, 1996), pp. 61–107.

18. Steel to FO, 11.10.1957, PRO: FO371/130732.

19. Maudling to Macmillan, 17.3.1958, PRO: PREM 11/2341.

20. Steel to Rumbold, 17.3.1958, PRO: PREM 11/2341.

21. Letter Macmillan to Adenauer, July 1958, PA/AA: PA 2/927. State visit to Bonn, October 1958. Macmillan, *Riding the Storm*, pp. 453–7. Henning Köhler, *Adenauer: Eine politische Biographie* (Frankfurt/Berlin: Propyläen, 1994), pp. 1007–10.

22. Details of the visit in Hans-Peter Schwarz, *Adenauer und Frankreich: Die deutsch-französischen Beziehungen, 1958–1969* (Bonn: Bouvier, 1985). See also F. Seydoux, *Dans l'intimité franco-allemande: Une mission diplomatique* (Paris: Edition Albatros, 1977), pp. 7–13.

23. Harold Macmillan Diaries (HMD), 9.10.1958, cited in Macmillan, *Riding the Storm*, p. 454.

24. HMD, 9.10.1958, cited in Horne, *Macmillan*, vol. 2, p. 110.

25. Steel to FO, 17.10.1958, PRO: FO 371/137378.

26. Forschungsgesellschaft für Auswärtige Politik (ed.), *Documents on Berlin, 1945–1963* (Munich, 1963), pp. 180–96. See also Sabine Lee, 'Perceptions and Reality: Anglo-German Relations during the Berlin Crisis, 1958–1959', *German History*, vol. 13 (1995), pp. 47–69.

27. Steel to FO, 14.2.1959, PRO: FO 371/145773.

28. For example, at a CDU party meeting he made some unfortunate remarks about Great Britain and British policy towards Europe. Steel to FO, PRO: FO 371/145773.

29. HMD, 28.5.1959, cited in Horne, *Macmillan*, vol. 2, p. 133.

30. HMD, 18.6.1959 and 27.6.1959, cited in Horne, *Macmillan*, vol. 2, p. 133.
31. Daniel Koerfer, *Kampf ums Kanzleramt* (Stuttgart: Deutsche Verlags-anstalt, 1987), pp. 187–277.
32. Reports of plans to establish *Bundeswehr* bases for training purposes in Spain caused concern across Europe, but particularly in the United Kingdom. See Herwarth, *Anglo-German Relations*, p. 514.
33. Hans Heinrich von Herwarth, *Von Adenauer zu Brandt* (Munich: Propyläen, 1990), p. 280.
34. Macmillan, *Riding the Storm*, pp. 317–18.
35. Ibid., p. 319.
36. Report about British attitudes *vis-à-vis* Germany, November 1960, PA/AA: LA 3/304/180.
37. Harold Macmillan, *Pointing the Way, 1959–1961* (London: Macmillan, 1972), p. 327.
38. Harold Macmillan, *Tides of Fortune, 1945–1955* (London: Macmillan, 1969), p. 648. PRO: CAB128/29 CC (55) 31 (9); CAB 129/81 C 112(56); CAB 128/31 C (57) 16(7).
39. PRO: CAB 129/74 C 83(55).
40. FO to Washington, 15.11.1958, PRO: FO 371/137333 and FO to Washington, 15.11.1958, PRO: FO 371/137334.
41. Steel to FO, PRO: FO 371/137336.
42. 'Berlin and Germany', a memorandum written by Sir Gladwyn Jebb, January 1959. Copy in possession of the author.
43. See also Macmillan's thoughts on NATO in the context of Franco-British relations, PRO: PREM 11/3334.
44. Report of the visit of the Prime Minister and the Foreign Secretary to the Soviet Union, 21 February to 3 March 1959, PRO: CAB 133/293, Top Secret Annex, p. 4.
45. Sabine Lee, 'Germany and the First Enlargement Negotiations 1961–1963', conference paper given in Oxford on 24 March 1996.
46. Oliver Bange, 'English, American and German interests behind the Preamble to the Franco-German Treaty, 1963', in Gustav Schmidt (ed.), *Zwischen Bündnissicherung und priviligierter Partnerschaft* (Bochum: Brockmeyer, 1995), pp. 225–80.
47. FO minute Hancock, 11.11.1958, PRO: FO 371/137334.
48. It is interesting to note, for instance, that at a meeting between Adenauer and Macmillan in early 1961 (just after another Khrushchev memorandum) neither European security, nor Berlin nor NATO were on the agenda. Report Hoyer Millar, 9.2.1961, PRO: FO 371/161127.
49. Shuckburgh to Caccia, 26.7.1961, PRO: FO 371/160480.
50. Harold Macmillan, *Pointing the Way, 1959–1961*, p. 408.

9 Perfect Peace? Macmillan and Ireland

Richard Aldous[1]

In April 1916, two young men put into action their beliefs about King and Country. Harold Macmillan had just returned to the Grenadier Guards at the trenches of the Western Front. He had been in London since Christmas recovering from wounds sustained at the Battle of Loos in which 60,000 fellow Guardsmen had died. He wrote to his mother from the Front:

> Many of us could never stand the strain and endure the horrors which we see every day, if we did not feel that this was more than a War – a crusade. I never see a man killed but think of him as a martyr. All the men . . . have the same conviction – that our cause is right and certain to end in triumph.

Meanwhile, on Easter Monday in Dublin, Séan Lemass was on the roof of the General Post Office surrounded by home-made bombs with slow-burning fuses and shooting at the British troops on the street below. This was the Easter Rising – symbolic opening gesture of the Irish Revolution which would conclude with the creation of an Irish Free State in 1921. Macmillan followed events in Ireland with disdain, observing from the front that:

> The scenes in Dublin seem to be very much like those in Paris during the Commune. The real trouble is that the Sinn Fein movement is, as well as disloyal, largely anti-clerical. Therefore one of the strongest powers over them is largely diminished or hampered in its operation.

Almost half a century later, when he and Lemass met as Prime Ministers of their countries, Macmillan could only muse in his diary:

> The Irish story is a queer one. . . . Hundreds of years of bitter quarrels . . . civil war among the natives following the complete surrender of the British – and now, peace – perfect peace.[2]

A quick examination of the index of Alistair Horne's excellent official biography reveals the obvious point that Ireland mattered little to Macmillan. The only reference to Ireland in volume two (1957–86) runs as follows: 'From Berlin, [President Kennedy] flew on to Ireland, and a warm-hearted but calmer welcome – and thence on 29 June to Birch Grove.'[3] Macmillan's view of Ireland was shaped by castles and books. He loved Lismore Castle in County Waterford, where his wife had grown up, and visited regularly. He had a profound respect for Irish literature and a particular admiration for Séan O'Casey. After O'Casey's death, Macmillan became very close to his widow, Eileen, and might actually have married her if he had not been too shy to pop the question. Rather touchingly, he believed Ireland to be 'the last happy country in Europe'.[4]

When Macmillan became prime minister in 1957, Anglo-Irish relations were cool. The public policy of successive British governments, Conservative and Labour, on partition had been consistent after 1922: the division of Ireland was an Irish not a British problem. Britain would support any arrangement made between North and South provided it did not interfere with British interests. The sympathies of governments after the Second World War, if they lay anywhere, were with the Unionists.

Attlee as Dominions Secretary during the Second World War had had very pointed views on Irish neutrality and, as Prime Minister between 1945 and 1951, he remained loyal to those from Northern Ireland who had fought in the war. In 1948, 100 left-wing Labour MPs, led by Tom Driberg, put down an amendment to the Representation of the People Bill asking for elections to the Northern Ireland parliament to be suspended until the problems of the Nationalist community were addressed. Attlee insisted that the Northern Ireland parliament was not subordinate and seemed to move beyond the 1920 Government of Ireland Act which had stated that 'the supreme authority of the Parliament of the United Kingdom shall remain unaffected and undiminished over all persons, matters and things in Northern Ireland'. Attlee's own view on the Union was unambiguous: 'no change should be made in the constitutional status of Northern Ireland without Northern Ireland's free agreement.' In other words, it was the people of Northern Ireland not the British parliament who should decide their future.[5]

Churchill returned to power in 1951 and, despite his ambiguous record on Ireland, the hopes of Nationalists rose.[6] He had said publicly on many occasions that he wanted an end to partition.

Back in office, however, Churchill sustained the view of the Attlee government that Britain could play no part in ending division. He continued to offer vocal support to Unionists, most notably in his leader's speech to the 1953 Conservative Party conference at Margate. Support for Unionism also came from Sir Anthony Eden, Churchill's foreign secretary and, in 1955, successor. On trips to Belfast he vigorously defended the Union and partition. The Irish Ambassador in London, Freddie Boland, despaired of him:

> From what I have seen and heard of him, I am inclined to think that he is not a friend of Ireland and that we are likely to find him very unsympathetic or easy to deal with on the partition issue.... In everything... affecting Ireland, he is just the ordinary Right Wing Tory – rather narrow, shallow-minded and self-righteous.[7]

If successive British administrations between 1945 and 1957 remained clearly pro-Unionist, Irish governments did little to encourage more enthusiasm for a united Ireland. In 1948, a Fine Gael-led coalition finally broke with the Commonwealth. Séan MacBride, foreign minister and former chief of staff of the IRA, summed up the republic's position on the division of Ireland in a speech to the Dail that could have been given by a frontbencher of any party between 1945 and 1959:

> That the partition of Ireland is a grievous wrong is a proposition which I do not need to put forward for the assent of any member of this House. Its injustice is recognised outside Ireland, among fair-minded people in many countries of the world including Britain itself, the perpetrator of the wrong. Like all acts of injustice, it is the source of many evils, for which there is no true remedy except the removal of the parent cause. Within the separated part of Ireland, under a government and parliament subordinate to those of Britain, there is no true peace.[8]

When Harold Macmillan succeeded Eden as prime minister in January 1957, Anglo-Irish relations were, in the words of a British minister, 'semi-detached'. Macmillan did not warm to Eamon de Valera (thinking him 'not very jolly') and, when the Taoiseach came to London for St Patrick's Day in 1958, their brief meeting was unproductive. As de Valera toured the country, he was regularly booed and pelted with vegetables. During a visit to St Patrick's Church, Soho, bottles were thrown (one of which hit the Irish Ambassador) and clashes in an angry crowd of several hundred ended in forty demonstrators being removed by the police. When de Valera left Britain, he took with him not just this noisy demonstration of hostility, but the clearly expressed view of the British government that 'Partition is the will of the majority in the six counties and it will continue to exist as long as they see no reason to change their minds.'[9]

By 1959, two years into Macmillan's premiership, all visible signs of Anglo-Irish relations were gloomy. When Macmillan visited Belfast shortly after his brilliant electioneering coup in Moscow he was accused by de Valera of hypocrisy. 'When Mr Macmillan went to Moscow we here wished him well, believing that he was engaged in a worthy mission trying to find a foundation for peace', the Taoiseach commented, '[but] we could have wished that his visit to Belfast had been promoted by such a spirit and that he was visiting our island not merely as the leader of a British political party preparing for a general election but as a statesman in pursuit here of the purposes which took him elsewhere'. But by 1959, de Valera was a fading political force. Almost blind and exhausted by forty years of active political life, he resigned from the premiership in the summer. His replacement, Séan Lemass, seemed ready to blow the 'winds of change' on the question of partition.

Séan Lemass, like de Valera, had an obvious Republican pedigree. He is thought to be one of the gunmen sent by Michael Collins to assassinate the Cairo gang on Bloody Sunday during the Anglo-Irish war and fought for de Valera during the Civil War. But Lemass was an altogether more progressive and modern-thinking man than de Valera. As Minister for Industry and Commerce in every Fianna Fail government between 1932 and 1959, he had been quietly reforming the Irish economy and encouraging industrial growth. He had long believed that the first steps towards accommodation between North and South would be economic rather than political, observing as early as 1953:

> The division of Ireland ... is beyond question an economic absurdity. It is the greatest handicap to progress and stability on both sides of the Irish border. Its disappearance would open up new economic possibilities from which all the Irish people would benefit. It is certain to disappear sometime – economic absurdities always do – and the sooner the better.[10]

During the Macmillan years, Séan Lemass attempted to 'woo' Northern Ireland and move Britain away from the view that the partition was a matter for Irishmen alone. He aimed to encourage economic co-operation between the Republic and Northern Ireland; to change the semantics of partition; and, finally, to use prospective British and Irish membership of the Common Market to overcome problems of sovereignty.

Economic co-operation between North and South was at the heart of Lemass's plan for an Irish settlement. He told the *Belfast Telegraph* on becoming Taoiseach that 'better relations can be fostered by practical co-operation for the mutual benefit in the economic sphere' and promised 'to discuss with the Six Counties government proposals as to how policy might be directed so as to ensure that the economic progress of both parts of the country will be impeded as little as possible by the existing political division'. In speech after speech he offered to enter talks with the Northern Ireland government. He summed up his position at the Oxford Union in October 1959:

> We have expressed our willingness to co-operate with Northern Ireland without, on the one hand, concealing our own ultimate hopes or, on the other hand, asking those in control in Northern Ireland to make any immediate concession to our view. . . . Apart altogether from our political aspirations, we think this is a policy of good neighbourliness.

'The British government', he hoped, would 'encourage progress on these lines.'[11]

The semantic change which Lemass made was simple but significant. Ireland had long been in the habit of referring to its neighbour as 'the Six Counties'. This emphasized their place in the traditional thirty-two counties. This was done, in the words of the Secretary of the Department of Justice, purely 'for propaganda purposes' with 'no precedent' in law. Successive Northern Ireland governments were offended by the description. On 23 May 1960, Lemass announced that the government would encourage the title 'Northern Ireland' rather than 'Six Counties'. This practice was followed in subsequent government statements and adopted as house style by *The Irish Times* and *Irish Independent*. As the British Embassy in Dublin reported to London, this 'will perhaps go some little way towards meeting the Northern Ireland government's prerequisite for official contacts, i.e. "recognition of the constitutional status of Northern Ireland".[12]

When it became clear in the summer of 1960 that Britain would apply to join the Common Market, Lemass recognized the political as well as economic benefits which would come from membership by both countries. As he later told delegates at the Fianna Fail *Ard Fheis*:

> Within the ambit of an European community, the similarities of economic opportunities and problems in North and South, and the advantage of concerning policies to deal with them will, we believe, help to sweep away some of the arguments which have been used to sustain partition.

Certainly in discussion with the Boston-Irish Catholic US President, John F. Kennedy, officials emphasized expectations that the Common Market would provide a means towards genuine accommodation. The Irish Ambassador told Kennedy in 1962 that 'there was a political aspect involved and that membership of the EEC by ourselves and by Northern Ireland would go a long way towards eroding partition'. The President thought this 'would be a wonderful way of ending partition'.

With the Taoiseach, his government and officials all hopeful that membership of the Common Market would break down barriers, it is easy to see why de Gaulle's 'Non' in January 1963 should have been so devastating. An opportunity had been lost, Lemass told the Commonwealth Relations Secretary, Duncan Sandys, and once again Ireland had been 'left out on a limb'.[13]

Officials at the Commonwealth Relations Office – which still dealt with Irish matters even after the 1948 Republic of Ireland Act – were impressed by Lemass. A biographical sketch sent by the CRO to Macmillan in 1961 judged that Lemass was 'less rabid on the subject of partition than most Republican politicians'. With or without irony, the unnamed official concluded that 'there is little of the typical Irishman in him. . . . He is sensible, courageous and cool-headed, a man of affairs with his feet on the ground.'[14] Sir Gilbert Laithwaite, permanent under-secretary at the CRO commented that 'I have always had the feeling that we could do business' with Lemass, adding:

> Already Mr Lemass, though in very general terms, has adjured his people to stop talking about Partition and concentrate on improving relations with the North.[15]

This favourable reaction to Lemass was echoed at the Home Office which had responsibility for Northern Ireland. By 1961, the Northern Ireland desk believed:

> The political atmosphere in the South is changing. This metamorphosis will be neither rapid nor dramatic. But already there have been signs that the Dublin government is anxious to move away from the negative attitudes of earlier administrations. The spirit of 1916 and 1922 is on the wane.[16]

Enthusiasm for Lemass led Whitehall officials quietly to explore the prospects for increased economic co-operation with the Republic. In February 1960, the Home Office told the Stormont government in Belfast that:

> It is impossible to be optimistic about the Republic's economic future. Our economic and social relations with them are probably closer than with any other country, foreign or Commonwealth. The Republic comes eighth in the list of our world markets and a depression there must to some extent affect our own prosperity. It would therefore be desirable to try, if we can, to find some way of helping their economy.

In practical terms, this meant 'full UK support price for store cattle and sheep imported from the Irish Republic'; London would subsidize livestock in the Republic as well as Northern Ireland. This was the first step on the road to trade talks between Britain and Ireland which began in September 1963 and reached modest agreement in 1965.[17]

Unionists, unlike senior civil servants, were unimpressed by Lemass. As early as July 1959, the Northern Ireland cabinet decided that 'the proposal for "limited free trade" with the Republic could not be supported on political grounds'. The following year, the Northern Ireland prime minister, Lord Brookeborough, publicly rejected Lemass's offer of economic co-operation:

> Why this insistent harping on economic co-operation? Whatever the advantages – and I cannot see them in practical terms – we do recognise that the fundamental objective of Mr Lemass is political. Co-operation of the kind suggested is the thin end of the wedge which given time, would be driven home to create an ever widening gap between Northern Ireland and Britain and

eventually split us from the United Kingdom economy. . . . If this sounds uncompromising, I can only say that it is intended to be so. One can't compromise on matters involving basic principles, for to do so would be a betrayal.[18]

This was not only the view of Unionists in Belfast. There were influences close to the government, and Macmillan himself, who were keen to protect the *status quo* in Ireland. The arrival of Séan Lemass as Taoiseach coincided with that of Knox Cunningham, Unionist MP for South Antrim, in 10 Downing Street as Macmillan's principal private secretary (PPS). As Alan Clark observed in his diaries of the Thatcher years, the PPS is someone whom a prime minister can 'confide in personally' and will pop 'round to Number 10 when all engagements are over . . . [and] go upstairs to the flat and drink whisky'.[19] Macmillan found Cunningham congenial company. He was a fifteen-stone, jolly Ulsterman who had won a rugby blue at Cambridge and reminded MPs more of a secret service-man than a political secretary. The official record of advice he was giving Macmillan on Ireland between 1959 and 1963 is almost non-existent, but if his stand after 1963 is a yardstick, it is unlikely to have been positive.[20]

After leaving Downing Street, Cunningham voiced consistently hard-line views on partition. He vigorously opposed the liberalizing policies of Terence O'Neill and was the only Unionist MP publicly to support Ian Paisley. Moreover, when O'Neill finally met Séan Lemass in 1965, Cunningham defied his own party in opposing the visit. Recent evidence also suggests Cunningham's involvement with the emerging paramilitary organizations. In particular, his friendship and financial involvement with William McGrath, the founder of TARA, excited controversy within Ireland. TARA helped orchestrate both political opposition against O'Neill and the original Ulster Volunteer Force bombings in the spring of 1969 that forced O'Neill from office. What Cunningham's activities after leaving Downing Street make clear is that there was at the heart of Macmillan's private office a trusted figure who later opposed any accommodation with the South and supported hard-line, possibly paramilitary, Unionism.[21]

Cunningham had access at the highest levels of government but he was not a major political player. R. A. Butler, however, was the most senior member of the government after Macmillan and, as Home Secretary, the minister responsible for Northern Ireland.

Liberal, reform-minded and committed only to the 'art of the possible', RAB was the epitome of the consensus politician. According to his official biographer, Anthony Howard, 'RAB simply lacked the buccaneering attitude to politics.' This is what makes a gung-ho attitude to Ireland so surprising. Butler was a personal friend of the Northern Irish Prime Minister, Lord Brookeborough, and often paid private visits to his country home, Colebrooke in Co. Fermanagh. It was during one such 'private' visit in December 1959 that he was taken to the site in Rosslea where an RUC officer had recently been killed in a terrorist attack. Whilst there, the Home Secretary launched an attack on the Irish government for failing 'to do their utmost to control those who are perpetrating these outrages'. At Belfast airport he told reporters that he would consider sanctions against Ireland to end terrorism, adding that 'It is most important not to have mere words but something that would have a real effect.' Butler was resolute in standing side by side with the people of Northern Ireland and declaring that 'your soil is our soil'.[22]

Butler's message was intended to reassure Unionist fears about the British attitude to terrorism. The IRA had been engaged in a campaign of terrorist activity in Britain and along the border between Ireland and Northern Ireland since 1956. The fact that IRA members were thought to be well-known in Ireland but remained free gave strength to Unionist arguments that talk of economic co-operation was the acceptable face of Irish republicanism. At the House of Commons in November 1959, the Ulster Unionist MP Sir David Campbell told Butler:

> The Ulster members [are] convinced that the Eire government could do more to help; while they appreciate that open pressure might be inadvisable they [feel] that sufficient pressure had not been applied behind the scenes. Eire received all the privileges of the Commonwealth and some of these could be taken away.

If action were not taken quickly, he warned, 'the Ulster members . . . might not be able to restrain their people'. It is no coincidence that Butler's threat of economic sanctions should have come just weeks after this Unionist warning.[23]

RAB's uncharacteristic bullishness in Belfast seemed to catch Macmillan by surprise and he called the Home Secretary to Number 10 from the airport. The *Daily Mail* captured the sense of bemusement:

MPs were asking: Has RAB been carpeted. The view was that Mr Butler had been indiscreet. The idea of Mr Butler's being on the mat at No. 10 Downing Street is doubtless putting it too hard. Nonetheless, Mr Macmillan must have been distinctly puzzled by the whole affair.

Puzzled or not, Macmillan clearly accepted that Butler was only expressing the general thrust of government policy albeit in a forthright way. The Home Secretary reiterated his case in the House of Commons on 17 December and made clear a desire that 'the people of Northern Ireland should feel they have this government behind them'. This keen interest in the affairs of Northern Ireland continued throughout his time as Home Secretary. It was at RAB's request that a Cabinet Committee was established for Northern Ireland and a Northern Ireland bill drafted to enlarge the competence of the Stormont government.[24]

Macmillan's own relations with Stormont were not as close as his deputy's but remained relaxed and friendly. When, in July 1961, he invited Lord Brookeborough for a weekend at Chequers, he told him that 'I like to see as much of my friends at home as possible.' The party that weekend included the Chancellor of the Exchequer and the Home Secretary. Although there was some discussion about the difficulties facing Belfast's heavy industry, there was no proposal to exploit trade routes across the border.

The seriousness with which Macmillan listened to Brookeborough contrasted strongly with any desire to consult Lemass. The tone of their meetings had been established at the outset. Lemass met the Prime Minister for the first time as head of government in the summer of 1959. During the forty-five minutes they were together on 13 July, Macmillan exuded disinterest and even boredom. He inquired after the health of de Valera and asked questions from his crib cards about Irish industry, agriculture and emigration but showed little inclination to discuss the practical or philosophical aspects of Anglo-Irish relations.[26] In the same month that Macmillan invited Brookeborough to Chequers, his private secretary, Philip de Zulueta, noted that the PM was trying to 'put Mr Lemass off' because he was too busy to see him. Although British ministers were taking a critical strategic decision on Europe, the PM's office did 'not think the delay need matter since our decision about negotiations will not be affected by the discussions with the Irish'. In short, receiving Lemass was a simple (if inconvenient) courtesy and Irish views were a matter neither of priority nor interest.[27]

By the final year of Macmillan's premiership there were signs of a thaw between Northern Ireland and the Republic. The IRA had announced a year earlier 'the termination of resistance to British occupation launched on December 12, 1956'. Lord Brookeborough had been replaced by the more moderate and liberal Terence O'Neill as Northern Ireland's prime minister. Even Knox Cunningham felt moved to write that 'there is a wind of change blowing in Northern Ireland'.[28]

Counterfactual history always ends up by running into the buffers but what happens next is a moment so quintessentially Macmillanesque that it is impossible not to imagine an alternative narrative. Macmillan had based so much of his understanding of international politics on the importance of personal diplomacy. Like Churchill before him, he believed that if the key players could get round a table together, they would achieve more than endless negotiations between diplomats. The problem for Macmillan's summitry had always been Britain's position of relative weakness to the two superpowers, USSR and USA. But in any discussion with Ireland, it would have been Britain who played the role of 'superpower'. Even America would have deferred to Britain not least because the new President, John F. Kennedy was, according to the Irish embassy in Washington, 'British inclined and . . . makes no secret of his firm attachment to Britain.'[29]

The scenario was simple enough. In April 1963 Terence O'Neill asked Macmillan for his personal support in inviting President Kennedy to open the Giant's Causeway during his visit to Britain and Ireland that spring. Macmillan agreed this 'would be a good idea' and undertook 'to consider what could be done'. In reality he did nothing and made no suggestion to Kennedy that he might visit Northern Ireland. The Irish Ambassador in Washington had already warned Dublin that raising partition 'now when Britain has so many pressing problems to solve is something he [JFK] would avoid'. But if Macmillan had raised the issue and tried to engineer a meeting between Lemass and O'Neill during Kennedy's trip? If Macmillan had thrown his full weight behind talks and taken advantage of the goodwill created? If he had used the prospect of a presidential visit to Northern Ireland and the emergence of the forward-thinking O'Neill to initiate political talks? It is inconceivable that Macmillan would have missed this 'summit' opportunity had he believed for one moment that Ireland mattered.[30]

When Macmillan came to power, the policy of the British government was one of upholding the Union unless Irishmen of both traditions showed any inclination for unity. When he left office, despite the efforts of Séan Lemass and, latterly, Terence O'Neill, to enlist his support in starting a talks process, that position remained unchanged. By the autumn of 1963, hopes for accommodation and reconciliation were already receding. The IRA cease-fire was increasingly fragile with the additional threat that, if violence resumed, British cities would be targeted. Although O'Neill did eventually meet Lemass during the Wilson years, his room for manoeuvre had already been squeezed by hard-liners. From 1968, policy-makers struggling to come to terms with the violence would look back wistfully to days when all in Ireland had seemed 'peace – perfect peace'.

NOTES

1. I am grateful to Professor Ronan Fanning at University College Dublin for his perceptive and encouraging comments on early drafts of this chapter.
2. Harold Macmillan, *Winds of Change* (London: Macmillan, 1966), pp. 78–9; Alistair Horne, *Macmillan*, vol. 1 (London: Macmillan, 1986), pp. 40–1; John Horgan, *Sean Lemass: The Enigmatic Patriot* (Dublin, 1997), pp. 12–3; I owe the final quotation to Peter Catteral of the Institute of Contemporary British History.
3. Alistair Horne, *Macmillan*, vol. 2 (London: Macmillan, 1989), p. 512.
4. I am grateful to Charles Lysaght for much of this information which comes from his conversations with Macmillan; Horne, *Macmillan*, vol. 2, pp. 604–5.
5. National Archives Dublin, Foreign Affairs, London Embassy, F132/1/2: Department of External Affairs to London, teleprinter message 3351, 25 November 1951; Boland to O'Driscoll, 26 September, 1951.
6. Churchill had sent the infamous Black & Tans to Dublin during the Anglo-Irish war and negotiated the 1921 treaty with Michael Collins.
7. National Archives, Dublin, Foreign Affairs, London Embassy, F132/1/2: Ambassador to Secretary, Department of External Affairs, 22 January 1952; Ambassador to Secretary, Department of External Affairs, 24 April 1954.
8. National Archives, Dublin, Department of Taoiseach, S15823A: Statement in Dail Eireann, 30 November 1955.
9. Macmillan's conversations with Charles Lysaght; *The Times*, 18 March

1958; National Archives, Dublin, Foreign Affairs, London Embassy, L116/16: St Patrick's Day celebrations, 16–19 March 1958. The innocence of the 1950s with regard to security is beautifully illustrated during this visit. The report of the trip included the tale of a threatening phone call which 'claimed that a bomb had been placed in the Embassy and necessitated a precautionary search of the premises by the Ambassador and Sgt. Cruise'.

10. Horgan, *Séan Lemass*, p. 17; National Archives Dublin, Department of Taoiseach, S14291A/3: speech by Séan Lemass to Ottawa Canadian Club, 25 September 1953.
11. *Belfast Telegraph*, 9 July 1959; National Archives Dublin, Department of Taoiseach, S9361 I/94: Speech by Séan Lemass at Oxford Union, 15 October 1959.
12. National Archives, Dublin, Department of Taoiseach, S15579A: Secretary, Department of Justice to Secretary, Department of Taoiseach, 28 October 1955 (Secretary is the highest ranking civil servant in a Irish government department and equivalent to the British rank of permanent under-secretary); *Irish Independent*, 24 May 1960; PRO (Kew), DO 35/7824: Dublin 107/18, G. D. Anderson to O. R. Blair (CRO), 7 June 1960.
13. *The Irish Times*, 18 January 1961; National Archives, Dublin, Department of Taoiseach, S9361 K/62: speeches by Séan Lemass at Fianna Fail *Ard Fheis*, 16 January 1962 and 20 November 1962; Ambassador (Washington) to Secretary, Department of External Affairs, 28 March 1962; PRO (Kew) Prem 11/4320: Record of meeting at CRO, 12 March 1963.
14. PRO (Kew), PREM 11/4320: Notes on personalities and officials.
15. PRO (Kew), DO 35/7853: PUS to Secretary of State, 3 July 1959.
16. PRONI (Belfast), CAB4/115, Cabinet Conclusions, 2 February 1960: *Economic Relations with the Irish Republic: Memo for Northern Ireland Government* (with covering letter from Austin Strutt at the Home Office).
17. PRONI (Belfast) CAB 4/115, Cabinet Conclusions 2 February 1960; see also PRONI (Belfast), CAB 9R/60/12, Cabinet Secretariat: Anglo-Eire Trade Negotiations.
18. PRONI (Belfast), CAB4/1097; Cabinet Meeting 9 July 1959; *Irish Press*, 31 May 1960.
19. Alan Clark, *Diaries* (1993), p. 57.
20. His unpublished memoir, *One Man Dog*, is in the possession of the Drapers Company, London, but remains closed. The record of his activities held by the PRO amounts to a handful of letters and notes. Richard Thorpe was shown *One Man Dog* by its author and uses it in his biography of Lord Home (London, 1997).
21. C. Moore, *The Kincora Scandal* (Dublin, 1996); Bill Graham, 'Kincora: The Tangled Web', *Hot Press*, May 1996; review of *The Kincora Scandal*, by Conor Cruise O'Brien, *Sunday Independent*, 21 April 1996.
22. Anthony Howard, *RAB: The Life of R A Butler* (London, 1987); *Belfast Telegraph*, 12 December 1959; *Daily Mail*, 14 and 15 December 1959; *The Times*, 14 December 1959; *Observer*, 13 December 1959; National Archives, Dublin, Department of Foreign Affairs, London Embassy,

F132/11/21: London Embassy to Dublin, Teleprinter message 3830, 19 December 1959; National Archives, Dublin, Department of Taoiseach, S9361/I/94: Taoiseach's comments on statement by Mr R. A. Butler, 31 March 1960; PRONI (Belfast), COM/60A//1/3/89, Butler to Brookeborough, 10 September 1959.

23. National Archives, Dublin, Department of Taoiseach, S9361/K/63: London Embassy to Dublin, Ambassador to Secretary of Department of External Affairs, 19 January 1963; PRO (Kew), HO 284/45: Private Office to Home Secretary, Record of meeting with Ulster Unionist MPs, 23 November 1959; Note of meeting between Home Secretary and Sir David Campbell and other UUP MPs, 24 November 1959.

24. *Daily Mail*, 15 December 1959; National Archives (Dublin), External Affairs, F132/11/21 London Embassy: Teleprinter message 3830 from London, 19 December 1959; PRO (Kew), PREM 11/3897: de Zulueta to Glanville, 21 May 1961; Briefing notes for visit of Lord Brookeborough in July 1961.

25. PRO (Kew), PREM 11/3897: Macmillan to Brookeborough, 3 June 1961; Note for the record, meeting of Prime Minister and Lord Brookeborough at Chequers, 17 July 1961; PRO (Kew), PREM 11/4320: Record of meeting between Prime Minister and Taoiseach, 18 March 1963, National Archives, Dublin, Department of Taoiseach, S9361/K/63: London Embassy to Dublin, Ambassador to Secretary of Department of External Affairs, 19 January 1963.

26. PRO (Kew), DO 35/7853: Record of conversation at 10 Downing Street on 13 July 1959 between the Prime Minister and Prime Minister of Eire.

27. PRO (Kew), PREM 11/4320: de Zulueta to France, 30 June 1961.

28. National Archives, Dublin, Department of Taoiseach, S1157 B/94: Unsigned memorandum from Department of External Affairs, 18 February 1963; PRO (Kew), PREM 11/4386: Knox Cunningham to Tim Bligh, 18 April 1963.

29. See 'A Family Affair: Harold Macmillan and the Art of Personal Diplomacy', in R. Aldous and S. Lee, *Harold Macmillan & Britain's World Role*; PRO (Kew), PREM 11/4386, Note for the record, meeting between the Prime Minister and Captain O'Neill, 22 April 1963; National Archives, Dublin, Department of Taoiseach, S9361/K/63, Washington to Dublin, Ambassador to Secretary, 19 March 1963.

30. PRO (Kew), PREM 11/4386, Note for the record, meeting between the Prime Minister and Captain O'Neill, 22 April 1963; Cunningham to Bligh, 22 April 1963; Cunningham to Philip de Zulueta, 24 April 1963; National Archives, Dublin, Department of Taoiseach, S9361/K/63, Washington to Dublin, Ambassador to Secretary, 19 March 1963; PRO (Kew), DO35/7853 & PREM 11/4320.

10 Dear Brendan and Master Harold

Charles Lysaght

In the cool summer of 1968, when I was beginning my research for a biography of Brendan Bracken, I was bidden to lunch at Birch Grove, the Sussex home of Harold Macmillan. When I arrived in a taxi, I found my host waiting at the door to greet me. He fussed about where I should put my briefcase and whether I wished to wash my hands. He poured me a glass of sherry and then took me out into the lovely rose garden his mother had created and told me all about it and about her. He shuffled up and down the same path about ten times before we went into lunch. 'I don't usually see people who are writing books' he told me, 'but I liked your letter.' He spoke affectionately of 'dear Brendan' as he called Bracken. But speaking as a publisher he rather doubted if there was a book in it now that all Bracken's papers had been destroyed.

And so the conversation ranged wider. He had been to Ireland that summer and had been charmed by the Waterford countryside where his late wife's Anglo-Irish relations lived; 'I expect you know them', he added. 'It's the only happy country left in Europe' he remarked, 'nothing seems to have changed; it's just like England used to be when I was young.' He recalled the Irish writers he had known in his publishing days: Yeats whom he felt was a poseur; Sean O'Casey whom he considered a saint; James Stephens whom he loved and mimicked with relish and Oliver Gogarty whom he thought was rather a fraud. 'All that great efflorescence in Dublin in those days' he mused, 'and now nothing, I suppose.' He spoke of De Valera's great integrity but thought he was more a Spaniard than an Irishman – 'He is not very jolly, is he?' he remarked. As we talked, he made regular attentive enquiries about my comfort.

We worked our way through the regular Macmillan lunch of paté, cold ham and salad and then raspberries, which he proudly told me were his own as he took a second helping. No, he did not remember when I reminded him that in 1914, when he was Treasurer of the Oxford Union, he had spoken at the Cambridge Union for Irish Home Rule. But he was pleased to recall all his friends who had died in the Great War. Ronnie Knox and one other were the only friends he had left at the end of it.[1] Only his ambitious and rather formidable American mother, who nursed him back to health after he had been seriously wounded, had prevented him from following Knox into the Roman obedience. He was clearly very exercised by matters religious.

His own conversation was wonderfully learned, full of ideas and literary and historical allusions. Brendan, he said, knew more history than anybody outside a university. When I asked if he thought Bracken was a depressive, he answered that all the Irish and Highland Scots are. 'That was why *we* drink'; he added, 'the English, they drink for sociability – at bump suppers and the like.' He himself had suffered from the most awful depressions all his life and the only cure he knew was to lock himself away and read Jane Austen and pray that he would not have to take any decisions until it passed. Certainly he had about him a lonely, melancholy air. 'I don't live in the world anymore' he said; 'when I go to London and see people, I get tired.' He shuffled around uneasily, moving from place to place as we talked. He wrapped himself in a rug when he sat down outside. 'Don't go yet', he said when I made a move. He showed me all the family photographs. I did not then know the sad story of his wife's infidelity, but I did notice that the only photograph on his desk was of his mother. There were also several shots of President Kennedy in the room. He spoke wistfully and romantically of Kennedy's visit to him only a few months before the fatal day in Dallas.

When the time came to go, he himself rang for my taxi. Before I left he counselled me earnestly: 'Don't pay too much attention to accounts of conversations. Brendan and Winston and Max Beaverbrook were always saying outrageous things just for the hell of it; it was a form of relaxation. The real business was done in writing.' So he waved me off, a solitary, forlorn figure standing at the door of his empty house, leaving me charmed and captivated by his grace and style but not all that much wiser about 'dear Brendan' whom I had come to discuss.

When I got to work on my book I discovered that, contrary to what the Chairman of the House of Macmillan, who had been my host, had said, the destruction of Bracken's papers was not an insurmountable obstacle to writing a biography as many of his letters could be traced in other people's papers. Brendan Bracken was such a good subject that another author ran up a book in a year and won the Whitbread Prize, despite failing to unearth much material that was relevant and available.[2] I also discovered an amount about Bracken's relationship with Harold Macmillan that the former Prime Minister had not recalled or perhaps had never known.

Their association went back a long way. In 1926 as a young Conservative Member of Parliament, Macmillan had written an article for *The Banker*, a journal that Bracken had founded and was editing for the publishers Eyre & Spottiswoode, to whose board he had been co-opted that year at the age of 24. It was entitled 'Our mediaeval system of local taxation' and contained proposals for relieving industry of the burden of rates. They so impressed the Chancellor of the Exchequer Winston Churchill that they were given effect in the Derating Act two years later.[3] In the 1929 General Election, as the country swung away from the Conservatives, Macmillan lost his seat in Stockton while Bracken entered the House of Commons as a Conservative member for North Paddington, having survived a Labour challenge for this key marginal by a mere 528 votes after a tempestuous contest. 'The ladies of easy virtue who abound in Maida Vale and are the remnant of the once powerful Tory party are still loyal to our cause', he wrote during the campaign to his mentor J. L. Garvin, the editor of the *Observer*, 'but I fear their ancient profession is but little encouraged by derating and some of our other admirable measures.'[4]

In October 1930 Tom Jones recorded in his diary a weekend at the Astors' house Cliveden, when both Macmillan and Bracken were among a group of young disgruntled Tories 'all angry with Stanley Baldwin'.[5] But they would have had little in common except this antipathy. Macmillan was on the left of the party on economic issues, flirting with socialism as a cure for unemployment and blaming the Governor of the Bank of England Montagu Norman and other bankers for the Great Depression. Bracken thought this was arrant nonsense and was on the right of the party, decrying state intervention and criticizing 'lush doles'. He was also allied to Churchill in opposing self-government for India, a measure Macmillan supported when he returned to the House of Commons in 1931. As Churchill became isolated on that and on his early appeals for rearmament, and blotted his copybook by a number of other misjudgments, notably over the Abdication, Bracken remained at his side, his only consistent supporter. 'We were' Bracken later boasted 'a party of two.'[6] Stanley Baldwin, the Prime Minister, in a rare moment of wit inspired by his cousin Rudyard Kipling, described

Bracken as Churchill's faithful *chela*. *Chela* was the Hindustani word for a disciple.

In those years Macmillan drifted out of Churchill's life, although they lived quite close to one another in the country. Apart from their political disagreements, it may be surmised that Macmillan did not relish the possibility of meeting Robert Boothby, his wife's lover, who was a frequent visitor at Chartwell, Churchill's home in Kent. Churchill, for his part, found Macmillan over-earnest and rather dull. He deleted Macmillan's name when it was among those on a list of possible candidates to restore the strength of the Other Club, a cross-party dining circle of which Churchill had been a founder (with F. E. Smith) and remained the presiding presence, and of which Bracken was secretary.[7]

It was the issue of appeasement that brought Macmillan back into the Churchillian world. Macmillan recalled being invited to Chartwell in late 1935 during the uproar about the Hoare–Laval Pact, the effect of which was that the League of Nations sanctions imposed on Italy for invading Abyssinia were undermined; Bracken was among those he found there.[8] During the debates on the Munich Agreement at the end of September 1938 Macmillan brought Hugh Dalton to a meeting of Tory dissidents at 8 Lord North Street, Bracken's house, where the possibility of making common cause with Labour was discussed.[9] There was, however, little enthusiasm for this among these dissidents who lay low during the following months as the Agreement under which the German-speaking areas of Czechoslovakia were conceded to Germany was still popular. On 17 November only Churchill, Macmillan and Bracken voted against the government in favour of a Labour Party motion to establish a Ministry of Supply.[10] In the early summer of 1939, as the policy of appeasement disintegrated, Macmillan listened with admiration to Bracken in the House of Commons when he revealed that the Chancellor, Sir John Simon, had acquiesced in the transfer of the Czech gold reserves to the German Government. 'Simon's combination of legalism and cynicism', Macmillan later wrote, 'disturbed the House. Even the government's most loyal supporters could barely stomach so shocking and discreditable an affair.'[11]

On 3 September that year war was declared. Churchill joined the government as First Lord of the Admiralty. Bracken became his Parliamentary Private Secretary. Macmillan remained on the backbenches dissatisfied with Chamberlain's leadership and prominent in a group pressing for Churchill to succeed. Back in office Churchill did not intrigue with dissidents, but his acolyte Bracken made it his business to keep in touch with them.[12] In May 1940 after the fall of Norway, Macmillan was among those Tories who voted against the government in a division that was the death-knell of Chamberlain's administration. The next day Macmillan met Bracken, who seemed happy and assured Macmillan that he, too, could be happy. However, at the last moment, Chamberlain tried to hang on. 'It's like trying to get a limpet off a corpse', Bracken told Macmillan as they waited anxiously before Chamberlain finally agreed to go.[13]

Macmillan and Bracken remained in close touch as Churchill formed his government. Bracken was in the thick of things, suggesting the right men for various jobs. 'The Boss's mood is one of profound anxiety', he confided in Macmillan.[14] Macmillan was appointed one of Beaverbrook's understudies at the Ministry of Supply. Later he became Parliamentary Secretary at the Colonial Office, where he was able to act as spokesman in the House of Commons as Lord Moyne, the Colonial Secretary, was in the Lords. However, in the autumn of 1942, the government was re-arranged and Oliver Stanley, a Member of the Commons, became Colonial Secretary. This effectively downgraded Macmillan. He was disappointed that the Prime Minister did not value him more highly and wrote a letter of resignation. He showed it to Bracken, then whom nobody, he later wrote, was closer to Winston Churchill.[15] Bracken advised Macmillan to hold his hand. A month later, in the aftermath of the American invasion of North Africa, Macmillan was appointed Resident Minister there and given Cabinet rank. This proved the turning-point in his political career.

It was not long before Bracken was voicing disappointment about the man he had helped. In March 1943, in his capacity as Minister of Information, he was telling W. P. Crozier of the *Manchester Guardian*, that he had 'hoped Macmillan would fight for proper facilities for us in respect of news, but as a matter of fact, he was doing all the Americans told him and getting nothing for us'.[16] A little over a year later, on 22 June 1944, Robert Bruce Lockhart who worked with Anthony Eden, the Foreign Secretary, and with Bracken, noted in his diary:

both Brendan and Anthony are up against Macmillan, Anthony because Resident Ministers are always a bit of a business to the F.O. and Brendan perhaps because he is a little jealous of the P.M.s recent marks of confidence in Macmillan.[17]

Bracken and Macmillan were both members of the caretaker government formed by Churchill at the end of the War in Europe after the Labour members resigned in May 1945 to fight the General Election. Bracken was First Lord of the Admiralty, Macmillan Minister for Air. Both lost their seats in the landslide to Labour and both were returned at by-elections in safe Tory seats before the year was out.

Early the next year Robert Bruce Lockhart noted a meeting with Bracken at dinner in the house of Cyril Radcliffe, the eminent barrister who had run the Ministry of Information under Bracken:

> Brendan was subdued, quite sober, but in good form. He gave a long account of the difficulties of the new government, but thought that the Tories were out for a long time and were foolish in their tactics. Contrary to the last time I saw him, he was pro-Anthony [Eden] this time; said Anthony was the only leader who could command Liberal votes in the country and informed us that Harold Macmillan and Oliver Stanley were intriguing against him and trying to oust him from the leadership. All this was very foolish.[18]

Bracken viewed with jaundiced eyes the efforts of Macmillan and others, notably Rab Butler, to move the Party to the left. On 7 October 1946 he wrote to his friend Lord Beaverbrook:

> 'The Tory Conference is over. It was an interesting affair. The neo-socialists like Harold Macmillan, who are in favour of nationalizing railways, electricity, gas and many other things, expected to get great support from the delegates who are supposed to be greatly frustrated by the result of the general election and successive by-elections.
>
> Rab Butler and the other moles engaged in research to produce a 'modern' policy for the Tory Party believed that Blackpool would be a paradise for the progressives.
>
> It turned out that the neo-socialists were lucky to escape with their scalps. The delegates would have nothing to do with the proposal to change the party's name. They demanded a real Conservative policy instead of a synthetic Socialist one so dear to the heart of the Macmillans and Butlers and it gave Churchill one of the great receptions of his life.

I know not whether the Tories' return to their ancient faith is likely to get us more votes at the four forthcoming by-elections. it certainly won't lose us any.'[19]

Unfortunately, not much detail survives on the inner conflicts of the Conservative Front Bench during these years in opposition. Bracken's views critical of state enterprise, high taxation and welfare handouts, and in favour of the creation of the right environment for entrepreneurs as the only way forward may have been precursors of Thatcherism but they were then regarded as politically impossible. But apart from occasional sniping at Front Bench meetings and in his 'Men & Matters' column in the *Financial Times*, Bracken made little effort to harness political support against the 'Chartermongers' as he described Butler, Macmillan and their followers.[20] His priority was that his old friend Winston Churchill should be Prime Minister again. Arguments about policy could await that event. Meanwhile, he devoted himself to wholehearted noisy opposition to bills to nationalize public utilities such as gas, and to general abuse of government ministers.

I have not been able to discover any record of how Macmillan viewed Bracken's activities in these years. Doubtless he shared the general expectation that Bracken would return to the Cabinet on Churchill's coat-tails and may have been apprehensive of the influence he would wield on economic policy. But they were friendly enough that on the day the Labour Prime Minister Clement Attlee dissolved the House of Commons in October 1951, Bracken, who was quite confident of a Tory victory in the ensuing election, was discussing Macmillan's ministerial prospects with him. Macmillan later recalled the encounter:

According to his account, Churchill intends to stay a year or eighteen months. . . . Eden will go to the Foreign Office; Butler to the Exchequer; Lyttleton to Production. What would I like? The Service Departments will be under-secretaries, as in war. One idea would be to have a permanent chairman of the Chiefs of Staff Committee – an American plan which we subsequently adopted. In this case I could be the Minister of Defence unless Churchill took the post himself. Alternatively there was Leader of the Commons. With Eden at the Foreign Office it would be impossible for him to act as Leader. Would I like this? And so the strange conversation continued.[21]

In the event, when Churchill became Prime Minister, Macmillan was only appointed Minister of Housing. He was bitterly disappointed and had to be dissuaded from declining. He did not foresee how it would help his political career. Bracken, for his part, confounded friends and foes alike by declining the Colonial Office or any other post, pleading that his recurrent sinusitis made it impossible. Shortly afterwards, he resigned his seat in the House of Commons, so bringing his political career to an end at the age of 50. He was created Viscount Bracken, but never took his seat in the House of Lords, which in his irreverent way he called 'the Morgue'.

However, he remained close to Churchill and his commentary in letters to friends, notably Lord Beaverbrook, on the activities of ministers, including Macmillan, is full of interest. At first, most of his ire was directed at Butler because as Chancellor of the Exchequer he failed to check inflation. In January 1953, when the government had been in office just over a year, Bracken wrote to Beaverbrook:

> Taking them all in all I should think that Monckton and Macmillan are the most successful Ministers. . . . Macmillan is desperately anxious to get out of the Ministry of Housing, but I don't think Churchill will let him go to his spiritual home, which is the Foreign Office. Alone among the press the *Times* newspaper has pointed out that when the Socialists bolted they left behind them no less than 216,000 unfinished houses. It wasn't difficult, therefore, to induce good housing returns during the first year of a Tory government. Conditions will be very different this year and so Master Harold is right to try to find alternative employment. It must, of course, be said that Macmillan has shown a great deal of good sense in his dealings with the public. Small touches, such as arriving on the scene after the floods in Devonshire, are very much applauded by the public, and rightly so.[22]

In March 1953 Bracken spent a weekend at Chequers with Churchill where Macmillan was a fellow guest. He reported to Beaverbrook:

> Success has turned Harold into a healthy heretic and has shed his defensive armour of respectability. He is now chock-full of fun and is looking for new fields to conquer. Agriculture is beginning to attract him – I can't think of a better man to stir up

that moss grown department and to create hell in its appendage the Farmers' Union. Under him more food would be grown and so too would budget deficits.[23]

A few months later, in June 1953, Churchill suffered a stroke, whose existence was hidden from the public and even the Cabinet as a result of a conspiracy among his close associates, among whom Bracken and Beaverbrook were foremost. There followed two years when Churchill continued to preside over the government although not really fit to do so and his heir apparent Anthony Eden (who was recovering from a botched operation) grew more and more resentful at being made to wait. Macmillan, alone among Churchill's ministers, had the courage to tell the old man that he should make way for Eden. Bracken appears to have resented this although there is no evidence that he himself actively encouraged Churchill to remain on as Prime Minister.

Writing to his Australian friend W. S. Robinson on 28 January 1955, Bracken described Macmillan, who had become Minister for Defence, as 'a very remarkable man, imaginative, amusing and possessed of a judgement which is almost always wrong'.[24] Macmillan had apparently asked Bracken about becoming Foreign Secretary when, as was about to happen, Eden succeeded Churchill as Prime Minister. He was apprehensive that Eden would interfere with him unduly. Bracken, on his own account, told him that 'Eden would keep a grip on foreign policy as strong as a vice.' 'Nevertheless', Bracken remarked, 'Harold is not deterred as he has always wanted the Foreign Office.' In March 1955 Eden succeeded Churchill and Macmillan became Foreign Secretary. By November of that year Bracken was telling Beaverbrook that Macmillan had become 'a pompous posturer' and would be a growing liability to Eden.[25]

In December 1955 Eden re-shuffled his cabinet by making Rab Butler Leader of the House of Commons and moving Macmillan to replace him at the Treasury. Writing to W. S. Robinson on 18 January 1956 Bracken remarked:

Perhaps the major reason for Harold's appointment was his temperamental incapacity for the Foreign Secretaryship. There was only one place to which he could be moved and that was the Treasury and if he had not been given that he would probably have been at a loose end in the House of Commons where he could create lots of trouble for the Government. Never since the days of Charles Townshend has there been a stranger appointment to the Treasury.

His apprehensions about Macmillan at the Treasury had not been assuaged by a press conference that Macmillan held shortly after taking up his new office; as he told Robinson:

> Our new Chancellor of the Exchequer is beginning well! He saw some of the moguls of the newspapers on Monday night and told them that in his judgment the bankers were a menace to the country. He recalled that he had been Member for Stockton-on-Tees for nearly 20 years and that nearly 20,000 unemployed had walked the streets because of the policies of Montagu Norman and the joint stock banks. He also told them that he had crossed the floor of the House of Commons because of the deflationary policies of the bankers and Baldwin's government and if this government followed their bad example he would be perfectly prepared to cross the floor again. Old Sir Oscar Hobson of the *News Chronicle* who is a financial troglodyte, and practically a teetotaller, had to be revived with brandy because no smelling salts were available in Whitehall.

Yet Bracken was not without some hopes for Macmillan in his new post. As he wrote to Beaverbrook on 17 January 1956:

> Macmillan may be the witch doctor we need – at any rate for a while will give the appearance of being one – and may in our present circumstances be the best possible boss for the Treasury. He is a person of very little judgment and I can't forgive him for his gross disloyalty to Churchill. But our need now is for a financial Mary Baker Eddy and Macmillan has plenty of affinities with that lady. And so let us hope for the best.[26]

Within the month there was a serious clash in the cabinet when Eden opposed Macmillan's proposal to cut food subsidies on bread and milk in order to help stem the continuing flight from the pound. Bracken wrote to Beaverbrook on 15 February 1956:

> Your prophecy that your former Under-Secretary would make trouble for Eden has been swiftly proved. He sent in his resigna-

tion yesterday on a cunningly contrived issue which would have gravely embarrassed his boss and would have given your former Under-Secretary the credit for being the only virtuous and strong man in government. A truce has been patched up, but how long it will last is anybody's guess.

Unfortunately for E. he has given this man a job which puts him plumb in the centre of the political stage and one may be sure that he will make the fullest use of his nuisance value.[27]

Beaverbrook replied tersely, as was his wont:

Be sure that Macmillan will make trouble if he has power. As long as he is kept in order he will be all right. When he gets up he will be all wrong.[28]

Bracken remained critical of the performance of the new Chancellor. Writing to W. S. Robinson on 20 April 1956 he remarked:

Macmillan's budget is a ridiculous affair which will do nothing to stop inflation. Unless he is prepared to offer prizes approximately equal to his opposite numbers in the football pool business his premium bonds may prove to be a flop.

Within a period of six months the British Government have twice increased profits tax and they do this at a time when they are exhorting British industry to equip itself with the best of modern plant. The new increase in profits tax is, of course, a feeble though costly effort to show the Trades Union bosses that the British Government have no love for employers or shareholders. To adapt a Biblical saying. 'If they do these things in a green tree what shall be done in the dry?'

When Mr. Gaitskell gets into Downing Street you can take it from me that company profits will be remorselessly socked and the Macmillan plus Butler precedents well supported.

When, in October that year, Macmillan put before the party conference a proposal for a free trade area with the six original EEC states, Bracken reported to Beaverbrook:

Harold Macmillan jumped the gun when he enunciated his wonderful Britain plus a part of Europe free trade area. Our government is so alarmed by the prospect of being left out of this curiously contrived arrangement that they are willing to toy with the idea.

There is, I am told, fierce opposition from industrial bosses who are large contributors to the Tory Party and I expect that Macmillan and Thorneycroft will battle for time.[29]

By this stage, President Nasser's seizure of the Suez Canal and its aftermath was dominating the political stage. Bracken was dubious about the practicality of using force against Nasser, but he could not help admiring Eden's toughness in so doing. On 5 November, while British troops were on their way to Egypt, he wrote to Beaverbrook:

> The socialists who thought he was a charming milksop now hold him to be a blood lusting monster. Vanity can be a great toughener.[30]

The following day the troops landed, but under international pressure, led by the United States, the British government declared a ceasefire. Bracken viewed Macmillan's gyrations during this period with some reservations. As he wrote to Beaverbrook on 22 November 1956:

> Until a week ago Macmillan whose bellicosity was beyond description, was wanting to tear Nasser's scalp off with his own fingernails. He was like that character in O'Casey's play who cried: 'Let me like a hero fall. My breast expanding to the ball'. Today he might be described as the leader of the bolters. His Treasury officials have put before him the economic consequences of the Suez fiasco and his feet are frost bitten.[31]

Eden was exhausted and took himself to Jamaica to recover, an action described by one of his biographers as 'a fatal mistake'. It meant that he was not in the House of Commons on 6 December 1956 to meet a motion of censure that was moved by the Labour opposition. Writing to Beaverbrook on the following day Bracken admitted:

> If it was a mistake for him to go away at the present time (and I now think it probably was) I was one of the people who advised him to go. It shows how poor an adviser I am! But as he told me that he fully intends to brazen this out, I thought he

might as well get physically fit before facing the litter of problems that lie ahead.[32]

Bracken persisted in his jaundiced view of Macmillan's performance in the crisis:

Macmillan is telling journalists that he intends to retire from politics and go to the Morgue. . . . His real intentions are to push his boss out of No. 10 and he has a fair following in the Tory Party. The so-called Canal die-hards think better of him than they do of Eden or Butler.

I still think you were right to back Eden. He is the best of the Tories. I don't say that is terrific praise, but it is something. The alternatives are the crackpot Macmillan or Butler, who is a curious blend of Gandi [*sic*] and Boss Tweed.

Eden resigned on 9 January 1957 to be succeeded by Macmillan. A fortnight later Bracken brought Beaverbrook up to date:

The main reason for Eden's departure is not the one circulated by politicians and the Press. The reason is political, but as it involves a secret stuffed with dynamite I can't put it in a letter. This seems melodramatic, but alas, it is only too true as you will agree when you hear it. If Eden had been of tougher fibre, he could, I am sure, have brazened it out.

Health, of course, played a part in the decision, but I think his illness is more due to the effect of mind upon body than to the patchwork done by surgeons and doctors.

Butler greatly fancied his chances of succeeding Eden, but they were blighted by the advice offered to the Monarch by Eden, Churchill and Salisbury. Most of the Tories in the House of Commons were against Butler. They blamed him for the Suez scuttle, whereas Macmillan had a far greater responsibility. Nor was Macmillan slow in his siege of Number 10. He let it be known that in no circumstances would he serve under Butler and he did some powerful private canvassing. Of Butler, therefore, it may be truly said in the words of Coleridge – 'For I have lost the race I never ran'.[33]

Two days later, writing to an old friend, the former United States Ambassador, Lewis Douglas, Bracken remarked:

It was quite inevitable that Harold Macmillan should succeed Anthony Eden. Butler had been too long on the halls as an inevitable successor and so the audience is tired of him. He is credited with highly contradictory characteristics such as being naive and sly. A large number of Tories regard him as a Fabian whose only policy is to steal the Opposition's clothes. This is not an unfair estimate of Butler's devious leftish approach to politics. He is not, of course, by nature a man of the left, but he holds the simple view that in a democracy the only method of maintaining and keeping power is to bribe the mob.

I greatly grieve for Anthony. He is above the ruck of politicians. He is a man of high ideals and many graces and has been exceptionally well liked by all sections of the community. His political misfortunes and his departure have been a great shock to the young Tories to whom the Party owes its last two electoral victories. They looked up to Eden and felt that he was an Englishman of rare qualities. Neither Macmillan nor any member of the present Government can hope to command anything like the affectionate esteem that Eden enjoyed.[34]

Bracken watched suspiciously for signs that Macmillan's government would abandon the policy of disinflation initiated under Eden. Yet, when the Chancellor Peter Thorneycroft raised the Bank Rate to a record level of 7 per cent and cut back on capital investment programmes in the autumn of 1957 so as to defend the pound, Bracken expressed fears that it would damage British industry.[35] Early in 1958 Peter Thorneycroft resigned with the other Treasury ministers because measures they had proposed to defend the pound were rejected by Macmillan. By this time Bracken was in hospital being treated for the throat cancer that was to prove fatal. He sent a handwritten note to W. S. Robinson from his hospital bed:

Thorneycroft's resignation has had a peculiar effect upon the government. They parted from him because they looked upon him as an arch-deflationist. The excitement caused by his going stirred them to declare that they intend to cut more deeply than he ever tried to do. And in so far as Macmillan will abide by any policy for long I believe they will try to do so.

Macmillan shrugged off as 'little local difficulties' the resignation of his ministers and took himself off on a tour of the Commonwealth.

In March Bracken received a letter from Lord Cobham, the Governor General of New Zealand, after Macmillan had been there:

> Harold ... was obviously tired, but wonderfully buoyant in face of all disaster: resignations, bye-elections, opposition attacks: – all seem to slide off him like the traditional water off a duck's back.

Bracken was not so impressed by all the results of Macmillan's tour. As he wrote to W. S. Robinson on 29 April 1958:

> As you may have read in the newspapers Harold Macmillan is talking about starting a bank for the whole of the British Commonwealth. What purpose such an institution may serve passes my understanding. When one tots up the meagreness of the gold and dollar deposits held by Britain on behalf of the whole Sterling Area the irritating question springs to mind 'What is the bank going to have by way of cash?' One thing is quite certain – they will never be wanting a supply of eager borrowers. We can rely upon Mr. Nehru to elbow his way to the top of the queue, and the self-governing Sambos of Ghana will not be far behind.

Bracken and Macmillan met in May at a dinner given by Beaverbrook in honour of the Prime Ministers of the Canadian Maritime Provinces. After the dinner Churchill spoke but cut his remarks short because, as he said, 'I am in the presence of my leader, the Prime Minister.' With equal delicacy and brevity Harold Macmillan paid tribute to Churchill. This exchange pleased the ailing Bracken and a fellow guest observed that his tired, worn face broke into a smile.[36] Before the summer was out he was dead. Among those who made the pilgrimage to say farewell as death approached was Harold Macmillan. He might well have reflected that it was Bracken's intervention when he was about to resign in 1942 that had set him on the road to becoming Prime Minister.

When my book of Bracken finally appeared late in 1979, the Earl of Drogheda, to whom Bracken had left 8 Lord North Street, gave a party there to mark the event to which he invited a number of Bracken's old friends and associates, including Harold Macmillan. I retain the picture of the old man, who was then eighty-five, seated in a low armchair having his hand stroked by the seventy-year-old Lord Drogheda, who sat on the floor beside him calling him 'Former Prime Minister' and begging him to speak. At last, he struggled to his feet. 'I have not read this book' he began, 'but I have read another'. Having recovered from this gaffe by promising to read mine, he went on to recall that it was in this very room, over forty years before, 'that Winston and Brendan and I plotted the fight against appeasement'. He remarked that they were days 'so like the present when danger was not recognised' and referred to Iran, Mozambique and the Horn of Africa. He said that like Aron with Moses, Brendan had held Churchill's arms high when he was in the wilderness during the thirties and the country owed him a very great debt on that account. He recalled Brendan's unique position in Churchill's life, how he would contradict Churchill during the War when nobody else would dare and the quarrels that ensured; 'it was rather like a quarrel between a happily married couple' he remarked. 'Most of us are pretty ordinary' he went on, 'but Brendan, he was different.' He spoke of how from humble beginnings Bracken had set out to improve himself and had pulled himself up by his own efforts. 'That was considered a good thing to do when I was young', he said. 'Now I suppose it would be considered wrong to aspire to belong to the privileged classes.' It was vintage Macmillan and we all lapped it up.

The next day I wandered in to the Carlton Club and found Harold Macmillan sitting in the reading room with my book open in his hands. He held it up close to his eyes as he read it. One finger was in the index and he was turning over pages as if looking up par- ticular references. When the opportunity offered, I thanked him for his words the previous night. 'Curious fellow, Drogheda', he replied, 'he never told me I had to make a speech.' We conversed for a few minutes. I said something about Bracken's background not being so humble as his mother was a university graduate and he replied that he was sure they were perfectly respectable people. A few weeks later, having read my book, he wrote to Lord Drogheda correcting an error in a footnote that he had spotted but commending it because it showed 'a sympathetic understanding of a strange and lovable character'. If he was hurt, as surely he must have been, by Bracken's caustic comments quoted in it, and the discovery that the affection he had expressed for 'dear Brendan' did not appear to have been reciprocated, he did not show it. That too was Harold Macmillan.

NOTES

1. On Knox (later Monsignor Ronald Knox) and Macmillan's friendship with him, see Alistair Horne, *Macmillan 1891–1956* (Macmillan, 1988), pp. 17–27, 31–4.
2. Andrew Boyle, *Poor Dear Brendan* (Hutchinson, 1974).
3. Horne, op. cit., pp. 80–2.
4. Bracken–Garvin correspondence, Humanities Research Center, University of Texas.
5. Thomas Jones, *A Diary with Letters, 1926–30* (Oxford: Oxford University Press, 1969), p. 274.
6. House of Commons Debates (29 June 1944) vol. 401, col. 928.
7. Churchill Papers.
8. Horne, op. cit., pp. 111–2.
9. Harold Nicolson, *Diaries and Letters, 1930–1939* (Collins, 1966), pp. 375–6.
10. House of Commons Debates (17 November 1938) vol. 341, col. 1210.
11. Harold Macmillan, *Winds of Change* (Macmillan, 1966), p. 569.
12. See Charles Lysaght, *Brendan Bracken* (Allen Lane, 1979), chapter 14.
13. Harold Macmillan, *The Blast of War* (Macmillan, 1967), p. 76.
14. Harold Nicolson, *Diaries and Letters, 1939–1945* (Collins, 1967), p. 85.
15. Horne, op. cit., p. 151.
16. Lysaght, op. cit., p. 224.
17. Kenneth Young (ed.), *The Diaries of Sir Robert Bruce Lockhart, 1939–1965* (Macmillan, 1980), p. 325.
18. Ibid., p. 520. However, the sentence about Macmillan and Stanley intriguing in the original diary is omitted.
19. Bracken–Beaverbrook correspondence (now in the House of Lords) published in Richard Cockett (ed.), *My Dear Max* (The Historian's Press, 1990), p. 58.
20. See Lysaght, op. cit., chapter 19.
21. Harold Macmillan, *Tides of Fortune* (Macmillan, 1969), p. 355.
22. *My Dear Max*, p. 135.
23. Ibid., p. 144.
24. W. S. Robinson Papers, University of Melbourne.
25. *My Dear Max*, p. 184.
26. Ibid., pp. 186–7.
27. Ibid., pp. 189–90.
28. Ibid., pp. 190.
29. Ibid., pp. 193.
30. Ibid., pp. 194.
31. Ibid., pp. 196.
32. Ibid., pp. 199.
33. Ibid., pp. 203.
34. Bracken–Douglas correspondence, University of Arizona. (Copies available in the Churchill Archives, Churchill College, Cambridge.)
35. Bracken–Douglas correspondence.
36. *Brendan Bracken, 1901–1958: Portraits and Appreciations* (1958), p. 47 (Sir Beverly Baxter MP).

11 Macmillan, the Second World War and the Empire

S. J. Ball

Harold Macmillan had a good war. His appointment as Resident Minister to AFHQ, Algiers at the end of 1942 made his political career. Macmillan himself commented in later life, 'my belief is, when you get a chance, take it. It was always my philosophy. Chance played such a role in my life – Winston, the war, Algiers, Housing ... made me Prime Minister.' With the exception of Housing the other three factors Macmillan identifies are, essentially, the same. His record as an anti-appeaser and relationship with Churchill meant nothing until he got his opportunity in Algiers. Churchill was ruthless with his junior ministers. Macmillan held two relatively unimportant junior ministerial posts at Supply and Colonies. In the autumn of 1942 he was effectively demoted and considered resignation. If he had done so there is little doubt that his political career would have been at an end.

The Algiers job became a godsend, but he was not first choice. His Guards contemporary, the Financial Secretary to the Treasury, Harry Crookshank, turned it down on grounds of ill-health. Neither was it an obvious route to the top. At the time he feared he was being sent to 'political Siberia'. The great advantage of the post was that it brought Macmillan 'into the loop'. Cabinet ministers in London who were not members of the War Cabinet or its Defence Committee were effectively excluded from policy formation. Macmillan's contemporary and superior at the Colonial Office, Lord Cranborne, had complained unavailingly to Churchill, whilst Dominions Secretary, that: 'I do not myself know what is going on ... most of the important telegrams are exchanged by you personally, either with Heads of State or with Dominion Prime Ministers.'[1] Another Guards contemporary, ahead of Macmillan on the political ladder, Oliver Lyttelton, had already pioneered the Minister of State role in the Middle East.[2] He later recalled that 'no other

162

office ... could present the same opportunities for usefulness, the same independence, the same authority. ... I was far enough away from my colleagues to be able to make up my own mind on critical occasions. My powers were wide and unchallenged and I had to spend little time clearing subjects with other ministers.' Yet it was hard to disguise that the terms of Macmillan's appointment were less than ideal. Although he became a Cabinet minister, this gave him the same status as Duff Cooper, a slightly older politician whose career was already in decline, when he was sent to Singapore. Macmillan later wrote: 'His status would be roughly parallel to that of the Minister of State in Cairo.'[3] Unlike him, however, the Minister of State in Cairo was a member of the War Cabinet. Nevertheless, Macmillan made a major success of his appointment. It turned him, in his mid-forties, into a glamorous figure in the Conservative party.

Although he carried out his wartime duties with skill and dedication there is no doubt that he arrived in Africa at the right time. Political gossip had it that Algiers presented a tricky situation. On 1 January 1943 Harold Nicolson recorded in his diary: 'Rothermere tells me ... Harold MacMillan [*sic*] has been hurried out immediately by aeroplane. He will have a difficult job.'[4] Macmillan, however, had the immeasurable advantage of acting within the context of military victory. From the victory at second Alamein and the successful launch of Operation Torch in November 1942, until D-Day reduced Italy to a secondary theatre in June 1944, Allied military operations had a large measure of success. Macmillan was associated with this success, most symbolically when he was invited onto the podium for the Algiers and Tunis victory parades by Eisenhower. Oliver Lyttelton, who had been the sole Minister of State in the Middle East between July 1941 and February 1942, was in position at a time of disenchanting stalemate and had left before a significant victory was achieved.[5] He was also unable to make political capital from his appointment. Alan Moorehead, the *Daily Express* correspondent in Cairo, noted that he was hard-working and respected but, 'his press conferences were so appallingly dull, his words so banal and evasive that it was impossible to put him before the public as a leader'.[6] During his tenure Lyttelton had to sort out the disorganized logistics system, an important but dull subject, and relations with the Egyptian government, whose pro-Nazi dealings had to be kept secret. In December 1943, when future command arrangements in the Mediterranean were being finalized, Macmillan noted, somewhat disingenuously, 'if there is one commander, there must be one Resident Minister . . . if I am not selected I shall be able to come home, and presumably Winston will give me something there'. Lyttelton, who was much closer to Churchill than Macmillan, had indeed been brought home to fill the key role of Minister of Production. Yet despite his excellent performance at the ministry between 1942 and 1945 it removed him from the political limelight. Richard Casey had arrived in the Middle East just before Cairo began to lose its strategic centrality to Algiers. Duff Cooper had been tarred by the fall of Singapore. Lord Moyne, having been demoted from Colonial Secretary to deputy Minister of State, only achieved widespread fame through his brutal murder by Jewish terrorists. It is not fanciful to believe that Macmillan's sensitivity to timing in 1959 was influenced by the start of his rise to power in 1943. As Robert Rhodes James has rightly noted it was: '[his] semi-independent role in North Africa that brought out his supreme negotiating and diplomatic skills with the Free French and the Americans. It also brought out an ambition that had not been noticed before by his colleagues. He had become, and was always to remain, a committed professional politician, with an eye on the main chance.'[7]

Anyone studying Macmillan's career cannot doubt that his two-and-a-half years with allied forces in North Africa, Italy and Greece was a formative experience. He spent just as long in this role as he did as Minister of Defence, Foreign Secretary and Chancellor of the Exchequer, the offices of state concerned with foreign affairs which brought him to Downing Street, combined. The world in January 1957 was very different from that of January 1943 and Macmillan had, to an extent, changed with it. He continued, however, to draw on the lessons of Algiers in his conduct of affairs. The elements of this experience which have been most thoroughly explored, and which Macmillan himself stressed, are his understanding of the 'special relationship' and his relationship with other world leaders, especially Eisenhower and de Gaulle. This essay suggests that wartime experiences coloured other areas of Macmillan's conduct of the Premiership, and, in particular, his attitudes to the Empire.

Both contemporary commentators and historians have been interested by Macmillan's attempt to redefine Britain's role as a global power and, within this overall context, the very rapid process of decolonization which took place during his second administration, between October 1959 and October 1963. Much can be explained by the 'strategic vision' that Macmillan developed in 1955–6 and reified during the Suez crisis. Britain needed to cleave more closely to the United States, make its power projection capabilities more impressive, discard the dead wood and cut a constructive and successful dash on the world stage. Most colonial territories came under the heading of 'dead wood'. Britain's most important colony, Malaya, had signed a defence treaty with the UK in January 1957, days before Macmillan became Prime Minister. Malaya became independent in August 1957. This prefigured a new kind of relationship of which Macmillan approved. After 1958, the timing of further moves to create this pattern of relations elsewhere rested largely on the interplay of Tory politics with international developments. In Britain the White Paper on massacres in the Hola camp in Kenya was published in June 1959 and the Devlin report on the suppression of riots in Nyasaland was released a month later. Just as importantly, French and Belgian moves to leave their African colonies made action inevitable.[8] In 1959, during talks with Michel Debré, Macmillan 'sympathized profoundly with French difficulties in Africa; . . . all the more because people were conscious that similar problems confronted HMG in, for example, Kenya and Nyasaland. . . . The problem of the multi-racial state remained . . . the $64,000 question in Africa, . . . similar difficulties confronted the Commonwealth and the French Community: in the case for example of both Algeria and Rhodesia the situation contained similar elements: there were important white communities and local coloured *évolués* who attracted the support of public opinion at home . . . there was no doubt that Africa was going to become the big problem.'[9]

Despite the obvious explanatory importance of politics in the late 1950s, however, Macmillan's experiences a decade-and-a-half before were far from being merely distant memories of a distant era. Macmillan drew a number of important long-term lessons from his wartime experience. They affected both his understanding of the nature of empire and his conduct of imperial policy.

Macmillan's own role as a semi-independent minister had been a golden opportunity. It was not an opportunity he wished others to repeat. He became aware how adventures in exotic climes could immeasurably increase a minister's prestige. Finding oneself under fire from communists and *The Times* in Athens had definite political advantages. His African and Far Eastern tours as Prime Minister were a reflection of this belief. Although Macmillan's most important prime ministerial summits were in Paris, Rambouillet and Nassau, he cannot have failed to reflect that white fur hats were ridiculous in both wintry Finland in 1940 and Moscow in 1959.

As prime minister he had little enthusiasm for imperial proconsuls; he preferred his colleagues safely under supervision in London and was irritated when they escaped. Duncan Sandys received few thanks for his personal presence in the Far East during the formation of Malaysia, although the intimate but hostile relations of the Singaporeans and Malayans in 1963 had points of comparison with intra-French relations in 1943.[10] Not for Macmillan the telegram Eden sent him during the Lebanese crisis: 'You are clearly the best judge since you are so much nearer the theatre than we are.'[11]

Oliver Lyttelton noted of Churchill: 'The Prime Minister was fond of applying to organisation the dictum of Napoleon ["*Une Constitution doit être courte et obscure*"] that constitutions should be vague.'[12] As Lyttelton had previously found in Cairo, Macmillan was to find in Algiers. There was no defined role for a politician on the loose. He had to push himself into an existing structure. Both Lyttelton and Macmillan succeeded in establishing themselves because of the political crises surrounding the Gaullist and Vichy French in North Africa and the Levant. The military authorities were glad to hand over their extremely complex wrangles, mainly over status, to a political figure on the spot. Allied military advances enabled Macmillan to expand his authority into Italy and the Balkans, effectively ousting Lyttelton's successor in Cairo, Dick Casey, who was 'liquidated' and sent out to become Governor of Bengal.[13] Yet even as he pushed out the boundaries of his authority, insisting that a political minister, 'must be in a position of greater freedom to initiate and criticize policy', Macmillan noted that this was not necessarily desirable. 'His relations with the Foreign Office and its representatives', he minuted Churchill, 'must always be somewhat delicate, sometimes even strained.... I am bound to say that I should myself sympathise with a Foreign Secretary who would prefer to rid himself of such an incubus and rely on more correct and perhaps more pliable instruments to carry out his policy.'[14] He always had a bad word for those in an analogous position to himself. Casey was '*very* pleasant – but not, I think, very clever.' Alternatively, he was 'intelligent but ill-educated, just has not got the experience. He is absolutely honest, patriotic and devoted. But he is weak.' Lord Moyne was 'charming and ineffective as ever.' General Louis Spears, Churchill's confidant and Minister in the Levant, was 'a clever man; but the trouble is that he has the qualities neither of the British or the French. . . . I cannot help thinking that being a popular hero in the Levant has rather gone to his head. I cannot believe he was ever so cheered and applauded in Carlisle!'[15]

Macmillan certainly chose more pliable instruments when he was Prime Minister. The post nearest in nature to that of Resident Minister in the 1950s was the Commissioner-General in Southeast Asia. Macmillan chose a minor politician, the former First Lord of the Admiralty, Lord Selkirk, for this post. He disliked Selkirk's attempts to approach him directly and the post was abolished at the end of his Premiership. On the other hand, Macmillan was extremely impressed by the performance of the military leaders with whom he dealt. He would escape to the calm of military headquarters. 'I cannot tell you', he wrote to Lady Dorothy in March 1943, 'what a delightful change this was from the continual atmosphere of strife, incompetence and intrigue which surrounds us in Algiers.'[16] In contrast to his dislike of regional 'czars', he firmly supported Mountbatten's introduction of unified military commands in the Near and Far East. Perhaps he remembered Churchill's post-prandial outburst en route to Cairo: '"you may take the most gallant sailor, the most intrepid airman, or the most audacious soldier put them at a table together – what do you get? *The sum total of their fears!*" (This with frightful sibilant emphasis).'[17]

As regards substance rather than process, the seeds of future policy were sown through Macmillan's insight that empires, whether formal or informal, were not independent entities. Indeed, they were not of primary importance to the European powers as anything other than the theatre of great power politics. Macmillan had rarely expressed a close interest in imperial affairs before the war and his sojourn in Algiers did little to ignite his interest. In May 1943, whilst still deeply involved in the political intrigues of Algiers, he heartily endorsed a paper by the Security Service officer Kenneth Younger, which baldly stated: 'North Africa, after all, is unimportant.' Younger went on to argue, and Macmillan agreed, that, 'now the Tunisian campaign is over the case for a "quiet life", the argument which carried Darlan to his short-lived tenure of power, is no longer convincing.' Yet the Resident Minister should not be concerned with the fate of the empire for its own sake. 'It is time now to look to France and the future of Europe. It is the task of Britain to ensure that future is decided not by the discredited remnant of the old ruling clique, not even by the liberal imperialists in Washington, but by the people themselves. In this, Great Britain,

as the only great power left in Western Europe, can have a decisive influence and has therefore a special responsibility.'[18] Younger
later went on to be Minister of State at the Foreign Office during
Attlee's government and Director of Chatham House during
Macmillan's prime ministership. In 1943 Macmillan agreed with him
that co-operation with France on imperial issues was merely a way
of securing co-operation in post-war Europe. His motivations were
thus subtly different from those of his Tory colleague, Duff Cooper,
who took over his responsibility for Anglo-French relations in January
1944. Cooper believed that 'we have surely enough native problems of our own to face without stirring up native problems for
others. I think we should try to help the French to rebuild both
their country and their Empire, and by our encouragement win
their friendship.'[19]

During his time in North Africa, Macmillan witnessed how imperial issues could sow the seeds of discord, needlessly in his view,
between great powers. He was as disturbed as Churchill, and at
one remove de Gaulle, by Roosevelt's patronage of the Sultan of
Morocco in January 1943. 'Things were not helped', he wrote of
the Casablanca conference and attempts to reconcile Giraudist and
Gaullist factions, 'by a dinner Roosevelt gave in honour of the Sultan
of Morocco on the very day that de Gaulle arrived at the Anfa
camp. It was a curious and impolitic manoeuvre. . . . The President
talked a great deal about colonial aspirations towards independence
and the approaching end of "imperialism". All this was equally
embarrassing to the British and to the French.'[20] Macmillan was
uneasily aware, however, that distrust of the processes of British
imperialism was probably justified. He used irony to explain this
distrust to Churchill.

> misunderstandings [of British imperial policy] are based on the
> curious way in which history seems to work out. Of course Mr.
> Gladstone repeated over and over again that we would leave South
> Africa, but somehow or other we got back there. Of course Lord
> Kimberley and the Little Englanders did their best to prevent us
> forming a Colonial Empire and to impede the efforts of Mr. Rhodes
> at every stage, but somehow or other Mr. Rhodes got the better
> of them. Of course a series of British governments declared their
> intention to leave Egypt, but somehow or other Lord Cromer
> brought us back there. We are always on the point of evacua-
> tion, but always return with greater authority. This, which ac-

cording to our political beliefs we regard either as the wicked and cruel fate that dogs us against our will to be a great imperial race, or know to be the mysterious workings of Providence, anxious always to give the British a second chance, the French believe to be due to more sinister, less hallowed and in any case less fortuitous causes.[21]

Conservative politicians of Macmillan's generation placed in similar positions lacked this sense of irony. Thus Oliver Lyttelton on Lord Killearn, Cromer's lineal successor: 'It became a popular criticism that [Sir Miles] Lampson was rough with the King of Egypt, that the velvet glove was threadbare, that he was dictatorial and still saw himself as High Commissioner. It was easy to make such charges, but equally easy to defend him and describe him, as I would, as a jealous guardian of his country's name and obligations, forceful and rigid only about essentials. Those who subscribe to this remember the sinuousities of some other British diplomatists in other countries, and whither they led us.'[22]

During his premiership it was hard to involve Macmillan in any imperial issue which did not have direct ramifications for domestic politics or relations with another great power. When, for instance, the Malayans suggested the formation of a federation with Singapore and British Borneo in June 1960, a move which had been British policy since 1948 and which the Malayan government had hitherto staunchly opposed, officials found it very difficult to engage the Prime Minister's attention. Despite the importance of this development for the region, an Anglo-American agreement, which allowed the British to stay out of Vietnam if the US was not called upon to involve itself in Malayan affairs, limited its impact on great power relations.[23] In June 1960 Macmillan was preoccupied by the collapse of the Paris Conference; in August 1961, when the move came to fruition, the Berlin crisis was at its height.[24]

Before his despatch to the Middle East, Macmillan had been under-secretary at the Colonial Office for ten months. Yet the empire he was to get to know most intimately was not that of his own country but that of France. During the war he was to have a powerful role in shaping the future of that empire in the Levant and North Africa. Macmillan believed that the empires were, in fact, dissimilar, accepting what Freya Stark had described to him as the incompatibility of the 'gradual assimilation or elimination as a ruling class of the *"indigène"* and "government by suggestion"'.[25] Nevertheless, the chance to see a major empire in crisis shaped the second set of substantive lessons he was to learn. France in the Middle East allowed him to develop some of his ideas about colonialism and its dangers. It showed him at first hand how imperial affairs could humiliate a great power. In 1944 he noted, pityingly, that the French 'entertain the pathetic belief that by insisting verbally upon France's greatness they make her in fact great again.'[26] Macmillan distrusted French imperial rhetoric. His successor as British representative to the French Committee of National Liberation (FCNL), Duff Cooper, could write that: 'To those who know M. Pleven and have savoured the mystic touch of his Breton ancestry, this highly coloured and spiritual concept at [the] Brazzaville [imperial conference] will not come as a surprise. But sometimes the dreams of the dreamer come true and I think the best in French colonial policy is well summed up by his own epigram ... *"une politique imperialiste de l'esprit"*.'[27] Macmillan, however, took a much less complimentary line on imperial mysticism. 'De Gaulle ... like so many mystics, is half-reactionary ... and half progressive, but ... is on questions of foreign and especially native policy fundamentally reactionary.'[28] Macmillan's analysis of de Gaulle's imperial policy was part of a wider lack of sympathy for the man and his ideas. Although he was sympathetic to the Free French movement he never really understood de Gaulle's conception of what France was or could be. He was always more comfortable with Jean Monnet and René Massigli. His favourite Free French generals were Catroux and Leclerc.[29] De Gaulle might admire M. Macmillan's *esprit délié*;[30] but he never made clear whether he regarded him as subtle or glib.

During the war Macmillan's thinking tended to have a *marxisant* slant taken over from his proposals for Britain's economic and social problems in the 1930s. His first sally into imperial affairs had been a remarkable paper written on Kenya whilst he was at the Colonial Office. In it he disputed the premiss that, 'the Highlands of Kenya are "a white man's country" in the same sense which other Dominions are to-day or the American colonies were in the 18th century' and that, 'on this analogy of American colonies, the claims to self-government of any substantial number of Englishmen who have settled permanently in a country cannot be resisted'. He believed that 'Kenya's future is to be a "white governed" country but not a "white man's country". We have before us the warning of the West Indies and the Southern States of America about the problems involved in a "plantocracy".' The implications of such a plantocracy were not appealing. 'Gradually the white stock will become contaminated by the effect of the climate or by some inter-breeding. But this decadent or slightly decadent people – not in-creasing largely in numbers by immigration – will be the proprietors of the land and all that implies. Surrounded by a native population [which] – if our medical and other services continue – will become increasingly crowded and land hungry. A clash is bound to come.' Macmillan's 1942 solution was to nationalize the land and to re-form agricultural production by creating state and collective farms. 'This would be based on the Russian system.'[31]

Macmillan's views were formed with no direct experience of Kenya. His knowledge was based on his wife's connections. His dislike of *colons* was reinforced by his sojourn in North Africa. There, white settlers had already shown the decadence he predicted in Kenya: they favoured the pre-November 1942 situation when business had been good and Jewish rivals could be persecuted.[32] Unsurprisingly, Macmillan tended to agree with analyses which portrayed North Africa in similar fashion to that in which he had characterized Kenya. Political action was shaped, indeed deformed, by the class basis of society. Kenneth Younger, for instance, saw wartime North Africa divided into five groups: rich colonial civilians; prosperous busi-nessmen from France led by Jacques Lemaigre-Dubreuil; military officers; the small bourgeois; and, finally, the Arab and Jewish na-tives. 'There is one significant gap', Younger concluded, 'a French or European working class is entirely lacking. . . . The absence of a European working class has left the field clear for the upper class elements, and in particular has removed any check there might otherwise have been on one tendency which is common to all the ruling and middle classes, civil and military – the overmastering terror of Soviet Russia and communism.'[33] Macmillan too found these 'upper class elements' distasteful. 'The chief of these was Jacques Lemaigre-Dubreuil. This man was a wealthy manufacturer of vegetable oil . . . an associate before the war of some of the Right-wing pressure groups, such as the Cagoulards. . . . Before the war, we irreverent young Conservatives had given to a number of the less attractive industrialists who sat on the Conservative side in this House of Commons, generally for very safe seats, the offen-sive nickname of the "Forty Thieves". Lemaigre-Dubreuil would have had a high place in this company.'[34]

Macmillan noted that Allied policy was too indulgent of such men and attitudes amongst the colonists: 'As for the principles of liberal democracy, the abolition of racial laws and so on, except in the less reputable part of Headquarters which is called PWB [Political Warfare Branch] and includes, therefore, as well as professional soldiers, professors, authors, journalists and the like who have put on the military uniform without acquiring the military outlook, the view held was that virtually any political development in North Africa was to be deplored as hampering the war effort.'[35] Yet he also had limited sympathy with 'professors, authors and journalists and the like', such as Stark and Younger. If the empire became too important to a nation, if, indeed, it became the nation, one would be caught between ultra-enthusiasts and liberal intellectuals. Although drawn to the latter, Macmillan developed a healthy distrust for both.

In 1959 he was to denounce the *trahison des clercs*, 'the attitude of certain British intellectuals, hostile to their own country, who attacked the whites in Africa and championed the blacks'.[36] In 1943 he had evinced little interest in the manifesto on political reform delivered to him by the Algerian writer Ferhat Abbas, 'a familiar type of nationalist intellectual', and did not protest when Abbas was placed under house arrest and the *Délégations Financières* was dissolved in September 1943. The main concern in his office was that, 'the eleven million Arabs of North Africa are bound to become increasingly vocal, and the French do not seem ready, either institutionally or psychologically to deal with (or as our American friends would say, to channelize) Arab Nationalism in North Africa.'[37] In November 1943 Macmillan maintained that 'We wish the pledges for Levantine independence given quite clearly in 1941 to be carried out. . . . the French must be told that in this liberal and progressive policy lies their only hope and that they must take this course or their Near East interests must inevitably go under in the end.' On the other hand, 'We must make it clear . . . to the Syrians and the Lebanese that we have no desire to see French interests in the Levant overthrown. . . . both the Syrians and (especially) the Lebanese must be deflated. They must be told that they cannot rely on us to help them eject the French, only to get a fair agreement as outlined.'[38] He strongly objected to the Casey/Spears line of threatening the imposition of martial law unless the Lebanese government, arrested by the French Commissioner, was fully restored to power.[39] 'Spears wants a Fashoda; and I do not.'[40]

The ambivalence Macmillan had developed about French imperialism during the war was reflected in his own imperial policies during his premiership. In essence his policy was based around the preferences of liberal Conservatives such as Iain Macleod and Reginald Maudling and symbolized by the 'winds of change' speech. Yet they were often deliberately offset by hard-liners such as Duncan Sandys and Macmillan's son-in-law, Julian Amery. As in 1943, Macmillan attempted to maintain a balance. 'The cruder concepts, whether of left or right, are clearly wrong', he told Walter Monckton, 'the Africans cannot be dominated permanently. . . . Nor can the Europeans be abandoned.' As Prime Minister the issue which took up most of the time Macmillan devoted to imperial issues was the fate of the Central African Federation. In Africa, despite the demise of Macleod, Macmillan tended toward the 'abandonment of the Europeans', the group he had found despicable in 1942. Where a *colon* population did not exist he tended to favour less liberal policies. In 1943 his preferred imperial relationships had been with Egypt and Iraq. 'Both these countries are now completely independent. We maintain no longer High Commissioners there, but Ambassadors. But we have special treaties freely negotiated, which guarantee to us the special rights which our past and present connections with these countries justify.'[41] In 1956–8 he continued to invest a great deal of hope in these relationships and was bitterly disappointed by their failure.[42] His hard line on the eastern Mediterranean in the 1950s was reflected by his willingness to sanction military action East of Suez, in Kuwait, Oman and Aden.

Macmillan was happy as Minister Resident. This much is clear from the diaries he chose to publish at the end of his life. His career blossomed and he was away from his unsatisfactory family. One could argue that his time in the Mediterranean had an unfortunate effect on him. As Richard Aldous has observed: 'He breathlessly recorded in his diary that the [Casablanca] conference had been "like a meeting of the later period of the Roman empire", and christened Churchill and Roosevelt "the Emperor of the East and the Emperor of the West". The experience remained with Macmillan: the idea of bestriding the world stage as a latter-day Churchillian emperor appealed to his highly developed historical tastes.'[43] Arguably, he did not learn enough from his experiences. He could see that 'France [in 1944] . . . now finds herself reduced to the rank of a third-rate Power, with a small population and slender resources compared with the giants that surround her.'[44] It was not an analysis he cared to apply to Britain in the early 1960s. On the other hand, although he later portrayed himself as a champion of de Gaulle, he had little time for Gaullism. He had, after all, believed that British officials needed 'the courage to deal firmly with de Gaulle if he behaved in an absurd way'.[45] British power had to be preserved, but not in the fashion in which de Gaulle, faced with a similar post-Suez *crise de confiance*, reinvigorated France. In 1943–5 and 1957–63, Macmillan spent as little time on empires and their subject peoples as possible. His lack of sympathy or understanding for both rulers and ruled was not unusual, but it did make his achievement fragile.

NOTES

The author would like to thank the British Academy HRB and the Faculty of Arts Research Committee, University of Glasgow for financial assistance in preparing this essay.

1. DO121/10A, Lord Cranborne to Prime Minister, 18 November 1941. (All documentary references are to files held in the Public Record Office, Kew.)
2. Olive Lyttelton, Viscount Chandos, *The Memoirs of Lord Chandos* (London: The Bodley Head, 1962), pp. 227–8 (hereafter *Chandos*).
3. Harold Macmillan, *The Blast of War, 1939–45* (London: Macmillan, 1967), p. 216 (hereafter *BW*).
4. Harold Nicolson, *Diaries and Letters, 1930–1964* (condensed edn; London: Harper Collins, 1996), p. 240. At the time Macmillan 'feared that the fact that Darlan had been eliminated might so simplify the French situation that a new Minister might not be needed' (*BW*, p. 218).
5. Erwin Rommel had arrived in North Africa in January 1941 and led his *Afrika Korps* to the borders of Egypt. Wavell was replaced by Auchinleck, but the latter's great November 1941 'Crusader' offensive failed to produce a clear military victory.
6. Artemis Cooper, *Cairo in the War, 1939–1945* (pbk edn; London: Penguin, 1995), p. 128.
7. Robert Rhodes James, 'Harold Macmillan: An Introduction', in Richard Aldous and Sabine Lee (eds), *Harold Macmillan and Britain's World Role* (London: Macmillan, 1996), p. 3 (hereafter *BWR*).
8. PREM11/2888, Dakar to Foreign Office, Tel. 34, 26 December 1959 (with Macmillan's comments).
9. CO936/562, Extract from Records of a Conversation between the Prime Minister and Foreign Secretary in Paris, 9–10 March 1959.
10. DO169/249, Duncan Sandys to Harold Macmillan, SOSLON No. 109, 5 September 1963; DO169/249, Kuala Lumpur (Sandys) to CRO (Macmillan), SOSLON No. 139, 11 September 1963; PREM11/4350, P. de Zulueta to Prime Minister, 11 September 1963.
11. FO660/40, Anthony Eden to Harold Macmillan, Tel. 2760, 23 November 1943.

12. *Chandos*, p. 228.
13. Harold Macmillan, *War Diaries: The Mediterranean, 1943–1945* (pbk edn; London: Macmillan, 1985), pp. 319–21 (hereafter *WD*).
14. PREM3/272/4, Harold Macmillan to Winston Churchill, 16 August 1944. Lyttelton came to a similar conclusion. 'Towards the end of my eight months in the Middle East it was quite clear that my relations with the Foreign Office were bearing the greatest strain.... Eden ... must at times have been inclined to send me a telegram to keep off his grass altogether.' Eden was and remained, however, a close friend.
15. *WD*, pp. 33, 305, 393. Spears was MP for Carlisle.
16. *WD*, p. 46.
17. *WD*, p. 295.
18. FO660/15, Kenneth Younger to Roger Makins (with Macmillan's comments), 12 May 1943.
19. Duff Cooper to Winston Churchill, 21 February, 1944. Quoted in Duff Cooper, *Old Men Forget* (London: Rupert Hart-Davis, 1954), pp. 322–3.
20. *BW*, pp. 250–1.
21. PREM3/182/6, Harold Macmillan to Winston Churchill. Lord Kimberley was Colonial Secretary between 1870 and 1874, when Cape Colony was granted responsible government, and between 1880 and 1882, during the first Boer war. Lord Cromer was Britain's chief representative in Egypt, under various titles, between 1877 and 1907.
22. *Chandos*, pp. 232–3.
23. FO371/175100, Minute by J. E. Cable, 23 September 1964.
24. CO1030/978, Lord Selkirk to Iain Macleod, 23 March 1961; CAB134/1949, text of letter dated 11 August, 1961 from Tunku Abdul Rahman to Prime Minister; CO1030/982, Lord Selkirk to Iain Macleod, 24 August 1961; CO1030/983, Lord Selkirk to Iain Macleod, 16 September 1961; CAB134/1949, GM(61)1st Meeting, 27 September 1961.
25. FO660/36, *The French Problem. Personal Notes by Freya Stark*, 18 August 1943. Stark had written four books on the Arab world before the war. She joined the Ministry of Information in 1939 and served in the Yemen and Aden. She arrived in Egypt in June 1940 and set up the Brotherhood of Freedom. This group was supposed to encourage democratic, pro-British and anti-Nazi sentiment amongst educated Egyptians: it had limited success. She moved to Baghdad in April 1941 and had recently returned when this paper was written.
26. PREM3/182/6, Harold Macmillan to Winston Churchill, 3 January 1944.
27. FO660/126, Duff Cooper to Anthony Eden, 26 February 1944. René Pleven was the FCNL's Commissioner for Colonies in 1943–4. 'I met Pleven first,' Macmillan recorded in his diary for 3 November 1943, 'at Hever, just after I had gone to the Colonial Office. We worked together a good deal over the West African Produce Control Board, of which I made the Free French members. I think he was grateful for the assistance I gave him in those days and (although he got rather excited by political events from time time) he has remained a staunch friend' (*WD*, p. 276).
28. PREM3/182/6, Harold Macmillan to Winston Churchill, 3 January 1944.
29. 'With our troops [in the Tunis victory parade] were General Leclerc's

regiment of Free French who . . . refused to march with the French, preferring the English for companions', *WD*, p. 91. Leclerc was the *nom de guerre* of Philippe de Hauteclocque. Twelve years younger than de Gaulle, he was killed in 1947. Georges Catroux, the head of the Gaullist mission to the Middle East, and subsequently the Governor-General of Algeria and Commissioner in the Levant, was already 66 in 1943.

30. Charles de Gaulle, *Mémoires de Guerre*, 3 vols (Paris: Plon, 1954–59), vol. 2, p. 93.
31. CO967/57, Harold Macmillan to Sir George Gater, 15 August 1942.
32. *BW*, p. 216.
33. FO660/15, Kenneth Younger to Roger Makins, 12 May 1943.
34. *BW*, p. 259. Lemaigre-Dubreuil controlled the newspaper *Le Jour*. He was Giraud's *chef de cabinet*, until he was ousted in the 'New Deal' of March 1943. He was assassinated by Moroccan *colons* in 1955.
35. PREM3/182/6, Harold Macmillan to Winston Churchill, 3 January 1944. In 1941 Oliver Lyttelton had been equally disturbed by a promise made by General 'Jumbo' Wilson to the Vichy authorities in the Levant which prevented the Free French from gaining access to their troops. *Chandos*, p. 252.
36. CO936/562, J1074/20 Record of Meeting between the Prime Minister and M. Debré at 10 Downing Street at 10 a.m. on 14 April 1959.
37. FO660/26, Roger Makins to W. H. B. (Hal) Mack, 3 April 1943.
38. *WD*, p. 305.
39. FO660/39, Resident Minister, Algiers to Foreign Office, Tel. 2445, 21 November 1943.
40. *WD*, p. 297. Casey, of course, disagreed. Lord Casey, *Personal Experience 1939–1946* (London: Constable, 1962), p. 148.
41. *WD*, p. 305.
42. Nigel Ashton, 'Macmillan and the Middle East', in *BWR*, pp. 37–66.
43. *BWR*, p. 13.
44. PREM3/182/6, Harold Macmillan to Winston Churchill, 3 January 1944.
45. FO660/15, Harold Macmillan's notes on a paper by Kenneth Younger, n.d.

12 Macmillan and East of Suez: The Case of Malaysia

John Subritzky

INTRODUCTION

Harold Macmillan assumed the Premiership amid the national trauma resulting from Suez. This crisis – synonymous with the post-war decline of imperial Britain – was an appropriate prelude to Macmillan's term as prime minister. For the next six years his foreign policy would be dominated by attempts to preserve Britain's world standing in an era dominated by the superpowers. In particular, he had to wrestle with two simultaneous influences which seriously undermined British power: a relatively low-growth economy at home and assertive, fiercely anti-European nationalism abroad. Change was inevitable. Under Macmillan's stewardship, the transformation of empire to commonwealth was sharply accelerated. Writing in his diary, Macmillan speculated at the time whether he was 'destined to be the remodeller or the liquidator of empire'.[1] It shall be argued in this essay that, at least in regard to east of Suez and the case of Malaysia, Macmillan's ultimate objectives were traditional, not revolutionary. He still wanted empire, but by more subtle and realistic means. Nevertheless, the cost to Britain of maintaining a 'world role' proved severe. Macmillan's plans for a greater Malaysia federation were strongly opposed by Indonesia, which announced *Konfrontasi* (Confrontation) of the proposed state in January 1963. Only a few months later Jakarta instigated a major guerrilla war in Borneo in an attempt to wreck plans for federation. By 1965 the Wilson government was deploying over 68,000 servicemen in the Far East, together with a fleet of over eighty vessels, including two aircraft carriers.[2] Confrontation slowly developed, therefore, into Britain's gravest colonial crisis of the 1960s.

BRITAIN AND THE 'WORLD ROLE' EAST OF SUEZ

During 1957 the policies of the Macmillan government, as they related to Britain's presence east of Suez, appeared to confirm a commitment to disengagement. On 31 August Malaya, easily the most valuable colony in the region, was granted independence. In addition, Britain's ability to reinforce its position in the Far East seemed dangerously compromised by the government's own reforms on defence spending. On becoming prime minister, Macmillan was clearly determined to reduce military expenditure, which he believed had reached unacceptably high levels.[3] Further, he believed that, in any event, the services wasted enormous sums on conventional forces and weapon systems which were no longer needed in the nuclear age.[4] Acting on these perceptions, he appointed the notoriously abrasive Duncan Sandys to push major reforms past the anticipated resistance of the Chiefs of Staff. The government's White Paper, released by Sandys in April 1957, encompassed many of the ideas Macmillan had held for some time. Most importantly, conscription was to be abolished, the armed forces' manpower to be reduced from 690,000 to 375,000 by 1962.[5] In future greater reliance would be placed on the nuclear deterrent to protect British interests world-wide. These forces would also be supported by small, but highly mobile air, land and naval units which would be responsible for colonial peacekeeping. Despite the opposition of the Chiefs of Staff, who feared the government was placing too much faith in nuclear rather than conventional technology, Macmillan and Sandys succeeded in forcing their ideas upon a reluctant military establishment. In particular, real progress had been made, or so it seemed, in adjusting British defence and foreign policy to the realities of the nation's reduced status in the post-war world.

None the less, as was so often the case with Macmillan, appearances were deceptive. The main dispute with the Chiefs of Staff was over means, not ends. Macmillan believed financial savings could be made from the defence budget without necessitating an abandonment of Britain's 'world role'. Indeed, during the late 1950s, the government reduced British air and land units in Europe, but only so that some of these forces could be re-deployed to the Middle and Far Eastern theatres.[6] It was evidently clear, therefore, that Macmillan had no intention of cutting, at least for the foreseeable future, Britain's remaining world-wide commitments.[7] This was especially so in Southeast Asia. Although formal independence to

Malaya was conceded in 1957, the Macmillan government had already secured a continued pre-eminent role for Britain through the Anglo-Malayan Defence Agreement (AMDA). By virtue of this agreement, Britain remained responsible for the external defence of Malaya and, in return, received the right to maintain and use bases in that country for this purpose. By the late 1950s AMDA had become a crucial means for both Commonwealth defence co-operation in the region and British support for SEATO. In 1959 Australia and New Zealand joined AMDA as 'associates', not being directly responsible for the defence of Malaya, but prepared none the less to deploy forces in support of British objectives. All three countries contributed units towards the Commonwealth Strategic Reserve (CSR), which was permanently stationed in both Malaya and Singapore. The CSR was co-ordinated by, and received its directives from, the ANZAM defence committee, which comprised representatives of the chiefs of staff from all three countries. According to these directives, the defence of the Malayan region was only the secondary objective of the CSR; its primary function was to support SEATO in deterring communist expansion further north in Indochina and Thailand. Britain's post-colonial relationship with Malaya, epitomized by AMDA, had become a crucial hub for continued close relations with not only the Australasian powers, but also the United States. Even more important than Malaya itself, however, was the still very extensive military facilities at Singapore. Bastion of Britain's remaining far eastern empire, the city-colony was experiencing, during this period, the same aggressive nationalism that was sweeping Africa and Asia. Such a movement, as the author of 'winds of change' well knew, could ultimately blow away the entire British and Commonwealth defence structure in the region.

DECOLONIZATION: SINGAPORE AND THE OPTION OF A GREATER MALAYSIA

Due to the strength of Chinese nationalist feeling the Macmillan government felt it had little option but to compromise and concede self-government to Singapore. Accordingly, in 1958, a new constitution was promulgated. Britain would retain ultimate responsibility for both internal security and foreign affairs, but in all other matters the local government would be completely independent. These reforms, however, did not pacify strong local feelings against continued British sovereignty. In the 1959 elections, the People's Action Party (PAP), led by Lee Kuan Yew, and campaigning on a platform of full independence, won a decisive majority. Although Lee's rhetoric quickly moderated once in power, many of his party demanded immediate British withdrawal. By 1961 tension in the colony had risen appreciably. Early in that year Lee expelled known communist sympathizers from the PAP. In response, these members formed the *Barisan Sosialis*, a strongly left-wing party which demanded unconditional independence from Britain and a socialist constitution for the new state. It immediately won widespread local support, particularly from organized labour. By July Lee was in a desperate situation, only holding a majority in the general assembly by virtue of the speaker's vote.

There is little doubt that Macmillan and his colleagues were very concerned at these developments. If Lee fell from power, and was replaced by the *Barisan Sosialis*, Britain's base on the island would almost certainly be crippled by industrial chaos. In such an event, the government would eventually be confronted by two dismal alternatives: either forcefully reassert direct rule from London or negotiate a phased withdrawal. Whichever option was adopted would almost certainly damage British prestige and, in the case of direct rule, require more resources than the government was willing to provide. On the other hand, the seriousness of the communist threat presented Macmillan with an opportunity for a third and far more attractive option.

Since 1945 British policy-makers had consistently argued that the most logical form of decolonization in the region was a union of Britain's remaining territories, starting with Malaya and Singapore.[8] This vision was re-emphasized by Iain Macleod, the colonial secretary, as recently as April 1961, when he urged Cabinet to adopt a greater Malaysian federation as 'the ultimate aim of UK policy'.[9] Unfortunately for the British, however, this idea had been strongly opposed by the Malays. Such a union, they feared, would totally upset the delicate racial balance in favour of the Chinese. Nevertheless, by 1961, the Malayan prime minister, Tunku Abdul Rahman, was himself becoming increasingly disturbed with recent developments in Singapore. In short, he feared that a predominantly Chinese communist state was about to be created on Malaya's borders. He was therefore receptive to the arguments of Sir Geofroy Tory, British high commissioner in Kuala Lumpur, that federation was the only realistic alternative. Further, in order to allay Malayan fears over the racial balance, the Macmillan government hinted that a federation could include Brunei and the Borneo colonies. This would ensure that the Chinese remain a minority in the new state. Mindful of Lee's precarious hold on power, the Tunku quickly adopted these proposals as his own. On 27 May he made a public statement in which he talked of an 'understanding' at some future date regarding a federation between Malaya and Singapore, together with British Borneo and the Sultanate of Brunei.[10] Although British officials had in fact made the initial suggestion, London conceded authorship to the Malays, hoping this would enhance the credibility of greater Malaysia with both the inhabitants concerned and world opinion in general.[11]

The Tunku officially forwarded his proposals to London on 26 June. Although British policy-makers strongly supported greater Malaysia in principle, they knew a number of major obstacles had to be overcome before it could be established. Firstly, it was necessary to obtain the consent of the inhabitants concerned. Whitehall realized this would not be easy. Preliminary enquiry suggested many people in Borneo did not want federation and were perfectly content with the *status quo*.[12] Secondly, and even more worrisome, was that AMDA would have to be renegotiated. The original treaty allowed the British to use bases in Malaya for Commonwealth defence, but not SEATO-related contingencies. The Malays, like many Asians, were suspicious of this American-led alliance and did not want to be associated with it. Accordingly, they suggested a simple extension of current arrangements to include Borneo and Singapore when Malaysia was established. In his letter to Macmillan on 26 June, the Tunku made it clear that the Singapore base, in particular, 'would no longer be at the disposal of SEATO but could be maintained as a base for the defence of the Commonwealth'.[13]

Deciding upon an official response to the Tunku's proposals revealed clear divisions within Whitehall concerning Britain's long-term future in the region. At one extreme were policy-makers who argued that the armed services must retain the unfettered use of the Singapore base. Regardless of Malayan sensitivities, SEATO was considered an essential part of Britain's far eastern strategy, especially as it provided for close co-operation with other Western allies, such as the United States, Australia and New Zealand. To allow Kuala Lumpur to dictate the use of its own base would seriously undermine Britain's credibility in the region with both allies and opponents alike. Such determination to retain the *status quo*, however, was not universally accepted throughout Whitehall. Noting the government's obvious desire to cut military spending, some officials pointed to greater Malaysia as providing Britain with an excellent opportunity to lessen its excessive commitments, and hence expenditure, east of Suez. This chance arose precisely because of the link between the Singapore base and Britain's military deployment in the region. It was logical that if the base was no longer freely available for British forces, then Britain's defence commitments would have to be reduced accordingly. Put simply, the greater Malaysia project could be used to initiate a process some officials believed was long overdue: a British disengagement from the Far East. Macmillan's response to the Tunku's letter, therefore, would ultimately turn on a single important and contentious issue: whether Britain should retain a significant role for itself east of Suez. As Cecil Gough, an official at the admiralty, explained on 28 September:[14]

> It cannot be automatically assumed that we must insist on retaining defence facilities in Malaysia. Whether or not this should be our aim depends on the answer to the following questions:
> (a) Are we willing to accept a bilateral arrangement whereby we assume in future a responsibility for assisting in the external defence of Malaysia?
> (b) Are we prepared to continue our military contribution to SEATO in much the same form and to much the same extent as obtains at present?

The most persistent advocate of retrenchment was the Commissioner-General for Southeast Asia, Lord Selkirk. He justified his radical views by pointing to Britain's diminishing ability to defend its overseas interests. 'The resources at our disposal', he warned Macmillan in August, 'have become less and less adequate to meet the commitments we still retain. The result of this is that we are stretched to the point where our strength might snap under the strain and indeed our present position would be highly perilous were it not for our basic dependence on the United States.'[15] To Selkirk the arguments in favour of disengagement were overwhelming. 'It has become apparent to me', he concluded, 'that we should have to lighten the load of our commitments in this area.'[16] His pleas were not ignored by the prime minister. During September Macmillan ordered, as part of Whitehall's deliberations on greater Malaysia, a review of British policy in the region.[17] Previously, maintenance of a substantial British base at Singapore was accepted without question. Rather abruptly, this was no longer the case. 'On grounds of finance', concluded Cecil Gough during a meeting of the officials' committee, 'it is imperative and urgent to seek reductions in our commitments and establishments outside Germany and we must therefore take a new look at our position in Southeast Asia and the Far East'.[18]

These pleas for change were opposed by a powerful Whitehall triumvirate. The Chiefs of Staff, in particular, demanded that the *status quo* be retained. Without unrestricted use of the Singapore base, they feared British forces would no longer be able to contribute effectively to the West's deterrence of communism through the SEATO alliance. This in turn would seriously damage relations with key allies, such as the United States, Australia and New Zealand, all of whom relied, to varying degrees, on a British military presence at Singapore. 'The fact remains', argued Julian Amery, secretary of state for air, 'that if we want to contribute to keeping the communists out of Southeast Asia, and if we want to maintain our influence with Australia and New Zealand on the one hand and the United States on the other, we must have the effective use of Singapore. Without it our influence in the region could sink to the level of France.'[19]

The armed services' were supported in their hard line by the senior political departments. At the Commonwealth Relations Office (CRO), officials were concerned at the effect any British disengagement, no matter how slight, would have on relations with Australia and New Zealand. Proposals concerning greater Malaysia, it must be emphasized, coincided with Macmillan's dramatic announcement in the House of Commons on 31 July that Britain would seek entry into the EEC. Both developments, without question, strongly reinforced antipodean suspicions that Britain was abandoning the Commonwealth for integration in Europe. Consequently, it was not surprising that both Australasian prime ministers personally emphasized to Macmillan the importance of retaining military facilities at Singapore with as few restrictions as possible.[20] Of the two dominions New Zealand, given its greater dependency on Britain for trade and military support, was particularly anxious. As the prime minister, Keith Holyoake, pointed out to Macmillan:[21]

Until now New Zealand's defence planning has been based almost without conscious thought on the assumptions that in any future war we should again be fighting side by side with you in all arms, our soldiers transported in British ships, serving alongside British troops under British higher command, using British equipment, operating from British bases and receiving British logistic support.... But if there is in fact no reliable British forward base providing adequate facilities from which to operate in the theatre of particular concern to us a vital link is missing and our assumptions will require fundamental review.

There was little doubt that any such review would recommend a tightening of relations with the United States, resulting in weakening further traditional ties with Britain. Holyoake himself hinted as much as when he concluded: 'in the circumstances we feel that we may be faced with the need for painful decisions with sentiment pulling us one way and material considerations another'.[22] Quite naturally, the CRO was eager to arrest this trend and allay antipodean fears that Britain was turning its back on old friends. They deemed it essential, therefore, that a substantial British military presence at Singapore be retained.

Officials at the Foreign Office (FO) held similar views. They were well aware, for example, that across in Washington, policy-makers were as opposed to British disengagement as those in Australasia. 'From a military viewpoint', outlined the US consul-general in Singapore, 'it is essential that the bases continue essentially as at present if the UK is to meet its commitments in Southeast Asia.'[23] On the other hand, 'removal of these forces would create a military power vacuum which, if not filled by the US, would be filled only by hostile elements'.[24] Consequently, American policy-makers favoured continued retention of existing British forces east of Suez, even if this resulted in London achieving financial savings through cutbacks to its forces in Germany. 'Many nations could reinforce Europe', explained CIA director Allen Dulles to officials in London, 'but by the accident of history only Britain could do the job in Singapore'.[25] Given the importance of Anglo-American relations to British foreign policy in general, the FO was also, not surprisingly, determined to preserve the *status quo* in Singapore against Selkirk and other like-minded revisionists.

At Downing Street Macmillan was undoubtedly influenced by the reasoning of the Chiefs of Staff and political departments. When the prime minister finally replied to Selkirk's letter in October he urged caution. Although Macmillan accepted that 'the need to adjust our policy is clear in the light of our reduced resources ... any solution to the problems of the area can only come about gradually'.[26] He was particularly concerned about relations with Australia and New Zealand, warning that 'we must not give them any cause to blame us for leaving them precipitely in the lurch'.[27] As a result, the government decided, after much deliberation, to maintain the *status quo*. Indeed, preservation of the Singapore base was now recognized as a prerequisite to British support for the greater Malaysia project. Consequently, Macmillan advised Australian prime minister Menzies on 16 November that 'we are in complete agreement with you that our objective must be to maintain intact the rights we at present enjoy in respect of Singapore.... We shall be seeking an agreement whereby we can fully discharge our commitments under the Manila Treaty [SEATO] and we shall reserve our position for further discussion if the Tunku cannot meet us on this at the forthcoming talks.'[28]

Fortunately for Macmillan the Tunku proved accommodating. At the Anglo-Malayan talks in November the Malayan delegation accepted Britain's need to use Singapore for SEATO purposes. Macmillan did not completely disregard, however, Selkirk's pleas for a reduced British presence in the region. By establishing greater Malaysia, Macmillan intended to release Britain from its responsibility for internal security in Singapore. This was by no means a minor task, as nationalist agitation in the city-colony required the presence of many troops. With this role being assumed by the Malays after Malaysia was established, Macmillan was confident that major savings could be made. Consequently, although air and naval forces would be retained at their existing levels, land forces were to be substantially reduced. In this manner, Macmillan hoped to have the best of both worlds: retain Britain's strong influence in the region through close relations with Commonwealth allies like Malaysia, Australia and New Zealand, but at greatly reduced cost. As Charles Baldwin, American Ambassador in Kuala Lumpur, neatly put it to the state department: 'UK objective will be to continue to play dominant role in local defense picture at reduced cost.'[29]

There is little doubt that Macmillan was well aware of the need for change. Traditional empire in Southeast Asia had become, by the early 1960s, both politically obsolete and economically wasteful. But there was also no retreat. As the evidence clearly shows, Macmillan was merely changing the means by which British power east of Suez could be preserved. He certainly was not prepared to challenge the traditional presumption that Britain was, and should remain, a global power. Even the New Zealanders, who probably had more to lose than anyone from British withdrawal, accepted that Macmillan's policies were intended to enhance, rather than undermine, Britain's world position. Reported the New Zealand high commission in London in November 1962:[30]

> It seems clear that the government regards entry into Europe not as involving withdrawal from her traditional world-wide interests, but as a means of strengthening her economy and political influence in order more effectively to sustain those interests. Thus, there is no reason, in our view, to suppose that entry into Europe would mean an accelerated withdrawal by the UK from her overseas defence commitments. The growing cost of defence may, in fact, oblige the government to take measures of contraction from time to time but we do not believe it is its policy to anticipate necessity by abandoning its global commitments and concentrating its defence effort into Europe.

Accordingly, during 1962, the Conservative government commenced preparations for the transfer of sovereignty. In order to ascertain opinion in the Borneo colonies Lord Cobbold, former governor of the Bank of England, was appointed to head a commission of enquiry. Despite their obvious preference for the *status quo*, Macmillan was determined to proceed with federation. The stakes were simply too high. Malaysia was viewed by British policy-makers as an essential means of not only reducing expenditure east of Suez, but also improving Britain's position in the region as regards Asian nationalism. By contrast, the consequences of failure could be disastrous. As Macmillan himself pointed out, 'if we are successful in achieving greater Malaysia this would relieve the British government of its most invidious and burdensome responsibilities in the area. If we failed, the problem of Singapore would become most urgent: at the next elections a situation might arise in which most of the British forces in the island would be required to defend their own base.'[31] As a result, Macmillan was impatient with colonial office objections that greater Malaysia was being unfairly forced on the Borneo peoples. On one such telegram from the governor of North Borneo, Macmillan wrote:[32]

> I am rather shocked by telegram no. 104 and the attitude it reveals. Does he realise (a) our weakness in Singapore, and (b)

our urgent need to hand over the security problem there? The whole mood is based on a false assessment of our power. If this is the CO point of view we shall fail.

Given Macmillan's strong views on the matter, it was not surprising that, in July, Lord Cobbold reported that, of the options available to them – continued British sovereignty not being one – the Borneo peoples favoured federation with Malaya and Singapore. In the meantime, HMG was in the process of withdrawing major land forces from Singapore, arguing that these units were for internal security purposes only and consequently were no longer needed because of the imminent creation of Malaysia.[33] Towards the end of 1962 plans for the establishment of Malaysia appeared to be progressing smoothly. It was precisely at this time, however, that Britain's careful plans for easing the new federation quietly onto the international stage became badly unstuck.

INDONESIA, CONFRONTATION AND THE CHALLENGE TO BRITISH POWER EAST OF SUEZ

Back in 1961, when plans for a greater Malaysia were first announced, Jakarta raised no objections. British officials happily concluded, therefore, that the most likely external objector to the project had been successfully placated. Their optimism proved both premature and misplaced. Since 1957 Indonesia's President, Achmed Sukarno, was a leader deeply committed to eradicating colonialism from Southeast Asia. He was strongly encouraged in this endeavour by the *Partai Komunis Indonesia* (PKI), then the largest communist party in the world outside the Soviet Union or China. The initial object of Sukarno's anti-imperialist crusade was not Britain but the Netherlands and, in particular, its continued sovereignty over West New Guinea. Sukarno claimed the territory as rightfully Indonesia's and, during late 1961, commenced a campaign to oust the Dutch from it. Generously supplied with modern weapons from Moscow, Sukarno cleverly engaged in brinkmanship with the Dutch, hoping international pressure would eventually force them to leave. By the end of 1962 it was clear he had succeeded. A settlement was reached by which West New Guinea would be transferred to Indonesia, provided a UN investigation confirmed that that was the wish of the local inhabitants. Crucial to Sukarno's success was the attitude of the United States.[34] Fearing Dutch obstinance could lead to war and, as a consequence, Indonesia joining the communist bloc, President Kennedy personally intervened in the crisis, effectively forcing the Dutch to abandon their last remaining Asian colony.[35] None the less, with his most immediate objective realized, Sukarno was now in a position to carry his vision of a post-colonial Southeast Asia to other parts of the region.

With the Dutch successfully ousted, the only remaining colonial power of any significance was Britain. Although it was preparing for decolonization, Sukarno was largely unimpressed with Malaysia. He complained, probably with some justification, that the proposed federation was neo-colonialist, ultimately intended to preserve rather than end British influence in the region. By the end of 1962 Indonesian hostility to Malaysia was becoming increasingly clear. Matters then reached a climax when, on 8 December, an attempted coup was mounted against the Sultan of Brunei. The Indonesians complained that, with the dispatch of Ghurkha troops from Singapore, Britain was again using brute force to destroy a legitimate indigenous movement.[36] For their part, the British believed Jakarta was covertly supporting the coup, together with subversive movements in Borneo which opposed federation.[37] With Anglo-Indonesian relations deteriorating rapidly, it was not long before Indonesia's opposition to Malaysia would become official. On 20 January 1963 the foreign minister, Dr Subandrio, declared that henceforth Indonesia would pursue a policy of *Konfrontasi* (Confrontation) against Malaysia. Unable to challenge British military power directly, this amounted to actively nurturing and then supporting a guerrilla insurgency in Borneo.

In London the belief that Malaysia had to be supported, regardless of Indonesian opposition, was accepted virtually without debate. Indeed, ministerial discussions focused on how Malaysia could be established, rather than whether this objective should be reviewed given Sukarno's declaration of Confrontation. It was also noteworthy that the role of the prime minister in decision-making concerning Malaysia had diminished. Although being fundamentally involved in providing the framework for greater Malaysia during 1961, Macmillan had, by 1963, essentially delegated responsibility for British policy to Commonwealth relations secretary Duncan Sandys and foreign secretary Lord Home.

Both these ministers, together with their departments, believed Britain had little choice but to honour its security guarantee to

Malaya. Indonesian subversion, it must be emphasized, was directed at Borneo, which was still a British colony. Further, British prestige was already fully engaged regarding the Malaysia project. While still having pretensions that Britain was, and should remain, a global power, policy-makers could not afford to have their plans destroyed by a country like Indonesia. It was also perhaps noteworthy that British elites personally despised Sukarno. They regarded him as an Asian Nasser, a rogue pretender, impatient to steal the Emperor's clothes. 'We are up against a man', wrote Lord Selkirk, 'with much of the instability and lust for power of Hitler and military forces, if not so efficient, at least comparable in size for the area'.[38] Macmillan himself particularly loathed the Indonesian leader. Observing in his diary Sukarno's vain liking for extravagant military uniforms, Macmillan described him as a cross between 'Liberace and little Lord Fauntleroy'.[39] Given these perceptions, therefore, it was not surprising that the Macmillan government was determined to ensure Sukarno failed in his attempt to destroy Malaysia before it had been established.

Despite their uncompromising support for Malaysia, the British were under no illusions as to the extent of the security problem facing them. In the first instance Indonesian hostility to Malaysia effectively reversed London's plans to reduce British forces at Singapore. 'We had hoped', pointed out private secretary Philip de Zulueta to Macmillan on 3 April, 'that as Malaysia's own forces were built-up, we would reduce our own. But the Indonesian threat has made this impossible. Our commitments', he concluded, 'so far from decreasing, will therefore increase'.[40] Put simply, Sukarno was deliberately undermining Macmillan's plans to perpetuate British influence in the region through a greater Malaysia federation. If the prime minister wanted Britain to remain a far eastern power, then the asking price to be paid was going to be far higher.

British policy-makers were also well aware that, by sponsoring a guerrilla insurgency in Borneo, the Indonesians could realistically continue with Confrontation for a reasonably long period of time. This in turn would consume ever greater British military resources. Indeed, in many respects, the overall strategic outlook for Britain was very bleak. 'This is a potentially formidable commitment', argued the Lord Privy Seal, Ted Heath, 'since Malaysia is practically encircled by hostile countries – Indonesia to the west and south, the Philippines to the east and the rickety structure of Indo-China to the north'.[41] Macmillan himself was very conscious of the possible danger. On 3 April he warned Lord Home that he doubted whether, if the situation 'really got out of control, Britain could deal with it single-handed'.[42] As a result, the prime minister believed it essential for Britain to obtain strong Australasian and, in particular, American support so long as Confrontation remained. 'Sukarno would only be stopped', wrote Macmillan in his memoirs, 'if he clearly understood that the Western powers were at one in opposing his acquisition.'[43] Unfortunately for the British, however, such assistance was not as readily forthcoming as they might have expected.

Across in Washington policy-makers were wary of British requests that the United States should apply concerted pressure on Jakarta to end Confrontation. Although the Kennedy administration supported the concept of a greater Malaysia in 1961, its readiness to offer any meaningful assistance to Britain in 1963 was tempered by a number of countervailing factors. Many in the administration feared that forceful Western action against Sukarno held the unacceptably high risk of not only open conflict but also pushing Indonesia into the waiting arms of Moscow. Such an outcome would be disastrous for American policy in the region and would completely undermine Kennedy's efforts to bolster the non-communist regime in South Vietnam. 'As they see it', wrote an official from the British embassy in Washington, 'they have enough trouble on their hands already in Southeast Asia without incurring the lasting enmity of so large a country as Indonesia'.[44]

For Macmillan, the fact of American non-involvement, although disappointing, was not disastrous. What disturbed him, and his colleagues, was Washington's inclination to appease Sukarno by offering him concessions in order to have Confrontation abandoned.[45] The British believed such tactics were very unwise; Sukarno was personally committed to destroying Malaysia. Concessions to him, they argued, would only encourage, rather than deter him, from obtaining this objective. In particular, the American attitude was disturbingly close to that over West New Guinea. It was viewed as critical in London that such a parallel not be established. 'We must avoid a situation', argued Fred Warner, head of the Southeast Asia department of the FO, 'where the Indonesians conclude that the American role over Borneo will be the same as it was in the New Guinea dispute, so that they will therefore push things to a stage where British forces will be committed to a prolonged struggle with Indonesia, in which the latter would enjoy significantly more support from the communist bloc than we shall from the Americans'.[46]

With the Americans proving difficult, the British had high hopes that Australia and New Zealand, at least, would actively support them in Borneo. Both Canberra and Wellington, however, had similar concerns to Washington. Neither wanted a violent break with Jakarta if it could be avoided. Australian policy-makers, in particular, were adamant that the country could ill-afford a hostile Indonesia backed by international communism. The Australasian governments were also very reluctant to adopt a position independently of the United States, even if it were in association with Britain. 'We have seen what happened to the Dutch', wrote Holyoake to Garfield Barwick, Australia's foreign minister, 'when they could no longer count on anyone's support against Indonesia'.[47] Consequently, both Menzies and Holyoake were reluctant to publicly align their governments with Britain during the early stages of Confrontation.

Despite receiving lukewarm support from Britain's closest allies, policy-makers in London were determined to establish Malaysia on time, regardless of Sukarno's objections. Eventually there was a delay, but only by a few weeks. On 16 September 1963 the federation of Malaysia formally came into being. The Indonesian reaction was bitter. Only two days later a crowd, probably acting with the acquiescence of the state authorities, attacked the British embassy in Jakarta, burning it to the ground. Simultaneously Sukarno intensified the guerrilla war in Borneo, requiring even further reinforcements to be sent into the region from Britain. There is no doubt that British officials were seriously concerned at the sharp deterioration which had taken place. There was no end in sight to Confrontation, a campaign that Indonesia could easily sustain for many years. 'At worst', warned Lord Mountbatten, chairman of the Chiefs of Staff, 'costs might well compare with those involved in the Malayan emergency'.[48] None the less, even with Britain's military resources being dangerously extended, there was no turning back by the Macmillan government. Britain simply could not afford to let Malaysia fall without dire consequences for its position – and prestige – as a global power. By September 1963 the two had become inextricably connected. 'This [Confrontation] will be a heavy burden on British resources', argued Warner, 'but we see no choice between supporting Malaysia and withdrawing from Southeast Asia altogether'.[49] Many Conservatives, including probably Macmillan himself, shared these sentiments. As one senior official concluded many years later, 'the Tories were always committed to imperial responsibilities and the world role ... their instinct was to hang on and not give up until they were convinced it was the only possible option'.[50] During 1963, at least, the inevitability of withdrawal had not yet been accepted.

CONCLUSION

Remodeller or liquidator of empire? That was the question Macmillan posed for himself when writing in his diary on becoming prime minister in February 1957. Certainly, it can be argued, especially with the benefit of hindsight, that greater Malaysia was an essential precursor to a British disengagement east of Suez. With power devolved to friendly local elites, and a stable federation established, the British were then in a position to quietly vacate the area.[51] The documentary evidence is clear, however, that Macmillan, at least for the foreseeable future, had no such intention. Admittedly, he realized that changes were long overdue. Traditional empire, in the form of direct rule from London, was no longer tenable. Singapore was a disaster waiting to happen, Chinese nationalist fervour threatening to explode into violence. The resources needed to control the situation were unsustainable in the long-term. The idea of a greater Malaysia federation, therefore, seemed a perfect solution to these problems. Responsibility for internal security in Singapore would be assumed by the Malays, thereby substantially reducing Britain's political and financial vulnerability in the region. Nevertheless, a strong British military presence would be preserved through AMDA and the Tunku's guarantees regarding the Singapore base. Britain, Macmillan hoped, would get the best of both worlds: pre-eminent influence at less cost to the Exchequer. These plans – or hopes – proved wildly over-optimistic, however. Sukarno, like Nasser in the Middle East, had no intention of allowing an ailing imperial power retain even a measure of its former glory and influence. The result was Confrontation, which critically undermined British objectives. Instead of releasing Britain from its more onerous imperial burdens, greater Malaysia drastically intensified them. The crisis remained unresolved when Macmillan announced his intention to resign as Prime Minister on 10 October 1963. It would ultimately be left to a Labour successor, Harold Wilson, to negotiate an end to a crisis which was proving, by 1965, to be an unsustainable drain on Britain's financial and military resources.

NOTES

1. Alistair Horne, *Macmillan, 1957–1986*, vol. II (London: Macmillan, 1989), p. 15.
2. John Darwin, *Britain and Decolonisation: The Retreat from Empire in the Post-colonial World* (London: Macmillan, 1988), p. 290.
3. Wyn Rees, 'The 1957 Sandys White Paper: New Priorities in British Defence Policy', *Journal of Strategic Studies*, vol. 12 (1989), p. 226.
4. Simon J. Ball, 'Macmillan and British Defence Policy', in Richard Aldous and Sabine Lee (eds), *Harold Macmillan and Britain's World Role* (London: Macmillan, 1996), pp. 67–8.
5. Philip Darby, *British Defence Policy East of Suez* (London: Oxford University Press, 1973), p. 107.
6. Ball, *Macmillan and British Defence Policy*, pp. 74–85.
7. A number of historians have stressed this point. See, in particular, Ball, *Macmillan and British Defence Policy*, p. 92; Turner, *Macmillan* (London: Longman, 1994), p. 272; Peter Clarke, *Hope and Glory: Britain 1900–1990* (London: Allen Lane, 1996), pp. 265–7.
8. See A. J. Stockwell, 'Insurgency and Decolonisation during the Malayan Emergency', *Journal of Commonwealth and Comparative Politics*, vol. xxv, no. 1 (1987), pp. 71–81.
9. Macleod to Cabinet, 7 April 1961, memo, PRO, DO 169/25.
10. J. A. C. Mackie, *Konfrontasi: The Indonesia–Malaysia Dispute, 1963–1966* (Oxford: Oxford University Press, 1974), p. 41.
11. Singapore to State Department, 16 June 1961, telegram, RG 59, central decimal file 1960–63, Box 2099, United States National Archives (USNA).
12. Brook to Macmillan, 17 April 1961, memo, PRO, Prem 11/3418.
13. Tunku to Macmillan, 26 June 1961, letter, PRO, Prem 11/3418.
14. Gough to Mackintosh, 28 September 1961, letter, PRO, DO 169/29.
15. Selkirk to Macmillan, 14 August 1961, letter, PRO, FO 371/159702, D1015/16.
16. Selkirk to Macmillan, 30 December 1961, letter, PRO, Prem 11/3866.
17. Committee on greater Malaysia, 27 September 1961, minute of meeting, PRO, CAB 134/1949, GM(61)1.
18. Ibid.
19. Amery, 4 October 1961, note, PRO, CAB 131/26, D(61)66.
20. Menzies to British High Commissioner Canberra, 28 August 1961, letter, PRO, Prem 11/3418; Holyoake to Macmillan, 20 October 1961, telegram, PRO, Prem 11/3422.
21. Holyoake to Macmillan, 14 December 1961, PRO, Prem 11/3866.
22. Ibid.
23. Singapore to State Department, 28 September 1961, telegram, RG 59, central decimal file 1960–63, Box 2099, USNA.
24. Ibid.
25. Amery to Watkinson, 2 November 1961, letter, PRO, DO 169/29.
26. Macmillan to Selkirk, 17 October 1961, PRO, FO 371/159702, D1015/26.
27. Ibid.

28. Macmillan to Menzies, 16 November 1961, message, AA, A1209/80, 1963/6544.
29. Kuala Lumpur to State Department, 24 March 1962, telegram, RG 59, central decimal file 1960–63, Box 2199, USNA.
30. Templeton to McIntosh, 2 November 1962, letter, Ministry of Foreign Affairs and Trade (NZ) (MFAT), PM 106/7/1.
31. Greater Malaysia committee, 21 March 1962, minute of meeting, PRO, CAB 130/179, GEN 754/3.
32. Goode to Colonial Secretary, 19 June 1962, telegram, PRO, Prem 11/3867.
33. High Commission Kuala Lumpur to CRO, 29 December 1961, telegram, PRO, Prem 11/3866.
34. For an excellent commentary of JFK's policy during this crisis, see Timothy P. Maga, *John F. Kennedy and the New Pacific Community, 1961–63* (London: Macmillan, 1990).
35. James N. Giglio, *The Presidency of John F. Kennedy* (Lawrence: University Press of Kansas, 1991), pp. 238–9.
36. Mackie, *Konfrontasi*, p. 121.
37. Selkirk to Foreign Office, 8 December 1962, telegram, PRO, Prem 11/3869.
38. Selkirk to Foreign Office, 20 December 1962, telegram, PRO, Prem 11/4346.
39. Horne, *Macmillan*, vol. II, p. 321.
40. de Zulueta to Macmillan, 3 April 1963, memo, PRO, Prem 11/4189.
41. Heath to Macmillan, 23 April 1963, memo, PRO, Prem 11/4347.
42. Macmillan to Home, 3 April 1963, minute, PRO, Prem 11/4347.
43. Harold Macmillan, *At the End of the Day, 1961–63* (London: Macmillan, 1973), p. 260.
44. Forster to Cable, 11 May 1963, letter, PRO, FO 371/169700, D1071/134/G.
45. Macmillan, *At the End of the Day*, p. 261.
46. Warner, 16 May 1963, minute, PRO, FO 371/169701, D1071/147.
47. Holyoake to Barwick, 4 February 1963, cablegram, MFAT, PM 420/2/3, Pt 2A.
48. Mountbatten to Thorneycroft, 30 September 1963, letter, PRO, Defe 4/161.
49. Warner, 29 May 1963, minute, PRO, FO 371/169702, D1071/172.
50. Sir James Cable, counsellor in the FO 1961–3, head of the Southeast Asia department 1963–6, interview with author, Cambridge, 16 September 1994.
51. For an outline on this argument, see Chin Kin Wah, *The Defence of Malaysia and Singapore: The Transformation of a Security System, 1957–1971* (Cambridge: Cambridge University Press, 1983), p. 60.

13 Macmillan and the Soviet Union
Sir Curtis Keeble

The global contest of ideology and power between the Soviet Union and the Western democracies set the tone for the conduct of international relations during a large part of the twentieth century. For successive British Prime Ministers it did much to establish the context within which their foreign policy had to be constructed and implemented. Many of them alternated between policies of confrontation and co-operation as they struggled to contain the twin threats of Soviet power and Communist ideology, while maintaining a working relationship with the Soviet government. David Lloyd George is identified with the abandonment of armed intervention and the first unsuccessful attempt to draw the new Soviet state into the international community. Churchill, his imagination fired throughout much of his political career by the threat and the challenge of Russia, moved from the anti-Bolshevik tirades of the twenties and thirties to the wartime military alliance, the nuclear confrontation of the Cold War years and the final attempt to forge some new understanding after the death of Stalin. Harold Wilson, to his final, sad years, never failed to recall his early trade negotiations with Mikoyan. Margaret Thatcher, coming to office after thirty-four years of Cold War, confronted almost immediately with the Soviet invasion of Afghanistan and as harsh as Ronald Reagan in her denunciation of the 'evil empire', could claim, as British Prime Minister, to have been among the first of the Western leaders to sense that with the arrival of Mikhail Gorbachev the time had come to end the decades of sterile confrontation. Yet so sterile had the relationship been that for most of those who occupied 10 Downing Street between 1917 and 1991 there had been little room for positive moves in the field of British–Soviet relations and of those initiatives which were undertaken few were fruitful. It is against this background that Macmillan's handling of the relationship has to be judged.

Now, as the century nears its end, the sharp images of confrontation with a formidable world-wide deployment of Soviet power and communist doctrine are quickly fading. In the popular memory of Macmillan the trivial and the grave come together in a jumble of impressions: the celebrated white hat acquired in Finland and worn in Moscow, the repatriation of the White Russians, Khrushchev banging his shoe at the United Nations, the Cuban Missile Crisis and the Nuclear Test Ban Treaty. Was there an identifiable single thread running through Macmillan's dealings with the Soviet Union?

In January 1957, when he formed his first government, the Soviet Union was arguably close to the apogee of its power. It had demonstrated in Hungary its ability and will to hold by force its wartime conquests. Beyond Europe it sensed the opportunities offered by the decay of Western imperial structures and it seemed ready, by a combination of armed force and doctrinal subversion, to extend a new Soviet imperialism throughout the world. The flaws in the structure were visible, but for most Western leaders, the threat of hostile Soviet power was only too apparent. As he confronted this power, what experience could Macmillan draw on?

Harold Macmillan was remarkable among British Prime Ministers in having taken a serious personal interest in the Soviet Union at a very early stage in his career. His interest was, in some ways, typical of his generation and to the end of his life he retained many of the instincts of that generation. These were the young men who, born into the gentle life of the well-bred comfortably endowed families of pre-1918 England, had survived, scarred by years in the trenches, to experience the disillusion of the post-war depression and the apparent inability of a capitalist system to provide adequately for the British people. There were few of them for whom Communism had any real appeal, but many felt that a political system which purported to harness all the power of the state to the welfare of the people at least merited closer examination. Macmillan summed up their feelings well when he wrote in *Winds of Change*[1] 'While the capitalist world seemed, to many observers, in decay if not in mortal agony, the Bolsheviks had apparently consolidated their power and stability. In the early years of my political life, Bolshevism was regarded in Britain with feelings ranging between contempt and fear. But by 1932 many British people were beginning to wonder whether, after all, the regime which had imposed itself over a vast part of the world's territory might not be worth careful and, if possible objective, study.'

At the end of 1929 the first Ambassadors had taken up residence in London and Moscow. On the first of January 1930 the

Daily Worker had been founded. And in September 1932, after a brief flirtation with Oswald Mosley's proto-fascist New Party, the young Macmillan, re-elected in the Conservative landslide of 1931, set sail on a Soviet ship at the start of a five-week exploration of the Soviet Union. He was accompanied by Allan Young, an ex-Marxist from the Clyde. In his memoirs he drew on letters written to his mother to describe the 'looking-glass world' which he found, a world 'where everything was the opposite of what one would expect'. Arriving in Leningrad, he spent some days in Moscow before travelling to Nizhni Novgorod and taking a river steamer for a 1,200 mile journey down the Volga to Stalingrad, visiting Rostov and Kharkov, returning to Moscow for further meetings with Soviet government ministers and officials and spending a final few days in Leningrad.

In a state of some mental turmoil, having just recovered from the nervous strains precipitated by Dorothy's relationship with Bob Boothby, and with his own political orientation still uncertain, he must have been in an impressionable frame of mind. There is no sign, however, that his remarkably thorough exploration of the Soviet Union led him to any definitive conclusions. He came with a questioning mind, hoping, as he said, to be able to read and study more intelligently in future what might be the developments in that bewildering scene. He left with few questions answered, but with impressions which he can scarcely have failed to recall in his later dealings with the Soviet leadership. His letters might have been written by almost any conscientious, independent-minded British visitor during the seventy years of Soviet power. As he made the standard circuit of housing developments, clinics, factories and collective farms, he commented on the sheer size of the projects, but expressed some scepticism about the gap between plan and reality. At an official function in Leningrad he had an opportunity to observe Stalin and remarked that so Bonapartist was the regime becoming that all evening the one subject of discussion was the identity and prospects of a young man sitting beside Stalin 'who had been thus singled out by the quasi-royal favour'. He records discussions about the prospects for British trade and investment, but only at one point is there a suggestion that there ought to be room for substantial improvement. Noting the shoddiness and the waste and suspecting the brutalities and tyrannies of a police state, he returned to Britain, 'stepping back from a kind of nightmare world into the world of reality', with no feeling of affection or admiration for the Soviet system, but with a deep impression of the good nature and kindness of the ordinary people.

His subsequent publications, *The State and Industry*, *The Next Step*, *Reconstruction: A Plea for a National Policy*, *Planning for Employment*, *The Next Five Years* and finally *The Middle Way*, show a concern that the state should involve itself actively in economic planning, but this owed much to his study of Keynes and little or nothing to his experience of the planned Soviet economy. There were, as he admitted in *Reconstruction*, points of similarity between his proposals and those of the Russian Communist or Italian Corporate state, but their political basis was wholly different. As he explained in *The Middle Way*, he sought a policy which would avoid both 'the intolerable restriction of a totalitarian state and the unfettered abuse of freedom under the old liberalism'.

As the European crisis deepened, Macmillan, preoccupied at first with Britain's own economic problems, showed a growing concern for the need to establish a firm front against the dictators. One might have expected him in this context to have taken a special interest in the position of Russia. Writing about it subsequently, his view was clear. In relation to Eden's visit to Moscow in the spring of 1935 he commented: 'Had something been done at that time to come to terms with Russia it is possible that an alliance could have been built which would have prevented the Second War.' But this was with the advantage of hindsight. At the time, he probably shared the view that Russia was 'at once too weak and too dangerous'. When, on the eve of war, the British Government made its half-hearted attempt to establish a tripartite pact with France and Russia, Macmillan does not seem to have joined publicly with Churchill and Eden who, in Parliament, were urging that the government should show a greater sense of urgency and purpose in the negotiations. In his subsequent treatment of the episode in his memoirs, arguing the case for a tripartite pact, he showed considerable sympathy with the Russian position: 'If Britain had grounds for suspicion of Russia, the reverse was also true. The hostility of the Western powers after the First War; the intervention in the Russian Civil War; the loss of territory imposed on Russia: none of these were forgotten.'[2] This understanding of the Russian obsession with security was a theme to which he was to revert at various stages.

Such sympathy as Macmillan had for the policy of Stalin's Russia in confronting the German threat must have been swiftly dissipated by the Nazi–Soviet pact of August 1939, the occupation of the Baltic States and eastern Poland and then, in the winter of 1939–40, the Russian attack on Finland. Among the British public, sympathy and admiration for the gallant fight put up by the Finns was matched by disgust at the callousness of the Russian attack and contempt for the incompetence with which it was pursued. Macmillan accepted with alacrity an invitation to lead an official mission to organize aid to Finland and to recruit an international volunteer force. Had he received more swift and determined support from Chamberlain's government, the result might have been to embroil Britain in war with the Soviet Union. Had he, on the other hand, been constrained by the responsibility of a ministerial appointment requiring a colder assessment of the longer-term British strategic interest, he could scarcely have responded so enthusiastically to the popular mood. As it was, the episode tells us more about the emotional half of his character, never wholly suppressed by the subsequent cares of office, than it does about his gradually evolving assessment of Soviet Russia.

In one respect, Macmillan's experience in Finland can scarcely have been absent from his mind when he was confronted, in May 1945, with the problem of the forced repatriation of Cossack troops and White Russians from Austria. He had in Finland been shown the bodies of a large group of Russian troops allegedly shot in the head or neck by their own commissars and he clearly had no doubt as to the probable fate of the Cossacks. His diary entry for 13 May reads: 'To hand them over to the Russians is condemning them to slavery, torture and probably death.' Macmillan's view, expressed in a brief conversation with General Keightley, the Allied commander responsible, was that they should, nevertheless, be handed back. The return of members of the Soviet forces who had been captured by the Germans had been agreed at Yalta. It formed part of a reciprocal arrangement under which British and other Allied prisoners of war in areas occupied by the Soviet army were also to be returned. In the confusion of the time, those handed back included not only the Soviet troops whose repatriation had been agreed, but also White Russians who could not properly be regarded as Soviet citizens, together in some cases with civilian family members. The incident has given rise to wild allegations about Macmillan's role and has been subjected to detailed investigation as well as legal proceedings. It does not, however, seem to have been a matter on which he believed that he was deciding policy or indeed to which he gave detailed consideration. For those who wish to pursue it, there is a very full and fair treatment in Alistair Horne's biography.[3]

It is in the early post-war years that we find the first major Parliamentary interventions by Macmillan on the question of relations with Russia. They are very much in character. By the beginning of 1946, less than a year after the victorious conclusion of the war against Germany, the alliance with the Soviet Union had disintegrated. Bevin had suggested a possible extension of the Anglo-Soviet Treaty to fifty years, but had, at the same time, warned Stalin that 'there was a limit beyond which we could not tolerate continued Soviet infiltration and undermining of our position'.[4] The deterioration in British–Soviet relations gathered pace and on 20 February 1946 Macmillan, opening a Foreign Affairs debate in Parliament, devoted some time to an analysis of the relationship. His theme was that, with the tripartite alliance virtually, if not formally, in abeyance, the time had come for personal and direct negotiation at the level of Heads of Government. What, he asked, did the Russians want? Were they returning to the expansionist policy of the Tsars? Was there to be a new imperialism or a return to the proselytizing fervour of international communism? Were military theorists back in control? Or: 'May it not be that the apparent Chauvinism of Soviet policy is a form of insurance, not of expansion, that security not imperialism is their instinctive goal and for this a new cordon sanitaire is being created . . . a kind of defensive glacis of small nations looking to the Kremlin for political and economic theory and to the local Russian commander for material support.' The purpose of Soviet policy might, he suggested, be 'not to dominate the world either as Russian imperialists or as militant international Communists, but to secure the soil of Russia herself against new outrages'.[5] At a time when public opnion was beginning to harden against Soviet policy, he was clearly disposed to look for a charitable explanation if one existed.

Macmillan's attitude at that time can be judged against the background of Winston Churchill's Iron Curtain speech, delivered at Fulton a fortnight later. Churchill, like Macmillan, recognized Russia's need for security and the need, too, for some understanding between Russia and the West. But where Macmillan posed questions, Churchill was more inclined to suggest answers and to speak of the Soviet Union as seeking not war, but 'the fruits of war and the indefinite expansion of their power and doctrine'. Where Macmillan called for tripartite discussion, Churchill called for Western unity and strength as the prerequisite for an understanding with Russia.[6]

It was not long before the deterioration in relations with the Soviet Union, coming to the brink of armed hostilities over the Berlin blockade, removed any hesitation Macmillan might have had as to the true nature of Soviet policy and the appropriate Western response. In March 1949 he spoke of Kremlin policy 'uniting in a single aggressive movement both the expansionist tradition of Russian imperialism and the subversive aims of international Communism' and, remarking sadly that 'we could not believe that the genuine friendship which we had honestly held out to our Russian allies could be so scornfully rejected', he called for the Cold War to be fought with as much energy and single-mindedness as the shooting war. Later that year, fearing another Rapallo, he was calling for closer European co-operation in the face of the 'persistent malignancy of Soviet policy', denouncing 'the peace of Communism, the peace of death, the peace of anti-Christ' and calling for the strengthening of Europe. He may have had his own half-apologia in mind when he said: 'What four years ago was a pardonable and even praiseworthy spirit of good will would now be criminal weakness.'[7] The confrontation had been joined and so it would remain until the death of Stalin and the accession of Khrushchev suggested to Western leaders that the time might be coming for a new attempt to establish a dialogue with the Soviet Union.

The early fifties saw a remarkably swift evolution of British policy, but it was some time before Macmillan was directly involved. In October 1951, when the Conservative government returned to power under Winston Churchill, the Korean War had brought the East–West relationship to a point of extreme tension, but by 1953, with the death of Stalin, it seemed that the time might be ripe for a new effort to improve relations. Macmillan at that time was busy restoring the Tory Party's standing in the country by building 100,000 homes a year. He had little time for the Soviet Union and does not seem to have been involved in Winston Churchill's controversial and abortive attempt in 1954 to establish an early dialogue with the new Soviet leadership. His brief period of office as Foreign Secretary under Eden in 1955 did, however, provide an early opportunity for him to establish his own direct contact, first at the ceremonial signing of the Austrian Peace Treaty and then at the abortive Geneva conferences on German reunification where, for the first time, he encountered Khrushchev, 'this fat, vulgar man, with his pig eyes and ceaseless flow of talk'.[8] At this stage the Soviet Union was an obstacle to German reunification, a looming menace to Western Europe and a growing threat to British interests in the Middle East, where Macmillan saw the threat that Pan-Arabism might become dominated by Communism and enable the Russians to 'turn the right flank of Europe'. The direct British–Soviet relationship did not take a high place in his immediate preoccupations at that time, but it was at Geneva that Eden invited Bulganin and Khrushchev to visit London. It was from this visit, carried out in the spring of 1956, that one can trace the route which was to lead through the dreary wasteland of the correspondence with the Soviet leaders to Macmillan's own visit to Moscow, the resolution of the Berlin crisis of 1958 and, eventually, the conclusion of the Test Ban Treaty.

The visit by Marshal Bulganin as Chairman of the Soviet Council of Ministers and Nikita Khrushchev as leader of the Communist Party was the first occasion since the Revolution on which the top leadership of the Soviet Union had visited a Western country. Macmillan had moved from the Foreign Office to the Treasury at the end of 1955 and had little direct involvement with the visit other than attendance at formal functions. As Chancellor of the Exchequer his main foreign policy concern at that time was with the development of the process of European integration, leading up to the Treaty of Rome and the attempt to reconcile Britain's Commonwealth and European interests. The Khrushchev visit does not seem to have made any marked impression on him – apart from the fact that, combined with Grace Kelly's marriage to Prince Rainier, it rather distracted public attention from his first budget. He commented that Eden thought it might be possible to do some business with the new Soviet leaders – not about Europe or Germany but over the Middle East – but there is no indication that Macmillan himself shared this view. The most that can be said is that the experience of encountering this strange pair at first hand may have whetted that curiosity which had inspired his first visit to the Soviet Union and have made him the more inclined, on becoming Prime Minister, to follow up the direct personal contact.

Then came Suez. It brought Macmillan to Number 10 with a shell-shocked government, a divided country and a deeply splintered relationship with the United States. He saw himself as faced with six major tasks: to restore confidence; to deal with the aftermath of Suez; to re-establish the relationship with the United States; to walk the economic tightrope; to re-appraise defence policy; and to manage the Commonwealth relationship. As such, the Soviet Union did not figure in this list. It was, however, to become a major element in the restoration of the British–American relationship. From that restored relationship flowed important consequences for defence, especially in terms of nuclear weaponry, and for foreign policy, not least in the hardening of French opposition to British membership of the European Economic Community.

In his memoirs Macmillan quotes with approval a letter, the existence of which he only discovered much later, sent by Winston Churchill to President Eisenhower in the aftermath of Suez. The whole theme of Churchill's letter was that if misunderstanding and frustration over Suez harmed the Anglo-American alliance, the Soviet Union would move into the dangerous vacuum in the Middle East, the North African coastline would come under Soviet control and Western Europe would be 'at the mercy of the Russians'. This was very much the argument which, with considerable success, Macmillan himself was to deploy in the course of 1957. It also matched, on the obverse, the Soviet analysis of the situation. The official history of Soviet foreign policy, published in 1980, noted with satisfaction: 'The years from 1957 to 1971 were characterized by further advances in the development of the world revolutionary process.'[9]

Macmillan's first opportunity came almost immediately, in the form of Eisenhower's initiative for a meeting in Bermuda in March. In his opening speech Macmillan said that they were meeting at a time which was critical in the secular struggle against communism. There could not, he argued, be neutrality in a war between two principles, one of which, communism, was evil. The immediate outcome of Bermuda was agreement on the stationing of American nuclear missiles in Britain and on the continuing of the nuclear testing which was necessary for Britain to develop its own capability in this field.

The Bermuda Conference was followed by a visit to Washington in October. It was during the period between the two meetings that Macmillan became increasingly involved in the problem of relations with the Soviet Union. At the time of the Bulganin/Khrushchev visit to Britain in 1956 there had a been a plan for a return visit by Eden in May 1957. This was on the table when Macmillan replaced Eden at the beginning of the year. By then the Soviet action in Hungary and their intervention over Suez had produced so hostile a reaction in Britain that one of Macmillan's first acts was to propose a delay until 'a situation may develop when a visit would be both welcome to you and timely from the world point of view'.[10] Bulganin's reply was noteworthy both for its speed and for its relatively positive content, looking forward to a meeting, stressing that the May invitation was still open, but agreeing to consider an alternative timing. The Bermuda agreements on nuclear defence policy must have rung some alarm bells in Moscow. Bulganin followed up his first letter with a vast ten thousand word document concentrating on disarmament issues, warning against the dangers of stationing American rockets in Britain and calling for an immediate suspension of nuclear testing. Between the Bermuda and the Washington meetings, the correspondence between Bulganin and Macmillan continued. In the course of it, Macmillan was careful to involve both his American and European partners. It was a difficult exercise, because this was a time when public opinion was becoming increasingly concerned about the dangers of a nuclear defence policy. The Russians were skilfully playing upon these fears, while insisting upon separating nuclear from conventional defence and maintaining their overwhelming superiority of conventional forces available for deployment in the European theatre. As the exchange progressed, Macmillan found it increasingly tedious. The letters were, he said 'interchanged with courtesy, but on a healthy basis of mutual distrust' and there was in Bulganin's lengthy epistles 'little that I did not already know or disbelieve'. Foreseeing that 'neither the interchange of a long and argumentative correspondence, nor the almost interminable detailed discussions of the subcommittee in Geneva would prove the real road to progress', he began to think of some 'bold initiative'.

It was against the background of this correspondence, of Britain's own nuclear weapons test programme and of the launch of the first Russian *Sputnik* that Macmillan went to Washington in October 1957, still within his first year as Prime Minister. Looking back at the 1957 records, it is clear that the *Sputnik*, seeming to symbolize the scientific and technical capability of the Soviet Union and its potential for sophisticated military developments, had a quite remarkable effect on thinking in both London and Washington. On 10 October Macmillan sent Eisenhower a long message, pleading for a re-examination of the ability of the two governments to meet the Russian challenge on every front, military, political, economic and ideological and seeking a co-ordinated effort. The President's response was encouraging: 'I believe that all countries that fear themselves threatened by communism or any other form of dictatorship look primarily to your country and to ours for the leadership they need. . . . It is necessary not only that the highest officials of our two countries are close together in these matters, but that this understanding and agreement should, to the greatest possible measure, extend to our two countries.' The message was followed quickly by the invitation to visit Washington. Informing his Cabinet colleagues of the President's invitation, Macmillan described this as a visit to consider how the collective strength of the free world might be mobilized. The United States government 'appeared to be convinced that, in order to counter the Soviet threat, of which the earth satellite was the most recent and the most spectacular warning, the whole structure of Western collaboration needed to be re-examined'.[11] The result of the visit was a formal British–American Declaration of Common Purpose which provided for joint measures of security against 'the threat of international Communism' and the 'danger of Communist despotism'. This was, in effect, a restoration of the close co-operation which had been established during the war and which, but for Macmillan, might have come to an abrupt end with Suez. It was a co-operation which operated in many areas, but, for Macmillan, the great prize was the promise of repeal of the McMahon Act and the consequent renewal of co-operation on nuclear defence. 'For the next decade', Macmillan wrote, 'Britain's problems in this immensely expensive and complicated area of scientific development of weapons were resolved.'

There is no doubt that Macmillan himself had been concerned about the threat of Soviet subversion, especially in the Middle East, and the invasion of Hungary in 1956 had demonstrated the readiness of the Soviet government to use military force in order to maintain its grip on the Eastern European satellites. A British nuclear defence capability was necessary as a counter to the pressure of the Soviet forces arrayed against Western Europe and there was, indeed, a broad identity of view between the British and American governments. On the other hand, as we have seen, the need to counter the Soviet threat had not figured in Macmillan's own list of his priority tasks on taking office and he had dismissed rather cursorily Bulganin's threat of a rocket attack on Britain at the time of Suez – 'We never took them too seriously.'[12] Certainly the correspondence with Bulganin made him focus on the relationship with the Soviet Union, but it is hard to escape the conclusion that, in restoring the British–American relationship and, in particular, securing the repeal of the McMahon Act and the promise of American co-operation in Britain's nuclear defence programme, Macmillan was shrewdly exploiting the sudden surge of concern in the United States about the Soviet threat. It would be wrong to say that he did not share that concern. Sharing it, he could the better exploit it.

With the American relationship restored, Macmillan could turn his mind back to the wider issues of peace and war, the 'fatigue and worry of the long-drawn-out struggle against Russia', and the need to work through negotiation for some easing of the tension. He had sensed – not that at the time of the Aldermaston marches it needed much acuteness of perception to do so – that the Russian peace campaign was playing upon very real public concern about the implications of a nuclear defence policy and he was ready to take an initiative with the Soviet leadership. Having spent the Christmas of 1957 brooding over the problem of how to handle the Russians and at the same time rally support among the Western countries and in the Third World, he sent a long thoughtful and very personal telegram to Eisenhower on New Year's Day. In it he deliberately raised questions rather than proposing a firm course of action, but he made clear the need to maintain the nuclear deterrent so long as the Soviet Union had its massive superiority in conventional weapons. This brought him to the argument against the McMahon Act.[13] At home he followed up with a Party Political Broadcast on 4 January in which he harked back to the courage and fortitude of the Russians during the war and the hope that, despite the profound differences, peaceful coexistence might have meant live and let live. Hopes had been dashed. But he was still ready, using any means, to try 'to clear away the rubble of old controversies and disagreements and then perhaps to get the path ready for a meeting of Heads of Government'. A reference to 'starting by a solemn pact of non-aggression' with Russia brought anxious queries from Eisenhower and Dulles and a typically nervous Foreign Office reformulation.

Macmillan's personal engagement with the problem of dealing with Russia had now strengthened to the point at which it was a leading foreign policy preoccupation. For a time, the correspondence with Bulganin and the consultation between London and Washington continued. Eisenhower accepted in principle a Bulganin proposal for a Summit Conference, but insisted that it would not be useful unless Foreign Ministers had first made some progress. Immediately after the broadcast Macmillan had the idea that he should write to Bulganin, offering to come to Moscow to discuss the agenda and procedure for further discussions. On a Commonwealth tour, he telegraphed Selwyn Lloyd: 'Somebody will try to break the log-jam one day. Why shouldn't we get the credit? If, as is very probable it all ends in failure to agree, we shall at least have gone through the necessary moral and intellectual exercises to strengthen our resistance.' With Butler chairing the Cabinet and Selwyn Lloyd arguing the Foreign Office case that a visit would be likely to 'provoke anxiety and suspicion among the Allies', it is not hard to reconstruct the discussion which was summed up in a minute that 'the Cabinet endorsed the view that it was inadvisable for the Prime Minister to propose a personal visit'.[14]

Telegrams went to and fro and when Macmillan returned to London he took the matter up again in Cabinet, referring to the public desire for progress in disarmament and trying to secure a less negative and uncompromising line than that advocated by the Americans. Eventually he sent a letter endorsing Eisenhower's view that any meeting of Heads of Government should be preceded either by a meeting of Foreign Ministers or by confidential diplomatic exchanges. But he was still concerned that Bulganin might get the better of these public exchanges. His wish, as he made clear in correspondence with Eisenhower, was that 'we should come forward as soon as possible with a constructive proposal that will put the burden firmly back on the Russians and be understood to do so'.[15] Taunted in Parliament about the government's slowness in securing a summit meeting, he could only take the line that he wanted a summit, but he wanted it to be successful.[16]

He had, however, to wait while the correspondence which had been initiated with Bulganin was continued with Khrushchev. As Britain, the United States and the Soviet Union pursued the different objectives reflecting the different stage each had reached in the development of nuclear weaponry and as the Western European countries strove to meet their own varied national interests and the pressures of their own public opnion, it was a frustrating exercise. This is not the place to analyse the sequence of Macmillan's moves in this multi-dimensional chess game, as he sought to complete the British nuclear test programme, while waiting for the US Congress to repeal the McMahon Act and meeting the specious Soviet declaration of a unilateral end to nuclear testing. The correspondence was still taking its frustrating course when, on 10 November 1958, Khrushchev injected a sudden new note of danger by a public announcement, followed by a formal note to the British, French and US governments, to the effect that the Soviet Union proposed within six months to end the Berlin occupation regime and to negotiate to establish a new status for West Berlin as a demilitarized free city. Since 1945 and above all since the 1948 Russian blockade, Berlin had been potentially the most dangerous point on the European fault line, a point at which a Soviet threat to the Western military guarantee of Berlin's independence from the East German regime could, if mishandled, trigger direct conflict between Soviet and Allied forces. Macmillan had already reminded Dulles of the celebrated minute by Palmerston on Russian policy – always to push forward its encroachments as fast and as far as the apathy and want of firmness of other governments would allow it to go, but always to stop and retire when it was met with decided resistance. Firmness was clearly necessary, but, as Macmillan wrote in his diary on 5 January 1959: 'Are we really prepared to face war over Berlin?' So it was that Macmillan decided, as Bevin had done a decade earlier, to take a lead, revive the outstanding invitation to visit Moscow and then proceed by way of Bonn and Paris to Washington.

The visit was planned and announced as an exploration, a voyage of discovery, not a negotiation, but even so considerable political capital was invested in it. Throughout the post-war years of confrontation with the Soviet Union, no British Prime Minister or American President had visited Moscow. The Soviet Union, under Khrushchev, had apparently thrown off some of the domestic barbarity of Stalin, but externally its combination of massive power with capricious policy gave no reason for confidence. Bonn, Paris and Washington accepted Macmillan's proposal with reactions ranging from serious concern to mild scepticism. The risk that it might be exploited for wedge-driving was obvious. The Berlin stakes were high. An airlift no longer offered a solution and the military option was unrealistic. To abandon West Berlin was unthinkable. To threaten was to risk a bluff being called. Yet why, unthreatened, should Khrushchev withdraw his ultimatum? As Macmillan wrote to Caccia, the British Ambassador in Washington: 'The whole art of dealing with an opponent who is indulging in brinkmanship consists of not allowing him to get into a position in which he has to choose between war and humiliating retreat.' At the least Macmillan wanted to leave no doubt in the public mind that every effort had been made to reach understanding and agreement and to ensure that

Western policy was based on as good an insight as possible into the basis of Khrushchev's policies. Beyond that he needed, without threatening, to make Khrushchev realize the gravity of the situation and, if there were any chance, to induce some move towards compromise. In this, against many expectations, he succeeded. What is more, by his success, he not only averted a possible disastrous clash over Berlin, but may have made just a fraction of difference to the very fine balance of forces which eventually tilted the Soviet Union away from a greater disaster over Cuba a few years later.

This was the high point of Macmillan's involvement with the Soviet Union and it is appropriate to consider the precise nature of his contribution. It was in essence that he recognized the need for direct contact with Khrushchev, that he had the force of character to establish it and that, having done so, he was able to inspire a degree if not of trust at least perhaps of respect. His action was, in some ways, akin to that of someone who is confronted with an armed man, isolated and holding a hostage at gun-point. Khrushchev had the arms. He had shown that he was prepared to brandish them and, in Hungary, to use them. Berlin was the hostage. The key to such a situation lies in the psychology of the hostage-taker. The essential is to talk. The Soviet leadership, brought up on Marxist–Leninist dogma, had held power by virtue of that dogma and, in power, had been fed with the same cliches which they had fed to others. They were isolated from any real understanding of the West. As leader of the Communist Party of the Soviet Union, Khrushchev had inherited massive power. By nature he had both the crudity and the shrewdness of the Russian – or, in his case, Ukrainian – peasant, capable of rational judgement in relation to his own field of personal experience and of wild irrationality in relation to anything outside it. Macmillan was swifter than other Western leaders of his time to recognize that with such a man there is a need for direct personal contact. In character and background he was as far removed as possible from Khrushchev, above all in terms of political and personal sophistication. Yet there was in Macmillan's character enough of the romantic to bring some glimmer of response from even so earthy and yet at the same time impulsive and emotional a man as Khrushchev. The enquiring spirit which had led the young Macmillan to pay his first visit to the Soviet Union was still unquenched by the cares of Downing Street. As he wrote in his memoirs: 'The visit would certainly be a great adventure; it might also be great fun.'[17]

An adventure this might be. Fun it might be. But there was a difficult political hand to be played. It called for cold, hard judgement and shrewdly calculated tactics. No statesman welcomes the prospect of returning empty-handed from a much publicized personal encounter and the Kremlin machine knew well how to play on the temptation for a foreign visitor to seek some superficial agreement at the price of ambiguity. Macmillan was careful not to arouse excessive expectations. In Moscow he was neither to be seduced by the flattery of a generous reception nor deterred by the abrupt change of tone from blandishment to bluster.

There was nothing remarkable in what he had to say to Khrushchev on Berlin. There was little which could not have been said through diplomatic channels and little, if any, room for actual negotiation. In any case, Macmillan did not have a mandate to negotiate for the Western allies. What his visit brought to Moscow was the fact of his presence and the force of his personality. After every courtesy had been shown to the visitor and all the conventional, well-worn arguments over Berlin had been exchanged, Khrushchev launched into progressively more intemperate attacks on British policy, including a reference to the unsuccessful talks with British and French delegations in 1939. Nothing, he said, had been done and war had broken out. If that should happen again Britain would bear the responsibility. Macmillan remained calm but firm. Khrushchev, pleading toothache, ostentatiously withdrew from a planned joint visit to Kiev. Macmillan, outwardly unflustered, continued with the visit and found that by the time of his return to Moscow Khrushchev had recovered his good humour. The final communique was an unremarkable document, recording that the use of nuclear energy for solely peaceful purposes and the conclusion of an interim agreement on ending nuclear tests were objectives which the parties had in common. On Berlin, disagreement on juridical and political aspects was recorded. But, silently, the ultimatum had gone. Instead, by agreement to the holding of a meeting of Foreign Ministers, a dialogue had been substituted. Unproductive though the dialogue was, it meant that the American, British and French rights in Berlin could be sustained until, three decades later, Germany was reunified. The visit also brought bilateral agreements on trade and on cultural relations. These, between them, helped to thicken the network of non-governmental contacts which over the years would gradually open the closed Soviet society to the Western world.

In his memoirs, Macmillan devotes a hundred pages to the Moscow visit. Gromyko gives it eighteen lines: 'Macmillan's term as Prime Minister was characteristic of the Cold War.... The atmosphere was none the less businesslike: nobody banged the table and a calm tone was maintained; but nothing was achieved. In all the results of that visit amounted to the fact that a senior guest had actually come and a meeting had actually taken place. That was all.' The contrasting treatment speaks for itself. In formal terms Gromyko, the supreme functionary, may have been right. The essentials of Soviet foreign policy were unchanged. The mood was still one of supreme confidence. In real terms, however, Khrushchev had perhaps learned more than he showed. At that time, confident, impulsive and uncomprehending of the West, he had the personal power to determine peace or war. Macmillan had thrown all he had into the visit. In the face of many difficulties and on occasion of great provocation he had handled the discussions with patience, firmness and skill. The years that followed demonstrated only too clearly how far the maturing of Khrushchev had yet to go, but at a critical point, Macmillan had helped him to pause and consider.

The Moscow visit had convinced Macmillan that there was no point in conducting a quibbling correspondence by means of replies to Soviet notes: 'I am quite convinced that we can have no effective negotiation with anyone but Khrushchev', he wrote in his diary.[18] The logic of this was that there should be a Summit Meeting. It seemed that the route to it had been opened up by the Moscow discussions and Macmillan must have felt that, as a result of the visit, he was uniquely well placed to bring it about. It was not long, however, before it was demonstrated to him with brutal effect that, skilfully though he had deployed a weak hand, the British role was at best only that of an intermediary in a tussle for supremacy between two superpowers. So long as the United States held itself aloof from direct contact with the Soviet leadership, Macmillan could take centre stage, enjoy the role and execute it with panache. The years which followed were to demonstrate the realities of power in the global contest.

When Khrushchev resumed his correspondence during the follow up to the Moscow visit, Macmillan recognized the Soviet tactic of driving a wedge between Britain and the United States. He was cautious in his handling of Khrushchev's proposal for a formal nonaggression treaty between Britain and the Soviet Union. He was at pains both to inform Eisenhower personally of his exchanges and also to do all he could to convince Khrushchev, from his long and intimate personal relationship with the President, that there was no risk whatever of the United States willingly embarking on a policy which would plunge the world into a nuclear war. It therefore came as a most unwelcome shock, causing him 'great annoyance – alarm – and even anger', when, in the summer of 1959, without any prior consultation, Eisenhower issued an invitation to Khrushchev to visit the United States that autumn, linking the visit to a possible Summit in Quebec. Macmillan recognized this for the turning point which it was. In his diary, listing the likely consequences of 'this foolish and incredibly naïve piece of amateur diplomacy', he wrote: 'Everyone will assume that the two Great Powers – Russia and U.S.A. are going to fix up a deal over our heads and behind our backs. . . . People will ask, "Why should U.K. try to stay in the big game? Why should she be a nuclear power?" . . . You and we have been made fools of . . . U.K. had better give up the struggle and accept, as gracefully as possible, the position of a second-rate power.'[19] However, within a very short time, mollified by Eisenhower and much gratified by public recognition that it was Macmillan's own action which had broken the ice, he recovered his composure, accepted the potential advantage of a Khrushchev visit to the United States and sent the President a character sketch of Khrushchev, pointing out that, while his intellectual formation had been entirely communist, he was open to influence; that, in a changing world the Soviet Union would have to change; and that Khrushchev's policies would need at least to appear to be more responsible, consistent and law-abiding. He was looking further ahead than he knew. But in the short term his renewed optimism seemed justified. In a more hopeful atmosphere, negotiations for a Nuclear Test Ban Treaty moved ahead and preparations were made for a quadripartite Summit in Paris in May 1960. Again, however, Macmillan was cautious not to arouse excessive expectations. A summit could not be expected to solve all the outstanding problems at a stroke. There had to be 'continued negotiations through a long and extended period involving a series of meetings'.[20]

The collapse of the Paris Summit, resulting from American incompetence in the handling of the U2 intelligence flight, the shooting down of the aircraft and Khrushchev's emotional and intemperate reaction, demonstrated only too clearly that, for all Macmillan's attempts to prevent the collapse, his earlier pessimism over Britain's role was justified. Eisenhower sent him a gracious little message of appreciation: 'No one could have tried harder . . . to bring about a degree of civilized behaviour in the arrogant and intransigent man from Moscow.' But no such message could hide the fact that his efforts had been in vain. It is interesting that, looking back many years later, Macmillan was inclined, as he had been in 1939 and 1946, to look for a charitable explanation for Russian behaviour. Had Khrushchev, perhaps, risked too much in his attempt to achieve co-existence and even co-operation with the West? Had the inept American handling of the U2 affair given genuine offence? Had he reacted partly under pressure and partly under a real sense of indignation? In Parliament, Macmillan's tone was one of gloomy perseverance. This was not the time to retire from the struggle, but rather to 'labour on patiently and with faith'.[21]

Whatever the explanation, the result seemed to be that Khrushchev was the more determined to brandish Soviet power and, in the response to it, Macmillan was no longer playing a leading role. Khrushchev continued to address to him and to other Heads of Government letters which Macmillan found 'long, argumentative, false and curiously boring', but this was little more than a routine propaganda exercise. They clashed at the United Nations, where a shoe banging interruption of Macmillan's speech did little for Khrushchev's international – and probably also domestic – standing. More alarming than his intemperate language was Khrushchev's action in bringing the Berlin crisis back to the boil by announcing a decision to conclude a separate peace treaty with East Germany and building the Berlin wall. Gloomy about the failure of the West to mount an effective response to the menace of Soviet power, Macmillan had already formulated his 'Grand Design' to develop a greater unity of purpose between Europe and the United States. In his diary[22] he wrote: 'We may drift to disaster over Berlin – a terrible diplomatic defeat or (out of sheer incompetence) a nuclear war.'

Throughout the later months of 1961 and the first half of 1962, the Berlin crisis waxed and waned, the exchange of diplomatic notes and correspondence with Khrushchev continued and the whole complex trial of strength between the Soviet Union and the Western powers took up much of Macmillan's time. Increasingly, however, he was turning his attention to the Western European dimension of policy. It was concern with the menace of Soviet power that led him, in his search for a unity of purpose, to see British membership of the EEC as part of the Grand Design. The application for membership made in August 1961 would probably have come at some point without the Russian spur. It might also have been successful rather earlier, had the Russian spur not led through the route of Anglo-American nuclear co-operation to De Gaulle's veto. But without the Russian spur the application might well not have been made in 1961.

In the event, the risk of armed conflict with the Soviet Union was at its highest in the autumn of 1962, when Khrushchev attempted to install nuclear missiles in Cuba. As a result of his close contact with President Kennedy, Macmillan felt himself to be at the centre of events: 'We were "in on" and took full part in (and almost responsibility for) every American move. . . . The whole episode was like a battle; and we in Admiralty House felt as if we were in the battle HQ.'[23] At this point, however, the trial of strength was a trial between the Soviet Union and the United States. For all that he may have felt himself to be at the battle HQ, Macmillan was there as a trusted, senior staff officer, not as Commander-in-Chief.

In relation to other aspects of the relationship with the Soviet Union – in particular to the Berlin crisis and the disarmament negotiations, Macmillan was acting as a principal. It has to be said, however, that his contribution received only the barest mention in memoirs such as those of Khrushchev or Gromyko. As the Berlin crisis ebbed, his final achievement was the signature on 5 August 1963 of the Nuclear Test Ban Treaty, 'one of the great purposes' which he had set himself. Just over two months later his Premiership ended.

Considered against the background of British–Soviet relations during the forty-year period from 1945 to 1985, the years of Macmillan's Premiership, from January 1957 to October 1963, were both turbulent and dangerous. They were years during which the Soviet Union was perceived as being at the peak of its power and influence and during which the aberrant megalomania and the impulsive conduct of policy by Nikita Khrushchev offered both the possibility of dialogue and the menace of open conflict. The great achievement of Western policy was that, through all the muddle, the contradictions and the misunderstandings, the global confrontation of power and ideology was so managed that open military conflict between the Soviet Union and the Western powers was avoided and no nuclear weapon was detonated in anger. In this process, for better or worse, the tone of the East–West relationship was set by the United States and the Soviet Union. British policy could often be a significant factor, occasionally crucial in terms of influence, but never dominant. The primary task of Western statesmanship in those years was to establish such a measure of contact with the Soviet leadership and to maintain such a degree of coolness and consistency as to pass safely through the worst tensions while the inevitable evolution of the Communist regime took its course. As Macmillan put it in Parliament, if war could be avoided, the offensive features of Soviet Communism might eventually became 'blurred, blunted and perhaps softened'.[24] For such a task to be successfully accomplished it was necessary, first, to understand Soviet Russia, the working of its system, the mentality of its leaders and the nature of its people. This, from his very first visit and throughout his political career, undeterred by the barrage of official Soviet mendacity, Macmillan sought to do. Understanding was the prerequisite. But, on the basis of understanding, realistic policies had to be constructed. These, in Macmillan's Premiership were the policies of the Cold War. They could not, in the circumstances of the time, have been any other. They amounted, in essence, to creating and maintaining an effective unity of purpose among the Western powers; resisting Soviet pressure; and seeking any opportunity to control and, by negotiation, to reduce the more dangerous areas of actual or potential conflict. It was Macmillan's achievement, that, pursuing these policies, he re-established British influence in the conduct of relations with the Soviet Union, maintained a measure of Western unity and kept the dialogue going until the worst crises had been weathered. Time was needed before his successors could begin to reap the reward.

NOTES

1. Harold Macmillan, *Winds of Change, 1914–1939* (London: Macmillan, 1966), p. 324.
2. Ibid., pp. 405, 595.
3. See Alistair Horne, *Macmillan, 1894–1956*, vol. I, pp. 252–78. I was personally involved in the repatriation of Russian prisoners of war by sea through Odessa in the early months of 1945. The circumstances were very different from those which prevailed in Austria, but they were part of the same pattern of muddle and confusion in Europe at the end of the war. There was the same priority task of securing the

repatriation of British and Allied prisoners and the same need for pragmatic decisions by the military commanders on the spot. I find Horne's account of the whole affair thoroughly convincing.

4. FO 371/56763/4065; CAB 133/82; FO 800/507/SU/45/7.
5. 419 HC Deb, 20 February 1946, cols 1164–66; *The Times*, 21 February 1946.
6. *The Times*, 6 March 1946.
7. HC Deb 463, 23 March 1949, cols 375–391; HC Deb 467, 21 July 1949, col. 1570; HC Deb 469, 17 November 1949, col. 2317.
8. *Macmillan Diary*, 22 July 1955, quoted by Horne.
9. Gromyko and Ponomarev, *Soviet Foreign Policy* (Moscow, 1980), p. 345.
10. Correspondence between the Prime Minister and Mr Bulganin, Cmnd 380.
11. CAB 128/31 CC 74(57) CC 76(57).
12. Harold Macmillan, *Riding the Storm* (London: Macmillan, 1971), p. 165.
13. FO 371 135279.
14. CC (8) 58.
15. *Riding the Storm*, p. 557.
16. 582 HC Deb, 20 February 1958, col. 1521.
17. Macmillan, *Riding the Storm*, p. 585. I have relied heavily on Macmillan's own account in his memoirs. In relation to the Moscow visit I have, however, been particularly grateful for the advice of Sir Patrick Reilly who was at that time HM Ambassador in Moscow.
18. *Macmillan Diary*, 8 March 1959.
19. *Diary*, 26 July 1959.
20. HC Deb 612, 27 October 1959, cols 77–80.
21. HC Deb 624, 30 May 1960, col. 1012.
22. *Diary*, 25 June 1961.
23. *Diary*, 4 November 1962.
24. HC Deb 582, February 1958, col. 1224.

14 Macmillan and Nuclear Weapons: the SKYBOLT Affair

Donette Murray

INTRODUCTION

When Harold Macmillan became Prime Minister in 1957 after the damaging Suez débâcle, he quickly identified two areas that demanded immediate attention: the economy and the 'special' Anglo-American relationship. Whilst financial constraints required the government to pursue a defence policy more orientated towards nuclear rather than conventional deterrence,[1] in the aftermath of the crisis two conflicting defence policy strategies emerged. On the one hand, Suez highlighted doubts surrounding the reliability of the American nuclear guarantee and encouraged dedication to an independent British deterrent force. It also succeeded, however, in reinforcing the lesson that American acquiescence was at least desirable, if not necessary, in order for Britain to consider unilateral action again. Thus developed in Britain a curious paradox – a policy of independence as a means of influencing the United States, retaining world-wide prestige and national pride that appeared to co-exist alongside a rhetoric of interdependence with the United States.

Macmillan attempted to convince the United States to restore the special nuclear relations that had originated during the Second World War, citing among his arguments Britain's nuclear progress,[2] the threat of Russian technological advances symbolised in Sputnik,[3] and the need for American help if Britain was to commit to a test ban agreement. Fortunately for Macmillan, the American President was committed to reversing what he personally believed to be the unjust McMahon Act restrictions that had prevented nuclear collaboration.[4] Success came in 1958 and the following year when the restrictions were amended. The restoration of the special relationship and the rebuilding in particular of defence relations, however, sowed the seeds of problems that would come to the surface within a few years. Increasingly faced with the unprecedented technological and scientific changes of the late 1950s, Britain was unable to credibly maintain her independent nuclear deterrent force and had to rely more and more on American information and collaboration. By 1960 the future of the last indigenous British weapon, BLUE STREAK, was being reconsidered and the difficulties in maintaining the dual policies of independence and interdependence were becoming increasingly apparent. In 1962 Anglo-American relations were in crisis and Macmillan was faced with fundamental choices to make about his nuclear weapons policy. The reason was SKYBOLT.

CAMP DAVID

> It is an intriguing story, full of forebodings and uncertainties, of high political stakes dependent on technological progress, of a chain of errors of judgement carefully kept from the public gaze and, finally, at Nassau, one of the great confrontations in the history of Anglo-American relations.[5]

The story begins at an earlier conference at Camp David in March 1960. The opening scenes of this drama gave no indication of what lay ahead. A light-hearted and friendly meeting between the British Prime Minister and the American President Eisenhower in the tranquil surroundings of the President's Maryland retreat was typical of the good relations the two leaders had managed to re-establish. Co-operation in the field of defence had been at the top of Macmillan's agenda since he had become Prime Minister. As the two men now talked about this, Macmillan confided some of his problems to his counterpart, the most pressing of which was that the shift from bombers to missile delivery systems involved a leap in technology that was increasingly beyond the British national capability.[6] In order to preserve the British-designed and manufactured V-bomber force as a credible deterrent by enabling them to penetrate Soviet air defences, a new generation Intermediate Range Ballistic Missile was needed. Such a missile, BLUE STREAK, was currently under development; however, all indications pointed to the fact that the missile would enter its operational phase obsolete. Moreover, the cost was proving to be prohibitively high.[7]

Macmillan's government had made the independent deterrent a high-profile policy. To now abandon what had become the visible embodiment of that doctrine without having an acceptable replacement was a worrying prospect for the Conservatives.[8] Fortunately Eisenhower was sympathetic to Macmillan's dilemma and offered his British counterpart a new weapon – SKYBOLT – currently under development for the United States Air Force.[9]

The SKYBOLT offer was a highly attractive proposition, especially in the eyes of the RAF.[10] The missile promised to extend the life of the British V-bomber force which was facing obsolescence by the mid-1960s, whilst reaffirming the position of the RAF, traditionally the service responsible for nuclear deterrence, and all at a bargain price. The agreement provided that the United States would undertake and pay for all the project's research and development costs, leaving Britain to pay for the number of missiles she then decided to buy.[11] With Macmillan's acceptance of this arrangement, Anglo-American relations had entered a new paradoxical phase – the British 'independent' deterrent was to be preserved through interdependence with the United States. SKYBOLT was the linch-pin.

CRISIS

Between the easy days of the Camp David agreement and the tense confrontational Nassau conference, a crisis unfolded. Moreover, it was one that was 'compounded', wrote David Nunnerley, 'of drama and deceit, of uncertainty and distrust, of muddled perceptions and disappointed expectations, of high political stakes both won and lost, of miscalculation and misjudgement, a phoney crisis', according to Nunnerley, 'that should never have been allowed to happen'.[12]

The SKYBOLT missile was an ambitious project by any standards, requiring the development and application of highly advanced and as yet experimental technology to be used to improve the credibility of the manned strategic bomber – the B-52. The rationale of such a mode of delivery was itself not without problems since the future of this particular weapons system was regarded by many as no longer assured.[13] It was, as Henry Brandon reported:

the most complex ballistic missile the United States had yet undertaken – more so than MINUTEMAN or POLARIS. The missile had to be launched over an altitude range of several thousand feet, to be able at high speed to resist shock, vibration and noise from a hostile environ and to be integrated in a unique way with the mothership which, with its computer system, contains about 130,000 parts.[14]

As it became clear by the beginning of the 1960s that the Soviet Union was building increasingly sophisticated anti-missile technology,[15] SKYBOLT's supporters were forced to redefine its role, arguing the need for a kind of 'tin opener' to knock out enemy air defences, thus clearing the way for other bombers and missiles.[16] This 'defence suppression' mission against enemy air fields and early warning radar systems was also highly attractive to the British whose ageing V-bomber force was similarly becoming increasingly incapable of high-confidence penetration of enemy defence networks. The SKYBOLT missile would give these bombers a 'stand-off' capability, enabling them to perform the difficult task of targeting strategic locations within the heart of enemy territory without running the risk of succumbing to interception.[17]

Despite the confidence of the USAF and the Douglas Corporation (SKYBOLT's prime contractor), Thomas Gates, the US Secretary of Defense under Eisenhower, was never happy with the 'drawing board proposition' as they called it, but nevertheless decided to approve the missile's development heavily influenced by the lack of operational missiles the United States was able to deploy and the uncertainty facing those currently in development.[18] Despite this decision, both men made no secret of their concern and frequently impressed upon their British counterparts the doubts and problems facing the project. Douglas told Harold Watkinson, the British Minister of Defence, shortly after the missile was given the official go-ahead, that SKYBOLT was 'in real trouble',[19] while Gates urged Sir Solly Zuckerman, the British Government's Chief Scientific Advisor, to warn the Minister that 'nobody would gain from making a political issue out of it', adding that attention was now shifting noticeably in favour of the Navy's *wunderkind* – the POLARIS Sea Launched Ballistic Missile (SLBM).[20]

Macmillan and Watkinson were concerned, the latter suggesting that they should begin work on a response should the Americans decide to drop the project. Macmillan was sufficiently worried to ask the Minister of Defence to prepare a memo on alternatives:

> if SKYBOLT should fail we shall have, on the basis of our present arrangements, no way of maintaining an effective means of delivery of the nuclear deterrent in the period 1965–70 . . . if you

think there is a real risk of SKYBOLT being abandoned soon, we must consider urgently what alternatives are open to us. There would be strong grounds for pressing the Americans to help us with a replacement, but we cannot do so effectively without some knowledge of the costs and timings involved.[21]

In conclusion, Macmillan advised that nothing should be volunteered to indicate either total dependence on the project or that Britain feared the repercussions of it being cancelled. The danger, recognized and duly noted for the record, prompted no more action for the time being. Meanwhile, in the United States, a decision to radically reduce SKYBOLT's funding in the last budget of the Eisenhower term virtually ended effective development and the future of SKYBOLT hung in the balance as American politics moved into limbo pending the outcome of the Presidential elections. In Britain, the Prime Minister and his colleagues held their breath and anxiously awaited an indication of what position the new Administration would take on the matter.[22]

KENNEDY

The new Kennedy administration initially backed SKYBOLT. Robert McNamara, the Secretary of Defense, was both worried about the current (and as yet undebunked) missile gap theory, and conscious of the fact that he was contemplating scrapping another star in the Air Forces' firmament – the B-70 bomber. Any attempt to cancel both programmes at once, the Secretary knew, would be tantamount to committing political suicide.[23] Ignoring a confidential report from a panel of experts recommending cancellation, McNamara instead allocated more funds to the project in the belief that Gates' reduction would not prove either way if the missile was to be a success or failure.[24] But as the year wore on SKYBOLT's future was again being questioned. Although McNamara was by now having doubts about the weapon he was not yet in a position to make a move against it. However, before the summer of 1962 had ended, McNamara's technical and budgetary aides were again urging him to close the project down recommending that it be dropped from the next budget in order to avoid a fight with Congress and the Air Force.[25] McNamara set the process of cancellation in motion, swearing his aides to secrecy lest the supporters of the programme find out and cause an ugly fight.[26] On 7 November 1962 McNamara met with President Kennedy and Secretary of State Rusk to tell them of his plans. In agreement, both men pressed upon him the importance of letting the British down gently on this and urged consultation. The Secretary of Defense himself volunteered to handle the cancellation, promising not only to tell the British but to go to London to negotiate a replacement deal for them.[27] Informing David Ormsby-Gore, the British Ambassador and Peter Thorneycroft, the Minister for Defence, McNamara then became embroiled in difficult budget details that prevented the Secretary from reaching Britain until 11 December.[28] Then, quite simply, all hell broke loose. McNamara and Thorneycroft met, argued and parted, shocked, confused and angry. As Ormsby-Gore wrote:

> suspicions, frayed nerves and bad temper became the order of the day. In such circumstances it behoved all in positions of authority to try and keep a cool head and strive to calm the atmosphere. The precise opposite happened.[29]

With no agreement reached it was left to Macmillan and Kennedy at Nassau one week later, to come up with a solution to diffuse the crisis.

CAUSES OF THE CRISIS

As Richard Neustadt discovered:

> Misperceptions evidently make for crisis in proportion to the intimacy of relations. Hazards are proportionate to the degree of friendship. Indifference and hostility may not breed paranoia; friendship does.[30]

There are three major factors that underpin the crisis: the different agendas being pursued by the US and the UK; a breakdown in communication between the two nations; and external events.

Different Agendas

The US government had decided to develop SKYBOLT as one of several weapons at a time when the only missile system it had fully operational was the ATLAS. Ambitious and complicated, the SKYBOLT missile would only have been useful for a tactical defence suppression mission if its development had been cheap and technically straightforward. However, since its inception in the late 1950s, the nature of strategic planning had completely changed as a result of the onset of the missile age, rendering obsolete systems that could not effectively penetrate enemy air defences in order to reach a target. During the course of its development, the missile proved anything but value for money and repeatedly failed when assessed against McNamara's 'cost–efficiency' yardstick.[31] It would, the Secretary explained:

> combine the disadvantages of the bomber with those of the missile. It would have . . . the bomber's disadvantage of being 'soft', 'concentrated', relatively vulnerable on the ground, and slow to target, . . . [it] would have . . . the lower payload and poorer accuracy of a missile, without the relative invulnerability and short-time to target of a MINUTEMAN or POLARIS.[32]

McNamara also had an agenda to rationalize of the Defense Department. While not exactly penalizing projects because of their complexity, he did target those that were incurring greatly augmented costs and time lags by refusing them the extra time and funding required to produce a viable system. Although the SKYBOLT system was far from technically impossible, according to Eugene Zuckert, the Secretary of the Air Force, 'the technical people downstairs had gotten Mr McNamara and the President in a bit of a bind by picking on the "technical infeasibility" or at least making dampening comments about technical progress in connection with SKYBOLT'.[33] To be fair to McNamara, the technical ins and outs of the weapons system was something he neither fully understood nor really cared about. Facing a defence budget of some $51 billion (the largest ever) and having spent $500 million on SKYBOLT already, the Secretary of Defense badly needed to jettison some excess dollars – SKYBOLT was costly, unpredictable and constantly late.[34] Instead of pumping more money into the project, McNamara knew that some two to three billion dollars could be saved if he pulled the plug now. Eventually, it was cost rather than feasibility that decided SKYBOLT's fate.

Within the administration opinions varied, not so much about the sagacity of abandoning SKYBOLT, but about what was to happen to the British independent nuclear deterrent as a result. For the most part the Pentagon, and particularly those in the International Security Affairs office, wished only to preserve the *status quo*. Many in the State Department, however, had very different ideas. Secretary of State Rusk, as Brandon remarked, 'was very passive', and seemed willing for McNamara to 'carry the ball', stipulating only that Britain should be given as much help as possible.[35] Many of his subordinates' thoughts, however, were more firmly crystallized, and ranged from providing assistance in a multilateral context to taking this opportunity to remove Britain from the nuclear club altogether.[36] As Rusk later admitted:

> British paranoia may also have been fostered by some in our own bureaucracy who wanted to use the cancellation to pressure the British to give up an independent force.[37]

In addition, major speeches made by senior American figures including Dean Acheson and Robert McNamara appeared to heavily criticize small independent nuclear deterrents, thereby increasing the suspicions of those in Britain.[38] It was clear that an element within the administration wanted Britain out of the nuclear club. What wasn't clear was how far this extended to official policy and the upper echelons of the Kennedy government. Even Macmillan himself was suspicious. He noted in his diary:

> it was difficult to suppress the suspicion that the failure of SKYBOLT might be welcomed in some American quarters as a means of forcing Britain out of the nuclear club.[39]

Outside State and Defense, the USAF and the Douglas Corporation had their own agendas, unashamedly based on vested interests. Both groups proclaimed until the weapon was officially cancelled in late December 1962 that SKYBOLT was a winning ticket, bound to succeed if given the necessary time and money to see it through a not unusually difficult development phase. The USAF, in particular, was fearful that cancellation of the project would effectively mean an end to any future the manned bomber might have.[40] With the B-70 virtually terminated, SKYBOLT was perceived in both Air Forces as a last ditch attempt to preserve their role as the nuclear arm of the deterrent.[41] It was not in their best interests to paint a gloomy picture.

Britain's position *vis-à-vis* SKYBOLT could hardly have been more different. Although Macmillan and both Defence Ministers, Watkinson and Thorneycroft, were well aware of the dangers involved in relying too heavily on the American missile, they nevertheless failed to take action to prevent a catastrophe should the project be dropped.[42] Despite remarks to the contrary, the fact remained that in theory and in practice, Britain's whole independent deterrent was tied up with the weapon. This worrying dependence should have been highlighted by repeated efforts by American officials to alert the British to the difficulties SKYBOLT was experiencing. Even though the most senior scientist in Britain, Sir Solly Zuckerman, was publicly blunt in his criticisms of the weapon, as Richard Neustadt discovered, 'it made no impact'.[43]

For Macmillan, reports of design problems and technical difficulties were something to be expected in such a complicated undertaking; not a new and worrying development. In order for SKYBOLT to be an effective deterrent for Britain, it only had to 'appear to work'. 'In English ears, a guidance system did not sound like a great trouble'. 'British purposes required only that the Russians *think* the weapon could be guided to a city' in order to fulfil the 'Moscow Criterion.'[44] Britain was not so much concerned with deterring the Soviet Union for it had the protection of the United States to meet this need, as it was with retaining some influence over American strategic decision-making and presumably over the targeting of the vast arsenal commanded by the United States.[45] Besides, Macmillan was assured, the SAC and the USAF were depending on the weapon as much as the British and since they were a formidable influence in the United States, traditionally dominating the Pentagon and receiving the lion's share of the defence budget; the fact that they did not appear to be anticipating trouble for SKYBOLT could only be interpreted as a good sign.[46] Even if cancellation was considered, Macmillan believed, Kennedy was an honourable man who would respect the 'moral obligation' to provide a replacement inherited from the tying of the 1960 SKYBOLT and Holy Loch agreements.[47] The Prime Minister also had other things on his mind. The Common Market negotiations were giving some cause for concern and his government had been long considering the possibility of offering de Gaulle some measure of nuclear-aid in order to smooth the way for an agreeable conclusion. Macmillan did not anticipate that the Americans would rock the boat at such a delicate time.

Thorneycroft also recognized the dangers inherent in a possible cancellation, even though he had come late to the story, inheriting the missile and the present problems from Watkinson. Ambitious at a time when the question of Macmillan's successor was very much open to debate, Thorneycroft knew that as the Minister for Defence he would be one of the first casualties if SKYBOLT were indeed to be cancelled. Unlike his counterpart in America, his power over the department and the armed forces was far from assured. Powerful RAF and Navy lobbies pressured the minister to support a course of action favourable to their interests. Thorneycroft was faced with two choices, neither of which appealed to him. He could either support SKYBOLT and take the blame for being incompetent both for allowing the British deterrent to become dependent on the United States and for failing have contingency measures in place. Or, he could denounce the American decision, declare that he had been told nothing to indicate that SKYBOLT was in trouble, and in private work to secure a better deal for Britain. Thorneycroft almost certainly had decided to do the latter by the time he had been contacted by McNamara. But he couldn't openly embrace POLARIS until SKYBOLT had been well and truly buried. As Neustadt remarked:

It would be tantamount to treason, selling SKYBOLT down the river.[48]

Instead, professing shock at McNamara's decision, Thorneycroft waited, and having privately set his sights on POLARIS, hoped that in the crisis atmosphere that was building up, Britain would get POLARIS and he would emerge politically unscathed.[49] Convinced that POLARIS was the only acceptable alternative, he tried to convince the Prime Minister to adopt a pro-POLARIS stance. Macmillan, however, had a lot more to lose. Having brokered the SKYBOLT deal, its cancellation at this point would reveal not only the fallacy of the independent British nuclear deterrent, but in doing so, could fatally undermine Macmillan's own position. Retention of the British nuclear deterrent as his biographer said:

represented a major plank of his political platform . . . the unrequited removal of SKYBOLT would be as if Britain were unilaterally disarmed.[50]

The future of the independent deterrent had been gambled on an unproved missile and when it became clear that SKYBOLT would be dropped by the US administration, Macmillan's government had no contingency plans to fall back on. The warnings he had received, far from galvanizing the Prime Minister into action, had served rather to immobilize him.[51] Unfortunately for Macmillan the alignment of his three key policies: independent nuclear capability; close Anglo-American relations and entry into the Common Market, was to coincide with SKYBOLT's demise. Aware that SKYBOLT was going to fall, he could do nothing until his meeting with de Gaulle at Rambouillet in a few days time for fear that the General might react negatively. The Common Market negotiations were reaching a critical stage that promised a decision one way or the other and the Prime Minister dared not show weakness *vis-à-vis* the Americans. Finally, Macmillan was also aware of the fact that Britain was just days away from completing the tests necessary to produce a nuclear warhead for the missile delivery system. Any action he might take ran the risk of upsetting this highly critical work.[52]

> McNamara's warning raised a horrid prospect: Pandora's box might open . . . the issue for Macmillan in November was how to sit on the lid.[53]

As the Prime Minister prepared for Nassau he knew that he should have heeded the warnings and taken action sooner to head off what was shaping up to be a very dangerous crisis. Depressed by his meeting with de Gaulle and as yet undecided about whether or not to try and save the SKYBOLT deal,[54] Macmillan calculated that the outcome depended on his own ability to stage-manage the negotiations.[55] Everything rested on his being able to appeal to Kennedy to honour the spirit of the 'Special Relationship'. However, the success of this strategy depended on the maintenance of an atmosphere of crisis and confusion until he, Macmillan entered to face Kennedy. He couldn't risk letting his plans become known, not least because if it were to be revealed that SKYBOLT was lost he faced dissension among the Services and the Cabinet. Indeed, Macmillan could not even be sure that a POLARIS deal would get the support of his Cabinet colleagues or indeed the country.[56] It was better, he reasoned, to return home with a *fait accompli* rather than risk being humiliated by a Cabinet split and damaging public opinion. Macmillan feared the repercussions of the renewal of the debate on the national nuclear deterrent. For some years, civil servants, Opposition and Conservative ministers as well as the Armed Services had been arguing over the feasibility and desirability of maintaining the British force. Any discussion prior to the Nassau meeting would almost certainly ignite this discussion and question whether this might be the opportunity to reassess the costly and for some, wasteful national obsession that embodied one of the central elements of Macmillan's foreign and defence policies. According to one Cabinet Secretary:

> for several months ... there had been growing an uncrystallized, uncanvassed, latent Cabinet sentiment against prolonging the effort to sustain the independent deterrent ... if a change had been put to the Cabinet ... especially if it involved more money, all those latent feelings might have crystallized *against* going on ... the hell with it ... the PM was not unaware of that.[57]

The years had seen the contradiction between independence and interdependence become increasingly obvious and difficult to rationalize. Macmillan had no desire to lose control now.

Breakdown in Communication

Failure to communicate effectively turned a relatively simple policy decision into a crisis in Anglo-American relations. This case study is special in that the misunderstandings, misjudgements and general confusion can be traced back to almost all levels of government, and in some cases, not only between British and American officials, but between American and American, British and British. As the crisis unfolded, too many conduits of communication rapidly became too few.

It has been argued (somewhat lamely by the British) that they were unaware of SKYBOLT's rocky past and precarious future. This would appear highly unlikely. Between technical teams, the RAF officers assigned to liaise with the project and Zuckerman himself, the reports reaching Britain about SKYBOLT were detailed and plentiful. Watkinson had repeatedly warned the Prime Minister that the project did not look very promising. His successor, Thorneycroft, was aware of SKYBOLT's probable fate from as early as his September meeting with McNamara.[58] Yet all three failed to communicate the potential for crisis to their American counterparts. It was only when Thorneycroft and McNamara met in December that the British Minister laid his cards on the table. But by this time, in an atmosphere of distrust and suspicion, a crisis was unfolding. Macmillan, on the advice of Ormsby-Gore, had not spoken directly to Kennedy about the matter, deciding that it was more sensible to wait for the Nassau *tête-à-tête*. Kennedy had really no idea his friend was in political hot water until he was on his way to the conference.[59]

Macmillan did stay in close contact with his Ambassador in Washington (although it has often been claimed that the Prime Minister deliberately kept him in the dark about his intentions).[60] Ormsby-Gore's advice was sought on several key matters including whether or not Macmillan should contact Kennedy directly. He was instructed to determine if the President would have any legal or Congressional problems that might prevent him from being able to offer a 'lend' of POLARIS submarines.[61] The Ambassador was also told to make sure that Kennedy would not make his decision public until he had first spoken to the Prime Minister.[62] Ormsby-Gore's job was to prepare the ground for a successful resolution of the crisis without giving away any clues about Macmillan's intentions. His was an unobtrusive role and it suited the Prime Minister's purpose for it to appear that the British Ambassador was not privy to his private thoughts on this matter. In contrast, Ormsby-Gore's American counterpart, David Bruce was much less active although this was not part of any Department of State strategy. Bruce received little by way of information largely because the SKYBOLT issue was being handled by the Department of Defense and not the State Department. Generally aware of the situation but without any specific instruction, the American Ambassador could do little besides send off telegrams warning of the volatile political situation in England.[63] Unfortunately, as was the case with numerous other reports, Bruce's fears failed to make much of an impact.

On the American side the breakdown in communication went further than David Bruce and failure to effectively communicate official policy was evident. Those within the State Department who wished to see the playing field levelled, and Britain removed from the nuclear club, could not come out and say this. Instead, they managed to influence key documents enough to make it appear to the British that this was a Kennedy–Rusk–McNamara agenda.[64] The USAF and the Douglas Corporation conveyed a rosy picture that was far from accurate, even until the final and so-called 6th successful test-flight[65] in order to preserve their own lucrative and prestigious positions.[66] With such confident reports coming from these sources, officials were understandably less likely to take notice of contradictory noises emanating from other sections of the US administration.

McNamara failed to effectively communicate his plans although he had his reasons for keeping these close to his chest. Because of SKYBOLT's supporters in Congress, the USAF and among the Joint Chiefs of Staff, McNamara could not openly set out his agenda without bringing upon himself the weight of these powerful bodies. Although he was in mind to cancel SKYBOLT certainly from August 1962, he could not say so even to his British counterpart who visited in September, for fear that the word would get out and catch him off-balance.[67] In fact, although Thorneycroft later complained that McNamara should have informed him earlier, the Secretary of Defense was only in a position to do so on 23 November when Kennedy officially approved the cancellation plan.[68]

> He could not tell them SKYBOLT was about to die, no matter that he had decided so, for this was not yet an Administration decision.[69]

McNamara again confused matters by emphasizing that the cancellation was for predominantly technical and financial reasons. At a distinct disadvantage as a result of their unfamiliarity with 'the new jargon emanating from the Defence community in Washington',[70] the British had trouble accepting the new procedures, facts and figures that their counterparts were claiming explained the cancellation decision. Aware that SKYBOLT was not a complete failure – the British then wondered if some other motive was behind the cancellation. McNamara's failure to ensure consultation had taken place before the story leaked only further exacerbated feelings of bewilderment and distrust.[71]

Kennedy had little to do with the crisis until Nassau. Many of his staff were aware that it was going to cause political fireworks, but all failed to effectively convey this message to him. Rusk, Bruce, McNamara, Bundy and Nitze all expressed concern that outright cancellation without prior warning or consultation risked dire repercussions for the alliance, but their concerns appear not to have reached the President.[72] Although McNamara was aware that the affair had crisis potential, certainly before his baffling encounter with Thorneycroft in December he was confident that the matter would be resolved with the minimum of fuss. This was largely due to a fundamental misconception about the original SKYBOLT deal. The Secretary believed that under the terms of the 1960 agreement, Britain was committed to assigning her SKYBOLT-armed V-bombers to NATO. He therefore expected to arrange a straight swap – POLARIS for SKYBOLT under these terms.[73] This pivotal mistake guaranteed confusion and chaos and for many in the administration created an opportunity that was not to be missed. The notion that the American Administration was intent on forcing Britain to relinquish her nuclear deterrent was a popular one. Macmillan and Thorneycroft both recognized the potential leverage that could be gained form emphasizing this apparent 'covert agenda'. Although the Prime Minister noted at the time in his diary that the behaviour of some in Kennedy's government was highly suspicious, he toned this down in a post-crisis entry that seemed to absolve the President and his top staff of any wilful wrongdoing in this area:

> it is also clear to me that they are determined to kill Skybolt on good general grounds – not merely to annoy us or drive Great Britain out of the nuclear business. But, of course, they handled things in such a way as to make many of us very suspicious.[74]

External Factors

No event in foreign affairs can fail to be influenced by or to influence other events unfolding around it. In the case of the SKYBOLT affair, it was the Cuban Missile Crisis in particular which played a major role. The Cuban affair not only delayed McNamara's plans, but it distorted perceptions and numbed usually sensitive antennae to a potential crisis that officials would otherwise have had under control. When the administration returned to the SKYBOLT issue after the euphoric but exhausting Cuban episode, the problem was not given the same consideration it might have received had the administration not been so distracted. As one official remarked:

> If there had not been a traumatic experience like the Cuban crisis, SKYBOLT would have seemed a big problem. But it didn't. Golf was the order of the day, not (more) missiles.[75]

Likewise, for Macmillan's government, other concerns seemed more troublesome than the admittedly disconcerting rumours reaching Whitehall about the probability of a cancellation. Macmillan's leadership had never looked so precarious. His popularity had declined badly over the past year and the domestic policies he had championed like the 'pay-pause' and entry into the Common Market, had not been well received. Alarming electoral defeats had prompted the Prime Minister to lose his characteristic *sang-froid*, axing a third of his Cabinet in a desperate attempt to retain the credibility of his government. This crisis barely over, Macmillan's reputation was further damaged by the furore in the British press over what they called the impotence of British power. This was demonstrated, it was alleged, by the lack of consultation by Kennedy during the Missile Crisis.[76]

Macmillan's many difficulties had resulted in a hardening of his position. Pushed into a corner by domestic problems and a cutthroat Press, the distractions of the Common Market negotiations, colonial problems in Africa and uncertainties facing the NATO alliance, the SKYBOLT crisis threatened to unbalance him to a degree he might well have survived in an earlier time. With less at stake politically, Macmillan's handling of the affair would arguably have been more low-key, focusing on technical rather than political issues. This, however, was now impossible. As he prepared to go to the conference he noted in his diary 'we shall have a difficult time with the Americans in Nassau'.[77]

NASSAU

As the Prime Minister stepped into the warm, inviting air of the picturesque Caribbean island, he wondered how things had become so perilous. Why hadn't Kennedy intervened? 'Everything depended upon it', he thought, 'the future of the Anglo-American alliance . . . the future of the Conservative administration, the future of Macmillan himself.'[78] Although Macmillan was under no illusions as to the difficulties that lay ahead, President Kennedy had only just been alerted to the gravity of the situation. Having invited Ormsby-Gore to fly down to Nassau with him, he quickly discovered the full extent of the problem and the possible repercussions for alliance relations if a solution was not found. The two men lost no time in getting to work on a proposal which allowed the US to withdraw from the project and Britain to retain it while splitting the research and development costs.[79]

But Macmillan had already seen the transcript of TV remarks Kennedy had made just days before criticizing the project. Even if he had wanted SKYBOLT, the Prime Minister knew that he could not accept a missile so publicly denounced by the President. 'The virginity of the lady', he told the Americans, 'must now be regarded as doubtful.'[80]

The atmosphere was tense as the two delegations met for the beginning of formal talks the next day.[81] Macmillan lost no time in captivating his audience by a skilled performance, describing in an emotional, eloquent and wonderfully phrased oratory, the story of the two great nations. He went to recall the recent agreement he had made with Eisenhower allowing the United States docking and service facilities in Scotland, reminding his audience that this agreement which had caused both he and his government considerable political difficulties, though not legally binding, had always been understood as a quid pro quo arrangement. In light of this, Kennedy had inherited, he suggested, a 'moral obligation' to provide a suitable replacement. Having established themes of friendship and betrayal, shared glories and hardships, and an indivisible common purpose, the Prime Minister set about demolishing possible American arguments for not giving Britain POLARIS. In response to the American fear that such an agreement might seriously jeopardize Britain's chances of getting into the Common Market, Macmillan replied confidently that 'the outcome of the Common Market negotiations would not be affected by decisions about nuclear delivery systems'; agriculture, he suggested, was the real stumbling block.[82] De Gaulle, Macmillan told the Americans, had understood clearly that the Prime Minister intended to ask for POLARIS as a substitute when they had met a few days previously in Rambouillet.[83] As for the other allies, it was foolish he told his audience, to conceive of any adverse reaction coming from that quarter as it was widely accepted, if admittedly not liked, that Britain and America had a special nuclear relationship dating back to the wartime Manhattan project.[84] Anyway, why should the NATO countries take offence at a switch from the 'lame horse', SKYBOLT, to what was now the favourite, POLARIS?[85]

Kennedy for his part, although not unreceptive to Macmillan's moving arguments, had come to Nassau with very little manoeuvring room on POLARIS. In the weeks leading up to the conference, divergent elements within the State Department had united in a passionate attempt to prevent Macmillan from wresting a POLARIS deal from Kennedy.[86] Unwilling to incur the combined wrath of these elements – and aware that there existed a very real possibility that to do so would rock the political boat at a delicate time – Kennedy resisted. The president was under immense pressure to avoid giving in to Macmillan's demands at all costs. Having decried the existence of small independent nuclear forces, argued against nuclear proliferation and repeatedly refused French requests for assistance in this field, by giving Britain POLARIS, Kennedy would be executing a very public U-turn in US policy. Not only did it risk endangering Britain's bid to join the Economic Community, but it would also reinforce resentment among NATO countries, especially France, of what was already perceived as the discriminatory Anglo-Saxon 'special relationship'.[87]

Another problem for Kennedy lay in the complications a POLARIS deal would have for the Multilateral Nuclear Force (MLF) proposal, a central element in his 'Grand Design' for Europe.[88] For some time his administration had been working on a formula designed to prevent nuclear proliferation and to stay what was perceived as a West German desire for a strategic nuclear role. This focus on multilateralism was in direct opposition to bilateral nuclear agreements and in particular to any agreement that would facilitate the continuation of the independent British deterrent. How could America hope to sell the concept of multilateralism to her European allies, the MLF proponents demanded, when one of the key players, Britain, had just received help to prop up her independent force?[89]

On the other hand, the President was deeply troubled by what might happen if Britain didn't get a deal. He was aware of the growing press criticism at home claiming that America was betraying her closest ally.[90] Kennedy also now knew that little consultation had actually taken place and recognized that being seen to renege on a deal could have serious implications for present and future relations with the other European countries. Moreover, if a solution was not found, Britain might turn for comfort to the arms of General de Gaulle or even West Germany.[91] If this happened (or the survival of the Conservative government came to depend on Macmillan adopting an anti-American stance), his administration's whole European policy would probably suffer a debilitating blow.[92] In the end Kennedy was reluctant to let his ally down. He had a high regard for Macmillan and the close relationship they had built up. If this crisis was allowed to get out of hand the President risked losing possibly the one leader he felt he could really talk to.[93] Macmillan played on these fears painting 'with something of a Churchillian palette', according to Brandon, 'the future of Anglo-American relations', emphasizing that while Britain would not renege on past arrangements with the United States, such intransigence would inevitably lead to a deep rift in relations between the two countries.[94] As Neustadt remarked, the President was facing:

> an impassioned older man embodying a valued weaker ally, who invoked in his own person a magnificent war record, an historic friendship, and a claim upon our honour – in Eisenhower's name – to say nothing of one politician's feeling for another. McNamara and Thorneycroft had spoken different languages; these two spoke the same.[95]

Having tried to placate the British Prime Minister with a range of other alternatives, in the end Kennedy gave in over POLARIS.[96] He offered the weapons system in a multilateral context and Macmillan accepted, providing that he was given an escape clause that was necessary in order for him the defend the agreement back home. The final agreement stated that the force would be used for:

> The international defence of the Western Alliance in all circumstances *except where Her Majesty's Government may decide that the supreme national interests are at stake.*[97] (my emphasis)

CONCLUSION

It was, as George Ball later wrote, 'a monument of contrived ambiguity'[98] that both sides could claim as a triumph. Macmillan had pulled off a remarkable face-saving exercise. He had gone to Nassau with little to offer and a great deal to lose. The Polaris agreement had secured the future of the British deterrent, against the express advice of the majority of Kennedy's advisers. With his nuclear policy broadly intact, he had preserved the central plank of his foreign policy – the special defence relationship with the United States and all at a bargain price. His personal diplomacy and skill in utilizing the 'special relationship' to get what he wanted from Kennedy whose government's dislike of national deterrents and nuclear proliferation dictated America's nuclear weapons policy was quite remarkable. Moreover, the Prime Minister had secured the deal without consulting the military men (Defence Chiefs and Service Heads) who were left to argue somewhat lamely after the fact that their preferences had not been taken into consideration.

Unfortunately, for Macmillan, although the Nassau agreement reaffirmed the special Anglo-American relationship, it presaged a year overshadowed by alliance problems beginning with de Gaulle's veto of Britain's Common Market bid and rejection of Kennedy's Polaris offer.[99] The 'independent' British nuclear deterrent had been preserved but the cost was as yet undetermined. Nassau highlighted the fact that the national deterrent was independent in name only. Provided by the United States and targeted in accordance with American plans, only the warheads would be British-made and even these were closely based on American designs. Moreover, Macmillan was faced with growing demands from the United States to participate in the multilateral force discussed at the conference and move away from an unrealistic and unnecessary independent stance. Nassau symbolized the apogee of Anglo-American defence relations and the successful restoration of the special nuclear bond severed after the Second World War. The triumph was short lived. Dissent and disagreement followed soon after.

NOTES

1. For Britain and nuclear weapons see: S. J. Ball, 'Military Nuclear Relations between the United States and Great Britain under the terms of the McMahon Act, 1946–1958', *Historical Journal*, 38:2 (1995); John Baylis, *Anglo-American Defence Relations 1939–1980* (London: Macmillan, 1981) and *Ambiguity and Deterrence: British Nuclear Strategy 1945–1964* (Oxford: Oxford University Press, 1995); Ian Clark, *Nuclear Diplomacy and the Special Relationship: Britain, Deterrent and America 1957–62* (Oxford: Oxford University Press, 1994); Lawrence Freedman, *Britain and Nuclear Weapons* (London: Macmillan, 1980); A. J. R. Groom, *British Thinking About Nuclear Weapons* (London: Frances Pinter, 1974); Martin S. Navias, *Nuclear Weapons and British Strategic Planning 1955–58* (Oxford: Oxford University Press, 1991); Peter Malone, *The British Nuclear Deterrent* (London: Croom Helm, 1984); Andrew Pierre, *Nuclear*

Weapons: The British Experience with an Independent Strategic Force, 1939–1970 (London, 1972); John Simpson, *The Independent Nuclear State: The United States, Britain and the Military Atom* (London: Macmillan, 1984).

2. Britain's first thermonuclear device was successfully exploded in May 1957.

3. *Sputnik* – the first earth-orbiting satellite – was particularly shocking to the West because it demonstrated that the Soviet Union was capable of constructing the technology necessary for long-range missiles, making the United States vulnerable to Soviet attack.

4. Dwight D. Eisenhower, *The White House Years: Waging Peace, 1956–61* (London: Heinemann, 1966), p. 219; *The New York Times*, 4 February 1960.

5. Henry Brandon, 'Skybolt', *The Sunday Times*, 8 December 1963.

6. CAB133/243 Commonwealth and International Conferences, 1960, Washington Meeting, PRO.

7. Britain had already spent £65 million and was facing an estimated bill of £600 million.

8. The decision to abandon BLUE STREAK had been taken on 24 February 1960 but only announced officially after Macmillan was sure he had Eisenhower's promise of a replacement. *The Times*, 14 April 1960.

9. The SKYBOLT or GAM-87A was an air-launched two-stage solid-propellant hypersonic ballistic missile with astro-inertial guidance. It had a range of approximately 1,000 miles.

10. The USAF had been in touch with the RAF about the missile since 1959. See *Aviation Week*, 22 February, 1960; *Space Business Daily*, 10 December 1962.

11. Memo, Dillon to PM, 29 March 1960, CAB 133/243, Public Records Office (PRO) London. In return, Macmillan agreed to Eisenhower's request for service and docking facilities for POLARIS. Although the PM had wanted more commitment on a future POLARIS deal, when this did not materialize, he backed down, content in the knowledge that this could be negotiated at some later date.

12. David Nunnerley, *President Kennedy and Britain* (London: Bodley Head, 1972), p. 127.

13. Sir Solly Zuckerman, Oral History, John F. Kennedy Library, Boston, p. 28.

14. Henry Brandon, op. cit. See also *Chicago Tribune*, 12 December 1962.

15. During the 1960s it was thought that anti-ballistic missile (ABM) systems could be developed which would track and destroy the incoming warheads of a nuclear attack. Although both the Russians and the Americans deployed such systems, they proved to be extravagantly expensive and essentially unworkable.

16. *The Times*, 9 June 1960.

17. Clark, *Nuclear Diplomacy and the Special Relationship*, pp. 281–4. See also *The Times*, 9 June 1960.

18. At the time, the US had only one operational missile – ATLAS – and it was unclear how those in development (MINUTEMAN, TITAN and POLARIS) would fare (Brandon, op. cit.).

19. Record of Meeting, 21 October 1960, PREM11/3261, MM 46/60.
20. Brandon, op. cit. See also Watkinson to Macmillan, 12 May 1960, DEFE13/195 PRO. POLARIS was a submarine-launched ballistic missile being developed for the US Navy.
21. Macmillan to Watkinson, 19 Nov. 1960, PREM11/3261 PRO.
22. Memo, December 1960, PREM11/3261 PRO; Record of Meeting, Gates and Watkinson, 12 December 1960, PREM11/3261 MM 54/60 PRO.
23. Roswell Gilpatric, Oral History, JFKL, p. 74. See also Richard E. Neustadt, *Alliance Politics* (New York: Columbia University Press, 1970) p. 37.
24. December 9 Memo, Box 273A–274, NSF, JFKL. See also John Newhouse, *De Gaulle and the Anglo-Saxons* (London: André Deutsch, 1970), p. 195.
25. Richard E. Neustadt, *Report to the President: Skybolt and Nassau: American Policy-making and Anglo-American Relations*, 11/63, Meetings and Memoranda, Box 322–323, NSF, JFKL, p. 4.
26. Neustadt, *Report to the President*, p. 9.
27. *Foreign Relations of the United States 1961–1963*, vol. XIII: *Western Europe and Canada* (Washington, DC: Department of State, Government Printing Office, 1994), p. 1085, Doc. No. 399.
28. Richard E. Neustadt Papers Box 19, Government consulting, Skybolt/Atlantic Affairs 12/62, Skybolt-Nassau (classified) Folder 2, JFKL.
29. Lord Harlech, 'Suez SNAFU, Skybolt SABU', *Foreign Policy*, vol. 1, no. 1 (Spring 1971), p. 49.
30. Neustadt, *Alliance Politics*, p. 72.
31. *Washington Post*, 21 December 1962.
32. Andrew J. Pierre, *Nuclear Politics: The British Experience with an Independent Strategic Force* (Cambridge: Cambridge University Press, 1972), p. 299.
33. Eugene Zuckert, Oral History, JFKL, p. 89.
34. *Washington Star,* 16 Dec. 1962; *Philadelphia Inquirer,* 28 December 1962; *Chicago Tribune*, 28 December 1962.
35. Henry Brandon, Oral History, p. 4; Clark, p. 361.
36. Telegram, London to State, 22 March, 1960 Box 1236 General Records of the State Department, Central Decimal File 1960–63 (RG59), National Archives, Washington, DC. This group known as the 'Europeanists' were a powerful element within the State Department. They believed that the 'special relationship' hindered the improvement of relations with America's other allies, notably France and West Germany.
37. Dean Rusk, *As I Saw It* (New York: W. W. Norton, 1990), p. 266.
38. Address by Acheson, 5 December 1962, Neustadt Papers Box 19 Folder 12/62 Skybolt Folder 2, JFKL and United States Information Service, United States Embassy, 16 June 1962.
39. Harold Macmillan, *At the End of the Day* (London: Macmillan, 1973), p. 343.
40. *The Times*, 27 December 1962.
41. As it turned out, the Air Forces' fears proved to be groundless. The B-52 bomber was still operational in the 1980s as were the British V-bombers.

42. Watkinson to Macmillan, 12 December 1960, PREM11/3261, PRO.
43. Neustadt, *Report to the President*, p. 20.
44. Neustadt, *Alliance Politics*, p. 41.
45. Pierre, *Nuclear Politics*, p. 93.
46. McGeorge Bundy, Oral History, p. 4. See also Neustadt, *Alliance Politics*, p. 62.
47. Telegram from Ormsby-Gore to Macmillan, PREM11/4229; Watkinson to Macmillan, 23 September 1960, PREM11/2941. See also Brandon, Oral History, p. 3.
48. Neustadt, *Report to the President*, p. 34.
49. Thorneycroft to Macmillan, 7 December 1962 PREM11/3716, PRO.
50. Alastair Horne, *Macmillan, 1957–1986* (London: Macmillan, 1989) p. 433.
51. Neustadt, *Report to the President*, p. 42.
52. Clark, op. cit., p. 349.
53. Neustadt, *Report to the President*, p. 44.
54. Macmillan was in a difficult position with pressure coming from the RAF and pro-SKYBOLT lobbies. According to Thorneycroft, out of a sense of loyalty and obligation to the RAF, SKYBOLT was still an option when the delegation headed out to Nassau (Thorneycroft, Oral History, p. 19, JFKL). Bligh recalls that the PM believed that it was better to 'try and play Skybolt along for another year to eighteen months in order to avoid political difficulties at home'. Note for the Record, 9 December 1962, PREM11/3716 PRO.
55. Note for the Record by Bligh, 9 December 1962, PREM11/3716.
56. Walt Rostow, Oral History, p. 102; Neustadt, *Report to the President*, p. 91.
57. Neustadt, *Report to the President*, p. 46.
58. Brief of 6 September 1962, FO371/166314; Memo 19 September, PREM11/3778. See also Zuckerman, Oral History, p. 28.
59. Neustadt, *Report to the President*, p. 89. Kennedy felt badly let down by his staff and complained afterwards that someone should have made sure he was informed. This is borne out by Bundy (Oral History, p. 4, JFKL).
60. Brandon, op. cit.
61. De Zulueta to Ormsby-Gore, 11, December 1962, PREM11/3716, PRO.
62. Neustadt, *Report to the President*, p. 49.
63. Ibid., p. 55.
64. Memcon, December 16, 1962 Box 317 meetings, NSF, JFKL.
65. Telegram, Ormsby-Gore to Macmillan PREM11/4229. See also Gilpatric statement, 22 December, 1962, Richard E. Neustadt Papers, Box 19–20 Skybolt/Atlantic Affairs, Statements and Clippings on Skybolt 1959–63. See also *Washington Star*, 30 December 1962.
66. Zuckerman strongly believed that those bodies fed their counterparts and contacts in Britain, as well as in the US overly sanguine and even false information about the missile's progress. See Zuckerman, Oral History, JFKL.
67. Neustadt, *Report to the President*, pp. 4, 61, 62.
68. Ibid., p. 22.

69. Neustadt, *Alliance Politics*, p. 41.
70. Nunnerley, op. cit., p. 132. See also Sir Solly Zuckerman, *Monkeys, Men and Missiles: An Autobiography, 1946–1988* (London: Collins, 1988), pp. 252–3.
71. Neustadt, *Report to the President*, p. 53.
72. Rusk felt it was essentially a defence matter and was happy to let McNamara handle it. While he was aware that it could cause problems for Britain, he failed to take notice of the warnings from Bruce that indicated that it had all the makings of a potential crisis. It is clear that despite warnings from some of his most trusted advisors, Kennedy failed to grasp the severity of the problem until his conversation with David Ormsby-Gore en route to Nassau.
73. Neustadt, *Report to the President*, p. 78; Adam Yarmolinsky, Oral History, pp. 61, 64, JFKL. This goes some way to explaining McNamara's confusion in London when Thorneycroft asked him for POLARIS without strings and seemed upset at the Defense Secretary's shock. McNamara was only informed of his error at a 16 December meeting re SKYBOLT! McNamara's unfamiliarity with the terms of the original agreement also meant that he was not aware that it contained an escape clause, inserted at the request of the British that allowed for cancellation of the project on technical grounds. Had he known, his job would certainly have been considerably easier.
74. Horne, op. cit., p. 441.
75. Nunnerley, op. cit., p. 137.
76. Not only was this politically damaging to the Prime Minister, it was also personally hurtful. In a Cabinet meeting after the crisis, he told his colleagues: 'we played an active and helpful part in bringing matters to their present conclusion, but in public little had been said and the impression had been created that we had been playing a purely passive role. It would not be easy to correct this without revealing the degree of informal consultation which had taken place; but this might be embarrassing to President Kennedy.' Rather than cause the President any trouble, Macmillan was content to let the matter pass without comment. The British press continued to harangue him about his role. CAB128/36, Minute 63rd conclusions, PRO.
77. Horne, op. cit., p. 432.
78. Nunnerley, op. cit., p. 151; Brandon, op. cit., p. 166.
79. Neustadt, *Report to the President*, p. 87; Harlech, op. cit., pp. 46–7; Note for Record, 1 August 1963, PREM11/4737. According to Neustadt and Ormsby-Gore, this 50–50 offer was never seriously intended as a solution. It would appear that its main purpose was to provide both Kennedy and Macmillan with ammunition for those who would criticise the dropping of SKYBOLT.
80. Record of Meeting 19 December 1962, PREM11/4229.
81. Nunnerley, op. cit., p. 153.
82. Record of Meeting: 19 December 1962, PREM11/4229.
83. Record of Meeting: 19 December 1962, PREM11/4229. Some controversy surrounds the Rambouillet meeting. The official British records show that while the two leaders spoke briefly about the SKYBOLT

problems, no mention was made, as de Gaulle latter claimed, of a joint Anglo-French nuclear force in place of continued Anglo-American collaboration. In spite of this confusion over a nuclear deal, Macmillan had returned from the meeting virtually certain that the French leader intended to prevent Britain from joining the Common Market. With this policy denied to him, it would appear that he made no mention of this in the hope that a deal with Kennedy might save the Anglo-American relationship and thus preserve at least one of his key policies.

84. Record of Meeting: 19 December 1962, PREM11/4229.
85. Record of Meeting: 19 December 1962, PREM11/4229.
86. Neustadt, *Report to the President*, pp. 23–31.
87. Note for Record, 1 August 1963, PREM11/4737.
88. The MLF proposal had been around for some time. First advanced by Robert Bowie as an alternative to General Norstad's MRBM scheme, the idea had been re-floated by the State Department under Kennedy. The proposal was for a mixed manned fleet (under Kennedy it became surface vessels rather than submarines), made up of participating NATO countries. The idea was that in such a fully integrated force, it would be difficult, if not impossible, for one nationality to dominate decisions or to seize control of the nuclear warheads in their possession. The scheme really took off after the Nassau conference in December 1962 and looked most likely to succeed in late 1963/early 1964. Almost universal apathy and opposition (with the exception of West Germany) eventually forced the Johnson Administration to drop the proposal in its entirety. Britain remained opposed throughout, agreeing only to participate in discussions about the force in October 1963, fearing that her continuing intransigence would only damage the 'special relationship'.
89. Memo by Bohlen, Neustadt Papers, Government Consulting, Box 19, Skybolt/Atlantic Affairs Folder 3, JFKL.
90. Neustadt, *Report to the President*, pp. 75–6. See also *Washington Post*, 15 December 1962.
91. Newhouse, *De Gaulle and the Anglo-Saxons*, p. 219. See also *Newport Press*, 13 December 1962.
92. Note for Record, 1 August 1963, PREM11/4737. See also *Wall Street Journal*, December 19, 24, 1962.
93. McGeorge Bundy, Oral History, p. 2.
94. Brandon, op. cit.
95. Neustadt, *Report to the President*, p. 91.
96. Kennedy offered among other things, another American missile uninspiringly named HOUND Dog. Record of Meeting: 19 December 1962, PREM11/4229 and a joint study group to be set up to analyse the problem. Neustadt, *Report to the President*, p. 87.
97. Nassau Communiqué: Bahamas Meetings: Texts of Joint Communiqués, Cmnd 1915 (HMSO, 1962).
98. George Ball, *The Past has Another Pattern*, p. 268.
99. Almost as an afterthought, Kennedy (and Macmillan) decided to make an offer of POLARIS on similar terms to de Gaulle which the General subsequently refused.

15 Managing Transition: Macmillan and the Utility of Anglo-American Relations
Nigel Ashton

The Macmillan years, 1957–63, have been described as some of the most intimate and successful in the post-war history of the Anglo-American 'Special Relationship'.[1] Perhaps only the degree of warmth of the Thatcher–Reagan relationship comes close to matching that achieved between John F. Kennedy and Macmillan in particular.[2] Indeed, the December 1962 Nassau Conference, when Macmillan snatched political victory and the independent nuclear deterrent from the jaws of defeat and humiliation has been called his finest hour.[3] Consider, then, this telephone exchange between the President and the Prime Minister a mere four weeks after the conclusion of the conference:

Macmillan	I say, did you enjoy Nassau? I loved it, didn't you? I thought it was awfully good.
Kennedy	Oh, which is that?
Macmillan	The Nassau meeting.
Kennedy	Oh yes – very good, very good.

Macmillan's official biographer, Alistair Horne, suffixes this exchange with the laconic observation: 'Kennedy's mind had evidently moved on.'[4] Perhaps, though, it points to one more general truism about the special relationship for which it would be unfair to blame Macmillan, and which is worth bearing in mind when examining his record in the field. In the post-war years, the Anglo-American relationship has always seemed more special and more important from the British than from the American perspective.

If one examines the relative international economic and political standing of the two nations in the period in question then the balance of their relations could not and should not have been otherwise. Britain's days as a pre-eminent world trading power were long since over. Her share of world manufacturing output by 1963 stood at 6.4 per cent compared to 35.1 per cent on the part of the United States.[5] Although the Empire and Commonwealth, together with her Permanent Membership of the United Nations Security Council, seemed to give Britain a standing in world affairs at the head of the second division of nations, just below the superpowers, the gap in prestige and influence was in fact a substantial and growing one. In terms of the crudest measure of power, Britain's total defence expenditure in 1963 stood at $5.2 billion compared to $52.2 billion on the part of the United States.[6] Moreover, a succession of retreats and symbolic defeats in the post-war years, ranging from the collapse of the Palestine mandate, through the Iranian oil crisis, to the Suez crisis, had created a *perception* of Britain as a nation increasingly unable or unwilling to project or maintain its power on the international stage. Such perceptions became as much the cause as the effect of a relative decline in Britain's international standing.

Macmillan held office at what was very much a transitional period in terms of Britain's international position as a whole, and more specifically in terms of the special relationship. Since it stands to reason that transitions are far more difficult to manage than the mere maintenance of a well-charted course we should perhaps adopt an appropriately less stringent standard in judging his handling of the Special Relationship. Before him stood three possible paths in international relations. The first was that of Empire and Commonwealth. If he bolstered Britain's commitment in this sphere he would please the Right of the Conservative Party and that segment of public opinion which was disenchanted with the Anglo-American alliance in the wake of the Suez fiasco.

The second path was that of Europe. Should he change tack and try to draw Britain closer to the union of the Six which was coming to fruition on the Continent? The perils of this path were evident. It would divide opinion within his own Party and the country as a whole, which was far from convinced that Britain's future lay in an 'ever closer union' with its European neighbours. Moreover, membership of the new Common Market which was in the process of being created might not even prove economically beneficial. Put simply, the scheme might not work. Forty years later the same dilemma resonates in different circumstances.

The final possible path was that of the Anglo-American alliance. Although the breakdown in relations over Suez might not make this a popular course in the short term, the legacy of close wartime relations, which had in part been translated into post-war international co-operation, seemed to make it an attractive course in the longer term. At the very least, Britain might be able to alter perceptions of her own decline through a renewal of her close association with the United States. Potential foes around the world would think much harder about challenging Britain if they knew that they could also expect to encounter steadfast US opposition. This was, at any rate, one lesson which could be drawn from the Suez fiasco. The Anglo-American course in foreign relations seemed perhaps the most appealing, and Macmillan could be forgiven for thinking that in any case a parting of the ways had not yet been reached. Surely he could continue to tread the path of the Special Relationship without turning his back on either Europe or the Empire? Events were to prove this judgement mistaken, but perhaps we should examine Macmillan's conduct of the Special Relationship, and the dividends he derived from it, before pontificating too much on the myopia of the course he chose.

To assess Macmillan's success in this field, let me propose five tests. First, and, it seems, most important, is how well the relationship functioned in periods of acute international crisis. In other words, how far was Macmillan able to influence the course of international events in a direction favourable to British interests through Anglo-American channels? Or, put another way, how far could Britain under Macmillan turn the projection of American power towards her own ends?

Macmillan's record here contains elements of both success and failure. For instance, one of the crucial theatres in shaping post-war perceptions of Britain's decline had been the Middle East. At the March 1957 Bermuda Conference, where much of the lost conviviality was restored to Anglo-American relations through the public camaraderie of Eisenhower and Macmillan, little was done to narrow the gap over Middle Eastern problems. As the *New York Times* reported, 'Administration officials privately said it would be unwise to overlook the importance of points on which differences remained or on which decisions were left open.'[7] Suspicions and differences persisted, despite Macmillan's attempts to rebuild relations with the President, and re-emerged in the response of the two countries to the Iraqi Revolution of July 1958. Publicly, the intervention of

American marines in Lebanon and British paratroops in Jordan was presented as a triumph of Anglo-American co-operation. Macmillan and Eisenhower exchanged open congratulations over the success of the supposedly combined operation, with the President noting that 'we can take special satisfaction in the complete understanding and splendid cooperation which was evident between our two Governments in these undertakings.'[8] However, in private the Americans had refused repeated requests for US troops to be sent to Jordan to stand alongside the British Paras. They had in practice treated the operations in Jordan and Lebanon as separate interventions.[9] As Macmillan himself acknowledged privately, the Anglo-American alliance had proven uncertain when put to the test in the Middle East.[10] On the other hand, one could still argue that in terms of international *perceptions*, it was more important for the US and Britain to have appeared to be acting in concert in the Middle East than for this to be the reality. Certainly, appearances in the summer of 1958 contrasted sharply with those of the autumn of 1956. Furthermore, Macmillan showed both in Jordan in 1958, and in Kuwait in the summer of 1961, that he had at least discovered the knack of ensuring American acquiescence in British action in defence of her interests in the Middle East. This, together with public protestations of support and co-operation, was perhaps all that was required from the Anglo-American alliance to bolster the British position in the region.[11]

Looking at the Macmillan–Kennedy years, the key international confrontation of the period took place over Cuba. Here, it must be asked how far Macmillan was able to influence the American President's handling of a major international crisis? Although recent research is sharply divided on the significance of Macmillan's role, there is a general consensus that his input did not substantially alter the course charted by the President.[12] This observation is not in itself all that significant, for it may well be that, as one historian has commented, Macmillan and Kennedy were in fact of similar mind as to the best way to deal with the Missile Crisis.[13] As to the importance of the support and counselling offered by Macmillan to the President there is a substantial divergence of opinion. One school of thought has it that Macmillan's role was to act as little more than an international Samaritan on the end of a phone line. He listened sympathetically to the President's telephone accounts of the decisions being taken in Washington, but was unable to influence them.[14] For historians of this school there is no evidence that Macmillan personally was able to do anything more than offer reassurance and solace to the President. Others, who include his official biographer, have argued that Macmillan's advice, understanding, and steadfast support helped to bolster Kennedy's resolve, and contributed to Khrushchev's decision to back down.[15]

Certainly, there seems little doubt that Macmillan's earlier decision to install David Ormsby-Gore, a close personal friend of Kennedy's, as British Ambassador in Washington, gave Britain a degree of access to the decision-making process in Kennedy's inner circle which was the envy of other Western allies.[16] Although it remains a matter of debate as to how significant an influence Ormsby-Gore exercised, his advice to the President over the question of how far to extend the maritime blockade around Cuba does seem important. Kennedy appears to have been convinced by Ormsby-Gore to move the blockade closer to Cuba against the advice of Defense Secretary McNamara.[17] This intervention allowed for a longer breathing space before any direct US Soviet maritime confrontation.

In the end, the verdict on the functioning of the special relationship over the Cuban question has to be one which recognizes that, for Kennedy, this was in the first instance a domestic American crisis. His first concern had to be with the security of the United States, and the survival of his Administration. It would be surprising if, in these circumstances, any outside power was able to influence his decision-making to satisfy its own interests. Taking this into account, the extent of the communication and consultation afforded Macmillan was indeed special.

In Indo-China too, although Macmillan was able to do little to influence either Eisenhower or Kennedy's handling of policy towards Vietnam, his advice over the problem of Laos, which confronted Kennedy in the first months of his administration, does seem to have had an impact. Laos was one of the four states which emerged in Indo-China following the 1954 Geneva Conference. Although supposed to be neutral, Laos' position was made precarious by the tensions between North and South Vietnam. During the course of 1959, civil war broke out between the central government and the Communist-backed *Pathet Lao* guerillas. By March 1961, the situation had deteriorated to the point where the new President Kennedy was under significant pressure from his advisers to contemplate full-scale military intervention. The case bears some similarities to that of Cuba in that the reservations Macmillan expressed at the Key West meeting about the nature and extent of operations proposed by Administration hawks seem merely to have reinforced Kennedy's own predilections. Nevertheless, by helping to forestall major military operations in Laos, Macmillan avoided the need for awkward choices to be made over any significant British ground force contribution. He also helped to avert the risk of a major superpower confrontation, leading one commentator to describe this as being amongst his finest diplomatic achievements.[18]

It is arguable, therefore, that Macmillan wrung about as much as could be expected from the Special Relationship in terms of its functioning in periods of international crisis. He was never going to be able to create a perfect uniformity of approach to every problem. For instance, differences persisted under both Eisenhower and Kennedy over issues such as Vietnam, the future of Berlin, and the handling of Arab nationalism. However, Macmillan avoided open breaches on the scale of Suez and was able to foster the appearance, if not always the reality, of two allies who would support each other in their respective times of trial. After the succession of blows which had eroded Britain's international prestige in the post-war years, there was something to be said for a period of greater stability underpinned by an apparent renewal of the Special Relationship.

In terms of my second test of the Special Relationship, its domestic dividends, one could also argue that Macmillan achieved a measure of success. Certainly, he was able to make use of the close relations he established with successive US Presidents to bolster the domestic standing of his government at several key junctures.[19] Here again, what seems to have been important as much as the substance of the Anglo-American relationship was its presentation. From the beginning of his premiership, Macmillan excelled in this. So, the pictures of Macmillan and Eisenhower strolling in friendly conversation at Bermuda in March 1957 were far more important domestically than the fact that beneath the surface major foreign policy differences remained unresolved. Similarly, although Eisenhower and his staff had major reservations about Macmillan's efforts to promote a great power summit during 1959,[20] Macmillan still managed to twist the President's arm to persuade him to visit Britain at the end of August 1959. At the beginning of the General Election campaign, Macmillan was able to bask in the reflected glory of Eisenhower's first visit to England since his wartime years as Supreme Commander of Allied Forces. The television pictures of the two leaders enjoying a cosy fireside chat, and Eisenhower's comments emphasizing the renewal of the Special Relationship, did no harm to Macmillan's re-election prospects.[21]

Finally, it seems clear that considerations of Macmillan's domestic position were at the forefront of the reasons why Kennedy eventually yielded to his demand for the Polaris nuclear delivery system at the Nassau Conference of December 1962. Here, surely, was a case where Macmillan's efforts to foster close personal relations at the summit of the Anglo-American alliance dug him out of a potentially disastrous political hole at home.[22] Kennedy proved willing to override the advice of his closest advisers in order to save Macmillan's political skin. Although some expected that the deal would still damage Macmillan domestically, once again his skilful presentation turned it into a dividend. It seems difficult to avoid the conclusion, therefore, that Macmillan wrung the maximum possible domestic political advantage from the Special Relationship, in sharp contrast to his predecessor in office.

The third test of Macmillan's handling of the special relationship must be its broader impact on other aspects of foreign policy. Here, we must return to the three possible paths outlined at the outset, and ask how far Macmillan's renewed focus on the Special Relationship hobbled him in his dealings with Europe and the Empire. These topics are dealt with elsewhere in this volume so the comments supplied here must of necessity be brief and impressionistic. In the simplest sense, the Special Relationship and membership of the Common Market were only incompatible because De Gaulle said they were. During the 1980s, when the Anglo-American alliance went through another of its periodic cycles of renewal under Prime Minister Margaret Thatcher and President Ronald Reagan, it was not credibly suggested that Britain must as a consequence consider withdrawal from the EEC. True, the renewed closeness in Anglo-American relations was indicative of a certain Euro-scepticism at the top in Britain. However, translating this back into the circumstances of the early 1960s, a degree of reticence and scepticism about the European project in high political circles in Britain was hardly sufficient grounds for the delivery of the French veto. Events at the Nassau Conference were no more than the pretext for De Gaulle's action. The fork in the paths of Europe and the Special Relationship only appeared due to the presence of a uniformed De Gaulle directing traffic.

As regards the Empire and Commonwealth, the Special Relationship proved to be far less of a hindrance in the Macmillan years than had previously been the case. This was largely due to the fact that Macmillan quickly came to the conclusion that Britain's interests were best served by moving swiftly to dismantle the African Empire. In contrast to the wartime tensions which had emerged between Churchill and Roosevelt over the former's refusal to grant early independence to India, neither Eisenhower nor Kennedy needed to chivvy Macmillan down the path to decolonization. There could of course be specific exceptions, such as the case of Cyprus, where Archbishop Makarios cleverly played to the US domestic audience in his campaign for the ending of British rule. Similarly, Anglo-American tensions emerged over the Congo Crisis. Here, Macmillan's concern was with the impact of the disintegration of the former Belgian colony on his precarious efforts to forge a Central African Federation. Kennedy, on the other hand, was preoccupied with the Cold War battle against the advance of communist influence in the Third World. Nevertheless, if one had to provide a brief blanket judgement as to the negative impact of the Special Relationship in the spheres of both Europe and the Empire it would be that this has been exaggerated. A renewal of the Special Relationship did not of itself seriously hamper Macmillan's conduct of policy towards Europe and the Empire.

My fourth test of Macmillan's handling of the Special Relationship is the personal relations established at the highest level – Prime Minister to President. Here, there is an interesting paradox. It would have seemed reasonable to predict that Macmillan would get along very well with his former wartime colleague, Eisenhower. Indeed, for much of Eisenhower's two terms of office this was so. Eisenhower greeted the replacement of Eden by Macmillan as Prime Minister with unabashed enthusiasm and, according to his biographer, Stephen Ambrose, counted Macmillan among the closest circle of his friends.[23] This friendship had of course been forged back in wartime days during Macmillan's tenure as British Minister with the Allied Forces in North Africa. However, Eisenhower seems to have drawn a clear dividing line between personal friendship and major affairs of state which became increasingly clear in the final eighteen months of his administration. Perhaps this division was a function of his military background. He could not allow major decisions of strategy to be clouded too far by particular personal attachments.

At any rate, Macmillan's efforts to cut a figure between the two superpowers before and after the 1959 General Election evoked considerable irritation on Eisenhower's part. This irritation first surfaced during Macmillan's visit to Washington in March 1959.[24] Although the Prime Minister went some way towards repairing the damage through his careful management of Eisenhower's visit to London in August 1959,[25] problems resurfaced at the failed Paris summit of June 1960. Here, the President was greatly piqued by what now appeared to be Macmillan's fair-weather friendship. The Prime Minister failed to back him up strongly in the face of Khrushchev's onslaught over the U-2 incident. Macmillan's attempts to salvage something from the wreckage greatly annoyed the President, who perhaps detected the continuing whiff of domestic political calculation in the background. At any rate Macmillan's efforts to persuade Eisenhower to beg Khrushchev to return to the negotiating table at the end of the summit drew an icy rebuke from the President.[26] As a postscript to this tale of what were, in the end, perhaps not quite so special personal relations, it is interesting to note that these two great friends apparently did not correspond directly for sometime after Macmillan left office. Eisenhower's explanation was that he had lost Macmillan's address.[27]

The Macmillan–Kennedy relationship, on the other hand, while far less predictable, became, for all its comparative brevity, remarkably close. Macmillan's efforts to build a bridge to the new President at the beginning of 1961 through his rather vapid musings on the 'Grand Design' seem, in the spirit of their later relationship, rather ironic. It was on the more fundamental level of a shared outlook on life, and a shared sense of its perversities that the two connected. During their earliest meetings, Macmillan's dry sense of humour evidently struck a chord with the new President who, in private, was wont to make remarks of his own in a similar vein. On the other hand, it is doubtful whether Macmillan knew what to make of another of the more prominent features of Kennedy's character: his womanizing. During one meeting between the two, Kennedy's attention evidently wandered, and, turning to Macmillan, he asked, 'I wonder how it is with you, Harold? If I don't have a woman for three days, I get a terrible headache . . .' Macmillan was apparently non-plussed.[28] Perhaps the problem was that while he frequently had his nose buried in the pages of romances, Kennedy was out conducting them.

For all their different experiences in life the Prime Minister and President were able to connect and communicate with each other remarkably effectively. Of course, there were occasions when the strength of their personal relations could not resolve disagreements over policy. Their final meeting at Birch Grove in the summer of 1963, for instance, was undoubtedly a failure. Nevertheless, cynics should not be allowed to denigrate the exceptional closeness the two achieved, leading Kennedy famously at Nassau to override all of his advisers to dig his friend out of a domestic political hole. Perhaps, then, the record of Special Relations under Macmillan at the highest level is one which on balance deserves to be described as a particular success.

This record, though, can only properly be judged when set against the concluding test of the Special Relationship under Macmillan. Agreements brokered using personal ties with the President might mean little if his close advisers, officials at a lower level, or political enemies, conspired to prevent them being put into practice. How well did the decisions taken at the highest level negotiate hurdles in Congress, and seep down through the various layers of the bureaucracy in London and Washington? Here, the record is rather mixed. Part of the problem seems to have been that, as Eisenhower put it in a moment of particular exasperation, Macmillan and his colleagues 'just didn't understand our parliamentary system'.[29] For instance, they placed far too great a weight of expectation on action the President could take without regard to the wishes of Congress. So, when, in the summer of 1958, Macmillan called on Eisenhower to mount a large-scale, ill-defined joint military action in the Middle East, the President cautioned him that this went far beyond the extent of anything he could do constitutionally.[30]

In terms of the Washington bureaucracy, although one could point to the nuclear field as one in which successful Anglo-American co-ordinating mechanisms were created, in other areas of defence and foreign policy senior advisers and lower-ranking officials did not always work together as their political masters intended. A good example of this would be the Working Group on the Middle East set up as a result of an agreement between Eisenhower and Macmillan during their talks in Washington in October 1957. Although the group produced an outline plan for joint Anglo-American military operations in Lebanon, such action was opposed by key figures in the US military and diplomatic corps. These included Admiral Arleigh Burke, the Chief of Naval Operations, and Henry Cabot Lodge, Ambassador to the United Nations. Their opposition no doubt contributed to the decision not to put the plan into action in the summer of 1958.[31]

As regards the Presidents' top advisers, under Eisenhower, British suspicions of Secretary of State Dulles were legendary. Mistrust of Dulles, according to Winthrop Aldrich, Ambassador to Britain at the time of the Suez Crisis, permeated the British Cabinet.[32] Certainly, the Secretary of State's handling of the crisis did little to dispel such views. Under Kennedy too, there were concerns about the tenor of advice on the Special Relationship given to the President by top aides such George Ball and Robert McNamara. The persistent British fear was that the President's advisers were working to force Britain into a Europeanist, multilateralist straitjacket. This judgement in fact does not seem to have been too wide of the mark.

On balance, though, these five tests of the Special Relationship suggest that Macmillan played what was a problematical hand in Anglo-American relations with a good deal of skill and a fair measure of success. Although criticized for his concentration on personal relations at the top, he was able to exploit these to achieve a measure of influence over US policy which Britain's relative international power and prestige would not otherwise have justified. Similarly, whilst it is true that the Anglo-American alliance was cited by de Gaulle as a pretext for blocking Britain's entry into the Common Market, the roots of the French veto lay in the General's desire for French domination of the EEC. The theory is impossible to test but it seems probable that neither closer nor more distant relations with the United States would have made any difference to the outcome of Britain's application to join the Common Market. After the débâcle of Suez, Macmillan's largely adroit restoration of the Special Relationship provided a degree of stability in what would otherwise have been a far more awkward period of transition. One would have to conclude by registering the verdict that, on balance, Macmillan was one of the more successful post-war British Prime Ministers in managing the special relationship during a period which threw up more than its fair share of international problems.

NOTES

1. R. M. Hathaway, *Great Britain and the United States: Special Relations since World War II* (Boston: Twayne, 1990), pp. 50, 70.

2. A. Horne, *Macmillan, 1957–1986* (London: Macmillan, 1989), p. 281.
3. Ibid., p. 443.
4. Ibid.
5. D. Reynolds, *Britannia Overruled* (London: Longman, 1991), p. 12.
6. P. Kennedy, *The Rise and Fall of the Great Powers: Economic Change and Military Conflict from 1500 to 2000* (London: Unwin Hyman, 1988), p. 384.
7. 'Detail Unsolved at Bermuda Talk', *New York Times*, press cutting, 25/3/57, Box 113, John Foster Dulles Papers, Seeley G. Mudd Library, Princeton, NJ.
8. D. D. Eisenhower, *Waging Peace* (London: Heinemann, 1965), p. 279; H. Macmillan, *Riding the Storm* (London: Macmillan, 1971), pp. 533–4.
9. N. J. Ashton, *Eisenhower, Macmillan and the Problem of Nasser: Anglo-American Relations and Arab Nationalism, 1955–59* (London: Macmillan, 1996), pp. 165–89.
10. Horne, *Macmillan, 1957–1986*, p. 98.
11. For further discussion of the Kuwaiti operation see: N. J. Ashton, *Eisenhower, Macmillan and the Problem of Nasser*, pp. 220–32; 'A Microcosm of Decline: British Loss of Nerve and Military Intervention in Jordan and Kuwait, 1958 and 1961', *The Historical Journal*, vol. 40, no. 4 (1997).
12. There is a substantial body of recent research on the Cuban missile crisis. Most relevant here are two contributions which look directly at the British role: G. D. Rawnsley, 'How Special is Special? The Anglo-American Alliance During the Cuban Missile Crisis', *Contemporary Record*, vol. 9, no. 3 (Winter 1995), pp. 586–601; P. G. Boyle, 'The British Government's View of the Cuban Missile Crisis', *Contemporary British History*, vol. 10, no. 3 (Autumn 1996), pp. 22–38.
13. Boyle, 'The British Government's View of the Cuban Missile Crisis', p. 36.
14. Rawnsley, 'How Special is Special? The Anglo-American Alliance During the Cuban Missile Crisis', p. 590; R. Lamb, *The Macmillan Years, 1957–1963: The Emerging Truth* (London: John Murray, 1995), p. 356; J. Turner, *Macmillan* (London: Longman, 1994), pp. 165–6.
15. Boyle, 'The British Government's View of the Cuban Missile Crisis', pp. 34–6; Horne, *Macmillan, 1957–1986*, pp. 382–4.
16. Horne, *Macmillan, 1957–1986*, p. 368; Lamb, *The Macmillan Years*, pp. 352–3, 356; Boyle, 'The British Government's View of the Cuban Missile Crisis', pp. 22–3; Rawnsley, 'How Special is Special? The Anglo-American Alliance During the Cuban Missile Crisis', pp. 588–90. Once again, Horne and Boyle argue that Ormsby-Gore's role was significant, while Lamb and Rawnsley contend the opposite.
17. Horne, *Macmillan, 1957–1986*, p. 369; Rawnsley, 'How Special is Special? The Anglo-American Alliance During the Cuban Missile Crisis', p. 588; Boyle, 'The British Government's View of the Cuban Missile Crisis', p. 26. At no point does Rawnsley manage to refute the specific contention that Ormsby-Gore swayed the President's decision to reduce the perimeter of the blockade.
18. Lamb, *The Macmillan Years, 1957–1963: The Emerging Truth*, p. 394.

19. This test relates to the specific political dividends of the Special Relationship. Depending on one's perspective, it could of course be argued that the survival of this particular government and the advancement of the national interest were not necessarily in harmony.
20. For Macmillan's summitry see R. Aldous, '"A Family Affair": Harold Macmillan and the Art of Personal Diplomacy', in R. Aldous and S. Lee (eds), *Harold Macmillan and Britain's World Role* (London: Macmillan, 1996), pp. 9–36; and R. Aldous, *The Last Summiteer* (Bangor: Headstart History Press, 1996).
21. Horne, *Macmillan, 1957–1986*, pp. 147–8; Lamb, *The Macmillan Years, 1957–1963: The Emerging Truth*, p. 59.
22. J. Melissen, 'Pre-Summit Diplomacy: Britain, the United States and the Nassau Conference, December 1962', *Diplomacy and Statecraft*, vol. 7, no. 3 (November 1996), pp. 678–82. Melissen's penetrative analysis reasserts the vital importance of personal diplomacy at the summit in resolving problems which are effectively intractable at lower levels.
23. S. Ambrose, *Eisenhower: Soldier and President* (New York: Touchstone, 1990), pp. 421–2.
24. Horne, *Macmillan, 1957–1986*, pp. 146–7.
25. Aldous, '"A Family Affair"', in Aldous and Lee (eds), *Harold Macmillan and Britain's World Role*, pp. 22–3.
26. Ibid., pp. 23–5.
27. Horne, *Macmillan, 1957–1986*, p. 588. It should be noted that Horne puts a very different gloss on this loss, and subsequent re-establishment, of contact.
28. Horne, *Macmillan, 1957–1986*, pp. 289–90.
29. Ashton, *Eisenhower, Macmillan and the Problem of Nasser: Anglo-American Relations and Arab Nationalism, 1955–59*, pp. 24–5.
30. Ibid., p. 171. It should be noted that ways around such constitutional limitations could be found in exceptional circumstances, as illustrated by one of Eisenhower's successors in office, Lyndon Johnson.
31. Ibid., pp. 152, 170.
32. Winthrop Aldrich, interviewed 15 July 1964, John Foster Dulles Papers, Oral History, Seeley G. Mudd Library, Princeton, NJ.

Index